Fired Up!

More Adventures & Recipes from Hudson's on the Bend

BY JEFF BLANK

WITH SARA COURINGTON

ART BY SHANNY LOTT

PHOTOGRAPHS BY LAURIE SMITH

FOREWORD BY LANCE ARMSTRONG

Credits

Book Design, Electronic Files and Print Management:
Nio Graphics, Inc. and Leslie Kell Designs

Food Photography: Laurie Smith

Chef Paintings: Shanny Lott,
paintings photographed by Andrew Yates

Color separations: Symmetry

ISBN 0-9766518-0-7

Manufactured in the United States of America

Acknowledgments

George & Dorothy Blank

Ron Brannon

Kelly Casey

Kitty Crider

Becky Barsch Fisher

Abel Garcia

Blas Gonzales

Jesus Caballero

Roger Joseph

Jesse Lemos

Collin & Sue Nelson

Molly Peck

Gert Rausch

Dale Rice

Mike & Pam Reese

Robert Rhoades

Eddie Safady

Pat Sharpe

John Siebels

Steve Smith

Rosemarie Sparmann

Courtney Swenson

Hudson's on the Bend is the restaurant on Ranch Road 620 that marks halfway between home and home on the old dam loop. It was one of the first rides I learned when I came to Austin in 1991. Ride out rolling and quiet Bee Cave Road, motor over Mansfield Dam on 620, turn onto Ranch Road 2222, hit the Tumbleweed hill, tuck and go for 60. Hilly and hard, the dam loop was the perfect carefree 50-mile midweek ride.

A lot has changed since then. The dam is now closed to traffic, and Hudson's feels like it's been engulfed by the growing city of Austin. The place that used to seem like it was in the middle of a three-hour expedition, now feels like part of the neighborhood. As the city has grown and matured, somehow the food has remained the same, the torchbearer for Austin. It's rooted in the wild game here; prepared with care, rustic and elegant; and made with fun and passion.

Since my first visit, it's the place that reminds me that I live in the greatest city in the world. The quiet Hill Country setting, the old ranchhouse that's sprawled to accommodate more and more people coming to love this place, it's become an anchor of mine that I ease into and enjoy food, family and friends. Somehow, someway, on every visit, the just right wine is pulled from the cellar to spark the meal into a fun, free flowing evening. Whether it's my first favorite, the hot and crunchy shrimp, or the rattlesnake I order every time I bring a European teammate with me, the food fits Austin, and it fits me, fresh quality, always interesting. Jeff and Shanny feel like family and Hudson's feels like home. And they've helped to make my homes. From Shanny's art to Ryan's designs (Austin architect, Ryan Street is Shanny Lott's son and has designed my homes in Spain, Dripping Springs and Austin), these people keep shaping the way I eat, live and enjoy life!

Now, I spend more and more time away from Austin, but even from afar, I stay connected to Hudson's. Maybe it's because I enviously hear about the Livestrong desserts, the yellow bikes out front pointing toward the sky during the mountain stages of the tour, or I'm regaled once again by one more friend from Austin raving about the last dinner they just had at Hudson's. I know that a night at Hudson's is more than a meal; it's an Austin experience: warm, laid back and unique. Jeff's even tried to get me to start cooking for myself, though I much prefer being his bartender and sous chef, I'm feeling pretty inspired. I'm leaning on this book to get me started. I hope I do him proud. I'm a little unsure about the cooking part, but pretty confident I can have enough fun in the kitchen.

So, I'll keep turning to Hudson's whenever I can, because it still marks the halfway point—halfway between my youth and the Austin I came to know years ago and halfway to home where ever I am. Enjoy this book and enjoy this food. I hope you become inspired to bring Hudson's into your home. And look out for the flames: that stuff is better left to the professionals!

Lance

Lance Armstrong

Alchemy

An ancient quasi-magical art through which practitioners sought a formula to cure any disease, confer eternal youth, and transmute base metals into gold (*New Illustrated Webster's Dictionary*). Turning base into gold—how better to describe the two processes of cooking and painting? Both disciplines take base materials and transform them into works of art. Jeff's art form has inspired eleven new paintings, nine of which are whimsical chefs conjured up by the sights and sounds of food festivals, fine dining, and travel experiences that come along with spending a lot of time with a chef. Two of the paintings are of what Jeff refers to as his "Magic White Coat." *Fresh Start* is how the coat looks at the beginning of an evening and *All Done* is what appears after the frenzy of the evening. I've taken this term from my granddaughter Hayden Hart Street. This is what she says when she is through with her dinner. By the way, she calls her grandpa "Craw Daddy" and he's hoping at last we have a child who will take over the restaurant when he is "All Done." I hope you enjoy these wonderful characters, and if you would like one of your very own, I would be happy to have a print made just the right size for you kitchen. Ordering information is in the Resources section of this book.

Blessings,

Appetizers

Antoinette Amuse'

Meet Antoinette Amuse', the ultimate food tease. She delights in titillating food foreplay. Here is a chef who knows where her talents lie and is not ashamed of her powers. She invites you into her boudoir to sample her creations and then sends you on your way, like a bad school boy. Don't try to make her your own; Antoinette belongs to the world. Besides, you need to pace yourself: this is just the first course.

Soups and Salads

Yin and Yang

These graceful twins each have a preference for cool and hot. Yin prefers to express herself with wonderful stews and soups. Yang prefers the chilly crispness of fruits and vegetables. What better chefs to represent soups and salads, for truly, the only thing separating these two foods is temperature. Yin and Yang, the epitome of equilibrium, can even flip roles and prepare a hot salad and a cold soup without loosing their balance.

Brunch and Holdiay Feasts

Big Chef Jolly

The first Christmas I spent with Jeff, he rolled out the most elaborate meal I've ever seen. He reminded me of the Ghost of Christmas Present from *A Christmas Carol*. He was Mr. Abundance: big and generous and so incredibly happy. That's the inspiration for this chef. May all your holidays be as full as ours.

Veggies

Freedom Fields

Freedom was raised by hippie parents on a commune in California. She moved to Dripping Springs in her early twenties to follow her dream of becoming a farmer. She has her own organic farm, aptly named Freedom Fields, where she grows veggies for all the great chefs in the Hill Country.

Meats

C.W. (Chuck Wagon) Goodknight

"First, you gotta catch a giant rabbit…to make the giant rabbit ravioli." Chefs are known to do a little exaggerating from time to time, as are Texans. C.W. is a chef who grew up rustlin' grub for cowboys. He learned to cook with whatever was available and to be creative about it. Rabbit never tasted so good!

Desserts

Co Co de Scharfenberger

Though she has no relationship to the wonderfully rich chocolate of the same name (different spelling: Scharffenberger Chocolates), she uses that product as often as possible. She stomped her foot in disgust when she found there were no recipes for chocolate desserts in this book (how rude). After consuming a few bars of the finest Belgian, she composed herself and recommended that you add some to the pecan pie.

Seafood

Felix the Fish Monger

Felix was a cat in a former life, and that's exactly who you want picking out your flounder, tuna, or salmon. Although he's not a chef, he's every chef's friend. He intuitively knows how to find the freshest and the finest. I guess the reward of having nine lives as a cat is getting to be a human the tenth time out.

Hill Country Libation

Oscar de la Cantina

Oscar's middle name should be Servicio. He represents the ultimate in attention to the customer. He, too, is not a chef, but where would the chef be without someone to deliver his creations to the table? Oscar was inspired by one of our gracious waiters; he will be happy to bring you the beverage of your choice.

*When you pour yourself down as rain on earth,
every living creature is filled with joy and
knows food will be abundant for all.*

Prashna Upanishad, 10

Table of Contents

Buffalo Quail Riding Jalapeño Cheese Grits

Crisp Asparagus Wrapped in an Ancho Cured
Salmon—Deep Sautéed in an Herb Crust atop
an Ancho Ginger Aioli

Duck Pot Stickers with a Pair of Dipping Sauces

Hot and Crunchy Oysters on Sesame Crisps with
a Mango Salsa and a Spicy Ancho Paint

Lobster Shooters aka Dirty Lobster Martinis

Mr. Pibb's Ribs with Sarsasparilla BBQ Sauce

Rain Forest and Tejano Ceviche

Seared Duck Liver atop Truffled Smashed Potatoes
with a Red Onion Apple Jalapeño Marmalade

Smoked Duck Diablos

Apricot and Butternut Squash Soup Spiked
with Thai Green Curry Topped with a Tea-Smoked Lobster

Caesar Atun atop Hearts of Romaine with a Mango
Vinaigrette With Parmesan Crisps

Coconut Curry Soup with Smoked Duck

Creamy Mussel Soup with a Spicy Jalapeño
and Cilantro Pesto

Fire-Roasted Green Chile Corn and Cabrito Stew

Gewürztraminer Poached Pear with an Herbed Goat
Cheese atop Arugula in a Sherry Vinaigrette

Hearts and Hearts Salad with Key Lime Vinaigrette

Hill Country Peach Salad with Spicy Candied Pecans, Pure
Luck Dairy Goat Cheese and a Balsamic Apple Reduction

Hot and Crunchy Avocado atop a Mango Jalapeño
Aioli with Ancho Paint

Iced Passion Fruit and Raspberry Soup Topped
with a Rain Forest Ceviche

Brunch and Holiday Feasts 88

American Bison Stuffed with a Blackened Turkey Tenderloin Served with a Peppered Cranberry Relish

Game and Wild Mushrooms Rolled in a Spicy Jalapeño Cilantro Crepe Topped with a Holy Mole Sauce

Holiday Hill Country Eggs with Smoked Wild Pig and a Basil Lime-Daise

Huevos Verde Broncos Topped with Rio Bravo Grapefruit Hollandaise

Malassadas with an Onolicious Sauce

Shrimp and Lobster in Saffron Crepes with a Brandied Lobster Sauce

Smoked Duck Potato Frittata

Tamale Cheese Pie with Smoked Quail Topped with Chipotle Mexican Crème

Meats 106

Giant Rabbit Ravioli in a Garlic Sage Ancho Butter

Chicken Fried Antelope with a Red Eye Gravy

Chuy's Hill Country Surf 'n Turf

Dos Gringos Tamales with Strawberry Raspberry Sauce

Espresso Rubbed Venison Backstrap with Jumbo Lump Crab in Chipotle Bock Beer Blanc Butter

Grilled Achiote Marinated Pork Chops Topped with a Watermelon Rind Chutney

Grilled Duck Breast Shingled with Seared Scallops in a Cranberry Chipotle Port Sauce

Texas Hill Country Wild Game Paella

Wild Lolli-Chop Salad atop a Macadamia Lemon Honey Dressing

Seafood 126

Giant Shrimp in a Masa Herb Crust Topped with a Cilantro Lime Butter

Grilled Salmon in a Gingered Corn and Herb Broth atop Baby Bok Choy with Shrimp Dumplings

Macadamia Nut Crusted Red Snapper with a Mango Butter Sauce

Mahi Steamed in a Banana Leaf with Herbed Lemon Wine

Really Expensive King Crab Legs and Lobster Salad

Sea Scallops Sautéed with a Saffron Cream in a Pumpkin Squash Cup

Spicy and Crispy Fried Oysters on a Bed of Spinach in a Bacon, Mustard, and Honey Vinaigrette

Tea Smoked Tuna in a Chipotle Gingered Shellac

Texas Jumbo Lump Crab Au gratin

An Introduction to Fired Up!

"Fired Up" is the much awaited volume two of the Hudson's on the Bend cookbooks. As was the case with *Cooking Fearlessly,* this book is about wild and great ingredients, professional techniques, a little chemistry, and even more fun. We hope that you have absorbed our first cookbook, *Cooking Fearlessly* and have adopted the "fearless" approach we preach! We are going to assume that you have, and with that said, let's go a step further and get "fired up" with more adventures and recipes from Hudson's on the Bend.

This book is also a celebration of Hudson's on the Bend Restaurant's twentieth anniversary. We want to share our enthusiasm for what we have been doing these last twenty years and some of the what-a-long-strange-trip-it's-been experiences we have enjoyed along the way.

Jeff Blank is the owner and chef of Hudson's on the Bend Restaurant outside of Austin. He has, over the last two decades, developed a Hill Country cuisine featuring game and fish—with an "extreme" approach, resulting in a taste as big and robust as Texas. Twenty years later, he remains "fired up" with his gusto for the Hill Country flavors.

"It is a big hearty taste," Jeff confesses. "If you're looking for something really mild, you're not going to find it here." All of our chefs and sous chefs really believe in big, full, round flavors and Hudson's on the Bend has benefited from a wonderfully diverse cast of chefs in the past twenty years: opening with the influence of that wild German Gert Rausch and his crew; a lengthy performance from Hal Sapadin, the New York Italian; the delightfully steadying influence of Jay Moore, our Okie; the feminine yet wily touch of Becky Barsch Fisher; the south of the border consultation provided by Blas Gonzalez; a little Disney World magic from Kelly Casey; and a lot of Robert Rhoades's truck-driving, skeet-shooting flavors on top of it all.

After Hudson's on the Bend had been open for four years, Jeff Blank and Jay Moore gave birth to the ever popular cooking schools. These have evolved from a regularly scheduled once a month class to at least four classes performed for private entertainment affairs per month. People have discovered that the classes are a unique way to get together for birthday parties, employee retreats/appreciation events, and customer business development gatherings. At the restaurant, we are resigned to the fact that "you can't please all of the people all of the time," but we have never had a single participant leave the cooking school without being completely thrilled with their experience. So far, we have "pleased all of the people all of the time." Because we have done so many cooking classes, our students are guinea pigs for our cookbooks. We have filtered all of these recipes through the students! If you can't come to a cooking class, grab our book, turn on the recommended songs, read the stories to get a little background, and "fire it up."

To our return readers and hard-core fans, we have repeated some things in this book from *Cooking Fearlessly.* Some things bear repeating. In the stories that accompany the recipes, we often mention "thievery." This is a practice that is common to all chefs. Oftentimes a chef will encounter a dish that is irresistible. It is a well-known law of the land that if you take an original recipe and change at least three of the ingredients, you can call it your own recipe. We have given credit to the original chefs of the recipes who became ours through this method.

In the years since the first cookbook, Chef Jeff Blank and his co-chefs at the Bend have continued to let their creative juices flow. Now it is time to throw away what your foremothers taught you about what you ought to eat, what tools to use, what goes with what, and even what might be edible.

"It is a big hearty taste," Jeff confesses. *"If you're looking for something really mild, you're not going to find it here".*

The Fearless Philosophy calls for exciting the taste buds in every corner of the mouth—sweet, sour, spicy, salty, and bitter. That's what we like to do with our cooking; get all the taste buds activated at the same time. The difference between an average cook and a great cook is the quality of the ingredients. It is our recommendation that you shop for fresh and organic as much as possible. "Cooking fearlessly" and being "fired up" evolved from the ability to access so much fresh regional product. For those without ready access to antelope or venison, recipes that feature exotic meats are presented with alternative ingredients. The "fearless and fired up" techniques, recipes and sauces can equally enhance chicken, beef, or bass. Or, if you'd like to try something a little wild, see our Resources section. Many things are available by mail these days.

"One can never know too much; the more one learns, the more one sees the need to learn more and that study as well as broadening the mind of the craftsman, provides an easy way of perfecting yourself in the practice of your art."—Augustus Escoffier

This book is dedicated to inspiring everyone to get fired up—from those who have never cooked to those who are pros. The philosophy challenges you to never leave well enough alone, adapt and conquer and when you find yourself getting too serious, stop and eat something.

Mystery History of Chef Jeff

Inquiring minds have frequently asked about Chef Jeff Blank's culinary upbringing. The staff at Hudson's has always ad libbed regarding his history. He was finally still long enough, a rare event, and the story was told.

Jeff's family came to Lakeway (a resort community west of Austin on Lake Travis) in a covered station wagon down a two lane road in the 1960s. They were part of the first 50 families that built homes in Lakeway. There is real pioneer running through his veins!

His restaurant career began in 1966 at the top of the marina steps at Lakeway Inn at the Beef & Bun Snack Bar. This restaurant was a true depiction of the life and times at Lake Travis in the '60s. They were open from Memorial Day to Labor Day every summer. This neck of the woods simply did not exist after Labor Day. Some of you probably remember when the drive from Austin to Lakeway was on a two lane pot-holed tar and gravel road. Among other uncivilized factors, there was not a large labor pool available in the area. Pierre Casselli* was the general manager at Lakeway Inn and he hired Jeff Blank to run the Beef & Bun. Jeff was sixteen years old at the time. Doesn't that make you shake your head and wonder about Pierre Casselli's judgment? Jeff was excited about the job for many reasons, none being the service industry. He has always been an avid water skier, and on most days, Jeff would disappear during the lunch rush for a quick skim across the lake! But on the more devoted, serious side, Jeff would then go upstairs and serve as a bus boy for the dinner hour in the dining room in the Lakeway Inn. Early on he demonstrated his knack for versatility with his ability to perform as manager by day and plate scraper by night.

After finishing high school, Jeff attended Oklahoma State University in the Hotel and Restaurant School. It was the only hotel and restaurant school in the region, as the culinary arts were a highly unrecognized industry at the time. In retrospect, he likens it to a "culinary wasteland" and confirms that he was simply in school to avoid Vietnam. He will never run for a political office and therefore feels completely comfortable in relaying his motives.

In 1969 Neil Armstrong landed on the moon, and Jeff landed in the Venetian Room at the Fairmont Hotel in Dallas. It was an amazing experience for him to be an active participant in the opening of a world class hotel. Now he was hooked on the adrenaline of the fine dining dinner rush! Jeff learned more in three months at the Venetian Room than he had in his three years of formal education in Oklahoma. This job ended when

> *"Life's journey is not to arrive at the grave safely in a well-preserved body, but rather to skid in sideways, totally worn out, shouting 'holy sh--...what a ride!'" —Anonymous*

the draft lottery came out and he found himself in the safe and comfortable spot of number 345. Feeling assured of a long life of freedom, Jeff left for Aspen, Colorado the very next day.

There he got a job as a night auditor at the Wild Wood Inn. This job was very similar to his beginnings at Lakeway at the Beef & Bun. His time in Aspen led him to where he is today. He was partying all night, showing up in the wee hours of the morn to punch in the room tax, pump up his air mattress and nap until he had to make the first wake-up call at 6:00 am. After the last wake-up call was made, he hit the slopes. Skiing always seems to be an underlying theme in his life. Once you get to know him, you can completely understand his passion for flying down a slippery slope with wild abandon at an extreme rate of speed. You guessed it—he eventually found himself studying with "Bill W," anonymously, of course.

After he wrapped up a winter ski season in Aspen, Jeff headed back to Austin to fill his days with water skiing. He landed a job in Lakeway as the maitre'd. He expected to live happily ever after, vacillating between Aspen and Austin, skiing his life away. While at Lakeway, Jeff met and worked with Gert Rausch. Gert, originally from Germany, was the executive chef at the Lakeway Inn. He was classically trained in the European hotel schools. Gert and Jeff were next door neighbors in the Lakeway employee housing, and there they had food parties where the dinner crowd was exposed to classic sauces, veal stocks, and much more European cooking. Gert introduced Jeff to the excitement the culinary world had to offer and gave him his first true taste of real food. Jeff gives Gert complete kudos for his enormous influence on his future. Remember, this was in a time when Steak & Ale was the finest dining available. So the preparations and combinations of flavors Gert was serving Jeff seemed from another planet.

One year later, a restaurant space opened up in Aspen. Jeff grabbed Gert and went west! They opened the Wine

Skin Restaurant in 1971 and made a go of it until 1978. The restaurant business in a ski resort is much like farming. If it didn't snow, the crop didn't come in. They had to shut 'er down. The life of a ski bum came to an end and Jeff found himself working for RG Maxwell's on Preston Road in Dallas, Texas, where he moved up to area director.

His next attempt at proprietorship was the San Antonio Broadway Oyster Co. in Alamo Heights in San Antonio, Texas. This was a doomed deal from the get-go. The Black Eyed Pea Restaurant had already tried unsuccessfully at this location. After three years, of standing in the middle of Broadway in a shark costume while wearing a sandwich board to promote the restaurant, he shucked that endeavor. From this experience, Jeff witnessed firsthand the soundness in the Howard Johnson three-part formula for success—location, location, location.

Jeff went back to the Hill Country to regroup. As he was driving down Highway 620 one day, he spied this little stone house for sale. George and Rebecca Rankin were selling their home. Jeff bought it for a song. (Apparently he witnessed the "location" philosophy but did not fully absorb it.) Jeff will forever be grateful to Bill Milburn, an Austin home builder, who fronted the money to him with nothing more than a "Hill Country hand shake." Twenty years later, the story has still not slowed down for Jeff. He is an extreme sport!

*Interestingly enough, thirty years later, Pierre Casselli's daughter and grandson have worked at Hudson's, and his son-in-law, Phillip Dubov, has been a Saturday waitperson at Hudson's for the past ten years.

"WHAT A LONG STRANGE

If you have ever
worked in a restaurant
in any capacity, you
know that it takes a
certain breed to remain
in the industry.
It is more akin to a
passion than a career.
The days are long,
the labor is very
manual, but the laughs
are plentiful, as the
following stories
will attest.

MANY KINDS OF FIRE POWER

COOKING WITH FIRE

Jeff has been known to enjoy a long tall flame more than the average red blooded male. This might explain the first cookbook. Yes, those hats really were on fire…FAQ.

As some of you may know, Hudson's serves as a restaurant and as a licensed packing plant for our gourmet sauce line. Jeff was preparing a double batch of Bourbon Vanilla Praline Sauce (try it on your family recipe for sweet potatoes) for the upcoming Christmas rush. This requires several gallons of brandy. In the name of safety, he went out to the driveway with the stock pot, propane burner, and three gallons of boiling brandy. When the brandy was lit, he was delighted by the eighteen foot flame that resulted! As Jeff was screeching with joy in the driveway, the sheriff drove by and screeched as well—to a halt. If you ever need assistance from Johnny Law, pull out the recipe for Bourbon Vanilla Praline Sauce and fire it up!

BIBLICAL FIRE POWER

Everything happens for a reason. One night at Hudson's, a customer came out of the ladies' room and announced to the hostess that there was an overflowing toilet. This started a chain of events that saved the restaurant. Had this flood occurred in the men's room, this story would have ended much differently.

There is an unwritten rule that the female host tends to the ladies' room and the male host tends to the men's room. The hostess is a do-it-yourself kind of girl, whereas the host is a delegator of chores. This seems like a petty detail, but it is really of the utmost importance to the story. The hostess went to look for the mop herself to take care of the mopping. If she had gone to the dishwasher, as the male host would certainly

RIP IT'S BEEN"

LAJITAS ▲ THE ULTIMATE HIDEOUT

have done, the dishwasher would have gone outside to get the mop and taken care of the situation. But, being the do-it-yourself girl, she went in search of a mop. First she went to the kitchen bathroom. No mop there. Then she went to the back shed. Bingo, there was an old discarded mop lying there with the mop strings smoldering in the flames of the hot water heater. Another thirty minutes and the restaurant would have been afire! God works in mysterious ways! Bless him for clogging that toilet as a cry for help.

Exactly one week after Hudson's had its near miss with the ultimate "fired up," The Ocotillo Restaurant, our sister restaurant in Lajitas, Texas burned down. Coincidentally, a mop caught fire in the water heater closet. They were unable to stop the fire before the kitchen completely burned down. The female hostess must have been off that evening.

HOT OFF THE PRESS

New York Times writer Elaine Louie visited Hudson's to write an article about the smokehouse. This was in the '80s when our smokehouse and wild game cooking was a novelty. Elaine flew in from New York and had only three hours to interview, photograph, and witness the entire smoking process. She expressed a desire to watch the procedure from start to finish. She wanted to witness the fire building in the smokehouse and follow the process until the meat went on the plate. But it takes several hours for the smokehouse to heat up. To speed up the process, Jeff threw lots of fuel on the fire. He was preparing an antelope leg stuffed with wild boar. He deboned the leg, stuffed it, tied it, threw it into the smokehouse, and then sat down in the lobby with Elaine to get it all down on paper. Jeff was facing the window, and Elaine had her back to the smokehouse. He could see the kitchen staff running back and forth from the kitchen to the smokehouse with five-gallon buckets of water. The smokehouse had heated up, and the roof was ablaze! Without Elaine ever being the wiser, the staff got the fire extinguished and kept the roof from tumbling down. She never knew how close she came to witnessing a new recipe: Antelope Stuffed with Wild Boar with a Bubbly Rooftop Sauce!

STAR STRUCK

ROCK 'N ROLL

In the 1980s, the Butthole Surfers, a Texas punk group, frequently came to Hudson's for dinner. Quite often they had a "Hollywood" type in tow. It was always an unforgettable experience for the other customers and the staff, as their arrival was much like that of a three ring-circus. After one extremely electrifying dinner, Jeff politely requested that it would probably benefit the other diners in the restaurant if the group would dine under the stars on our patio.

One night, an extremely large group of them arrived. They took a seat in the lobby to wait while the hostess went outside to set up a table that would accommodate the enormity of their group. Out of their crowd stepped Johnny Depp. In true "Don Juan DeMarco" style, he gallantly accompanied her to the patio and helped with his "Edward Scissorhands" to set up the table. The hostess felt like "Joon" and he her "Benny." Only in Neverland does this kind of chivalry occur. Yo ho and a bottle of wine, the "Pirates of the Caribbean" wined and dined and made merry at Hudson's.

INQUIRING MINDS

FAQ: do famous people dine here? Among the famous that have crossed our threshold are Tommy Lee Jones, Elizabeth Montgomery, Robert Foxworth, Olivia deHaviland, Johnny Depp, Dixie Chick Natalie Maines, Lance Armstrong, Dan Rather, Willie Nelson, Akeem Abdul Jabar, Earl Campbell, Peri Gilpin, Albert Brooks, Emmitt Smith, Farrah Fawcett, Tom Landry, Mack Brown, Pat Green, Bob Schneider, Rick Perry, George W. Bush, Lady Bird Johnson, Ann Richards, Barry Switzer, Dennis Quaid, Ray Benson, and Turk Pipkin.

15 MINUTES OF FAME FOR ALL AT HUDSON'S

Dinner at the Governor's Mansion

Honoring the president of Mexico, Vicente Fox

Featuring Hudson's on the Bend

Austin, Texas

Wednesday, November 5, 2003

8:00 p.m.

This affair was much more than a simple catering event for the staff at Hudson's. Blas Gonzales and Molly Peck, chefs at Hudson's, went to the Governor's Mansion with Jeff to cook the dinner. One week prior to the happening, Kitty Crider came to the restaurant to interview Blas about the upcoming dinner. She wrote a two page article with lots and lots of pictures of Blas. It was Blas's first fifteen minutes of fame. (We are sure that he has many more in his future.) In addition to the *Austin American Statesman's* coverage of the fan fare, Blas was thrilled at the opportunity to serve Vicente Fox! Blas is originally from San Luis Potosi. In his hometown, El Presidente Fox is greatly beloved and regarded as a savior of Mexico.

This was a landmark visit for the State of Texas, as well. It was the first time President Fox had visited the Governor's Mansion. Because it was post-9/11, the security was intense. The Mexican Secret Service, the United States Secret Service, and the Texas Secret Service had to do a security check on everyone attending and serving this event.

After successfully serving three courses, the staff was packed up and ready to roll. Jeff began to look for Blas, who had quietly disappeared. He found Blas cleverly positioned at the backdoor in an attempt to catch Vicente Fox as he exited the Governor's Mansion. Blas had seen the limo pull up to the backdoor and knew that this was the direction Vicente would be leaving the house. Sure enough, the president headed toward the limo in the path that Blas had predicted. The security guards pushed Blas and Jeff away from El Presidente as he passed them. Governor Perry and Jeff made eye contact, and the governor read the desperation of the situation in Jeff's eyes. He escorted Jeff, Blas and Molly past the security and introduced them to Vicente Fox. Jeff explained to the President that Blas, had been in charge of preparing their meal. Blas and Vicente went on to discuss Mexican soccer, San Luis Potosi, and a variety of common interests. From Jeff's view, it was the most animated and comfortable he had seen the president the entire evening. As Blas was chatting with Vicente, Jeff's cell phone rang—it was Shanny. She was watching the 10 o'clock news and was witnessing the exchange, LIVE!

Molly also got her fifteen minutes of excitement at the onset of the evening. Molly is a graduate of Texas A & M (an Aggie sister to Rick Perry). Molly wanted an autograph from the most famous of all Aggies—Governor Perry. Jeff introduced Molly to the Governor as "our little aggie," as she is quite small. They reminisced about their great college lives. Then he took her by the arm and escorted her to the front porch where the honor guard from A & M was lined up in preparation for the sword formation ceremony that Vicente Fox would walk through upon his arrival. Rick Perry said, "Men, this is Molly Peck. She is the cook at the best restaurant in Austin. If you are looking for a girlfriend that is a great cook, Molly is your girl!" Molly was still blushing when she returned to the kitchen.

This entire experience was filled with many memories. The governor's office sent a beautifully framed montage of pictures with Blas, Molly, Jeff, the Mexican president and First Lady, and Governor Perry. We have this lovely memorabilia hanging above the podium at the front door at the restaurant. In this photo, there is a striking physical resemblance between Vicente Fox and Saddam Hussein. More often than not, people will politely say, "Oh, look. It's Saddam Hussein," which always causes the hostess to giggle and reply, "This was his last meal before he went into the spider hole."

LIVESTRONG

Shanny's dad was a painter. When he died, Shanny found a photo that he had taken of a red picnic table. Obviously, he had intended to paint it. Since he didn't get to it, Shanny painted it for him. Jeff's immediate reaction to the painting was "Oh, great, another four top." He and Abel ran to Home Depot and immediately constructed four red picnic tables. The initial function of these tables was to serve after-dinner drinks and cigars to our diners in the backyard with the accompaniment of the cicadas. The cigar craze came and went, and the tables had become lonely in the backyard.

Jeff decided to use the tables in the front yard for creative marketing. His next inspiration came from Lance Armstrong. He was attempting his fourth win at the Tour de France. Jeff was then further motivated by Donald Judd, a sculpture and a minimalist who uses repetition with a theme. He bought four bikes and sprayed them yellow and attached them to the red picnic tables in the front yard with a sign that read "Go Lance Go...A Real Texas Hero." For every year that Lance has raced in the Tour de France, Jeff has added one more table and one more bike.

For Lance's sixth Tour de France attempt, Jeff bought the Livestrong bracelets and used them as a garnish on the "Go Lance Go" dessert. This dessert was a cookie/cake/custard bicycle. We would love to share this dessert recipe with you, but, unless you have a commercial kitchen with a support staff, it is an overwhelming process. So come by Hudson's next year during the Tour de France and enjoy a dessert with a bracelet to show your support for Lance and the fight against cancer.

RESTAURANT DIETS

MIRROR, MIRROR ON THE WALL

Jeff was asked to cook in the Conde Nast Café. This is a $60,000,000 employee cafeteria. That's right; employees only! The eatery is designed by the renowned architect Frank Gehry. Jeff and Shanny were very impressed with Mr. Gehry's design, from the kitchen to the "Earth, Wind and Sun" motif in the cafeteria to the full wall of "fun house" convex mirrors at the exit that produce the illusion of a 30 pound weight loss. These mirrors were the high point of Jeff's visit to Manhattan. He stood in that illusorily "happy" corridor for a full twenty minutes admiring every angle of his slender frame!

DROP THE POUNDS, ONE SLICE AT A TIME

Late one night (3:00 a.m.-ish), Jeff got a call from the alarm company notifying him that the alarm at Hudson's had been activated. He stumbled out of bed and went to the restaurant. Because his home is a mere 2.5 minute drive to Hudson's, he arrived at the restaurant before the sheriff. After determining that the alarm was caused by an innocent air draft, he went to the walk-in cooler and grabbed a delicious piece of Chocolate Intemperance (this recipe is in the first cookbook, *Cooking Fearlessly*, www.hudsonsonthebend.com). Certain of the safety of the restaurant and content, with his snack in hand, he opened the door to leave. He was greeted with the words "Drop It!" and a gun barrel pointed at his face and the local sheriff at the other end of the gun! You bet he dropped the cake. This diet method is 100% guaranteed to help one and all drop pounds.

MISCELLANEOUS

VALENTINE'S DAY MASSACRE OF '99

The Valentine's Day Massacre of 1999 still makes the wait staff shake and convulse. As you all know, Valentine's Day is one of the biggest nights of the year for restaurants. We had a brand new reservations manager who was instructed to presell tickets for the event. No one was overseeing her reservations strategy. Come to find out, there was no strategy. She booked 250 people at 7:00 p.m. We got the first 100 people seated without a hitch. They sat down for a long, romantic dinner. The other 150 people sat outside in the February chill in their strapless gowns. As you can imagine, these were 150 of the angriest people you have ever seen in your life. If you, dear reader, were a participant in this "massacre," we sincerely apologize, and we will regret, forever, what we did to your most romantic day of the year. To date, any diner who comes in and mentions that they were here for Valentine's Day of 1999 gets an apology and a complimentary dessert.

HOW MANY MILES DO YOU GET TO THE GALLON?

Jeff and Shanny were building their new home at Lake Travis. Shanny's son, Ryan Street, provided the architectural design, and it was turning into a work of art. In keeping with all of the unique design elements of the house, Jeff and Abel converted an antique stove into a Harley Davidson for the kitchen.

Jeff had stumbled on a vintage 1860 coal burning stove at a garage sale in South Austin. He purchased the rusted heap for $150. Abel, Jeff's better half, took the stove apart and recognized that the inner workings for a commercial Wolf gas range could be installed into the coal burner to modernize it. Jeff took some of the pieces to be enameled cobalt blue. The remaining parts he took to a motorcycle chroming shop in South Austin to be sparkled up. Jeff was walking out of the motorcycle chrome shop on St. Elmo Street with newly chromed parts sticking out of a box when two burly Harley riders said, "Hey man, what you got there?" He replied, "It's my stove." He giggled and explained that he had it bored out, so it would cook the fastest and the hottest! Retelling the story to Shanny, Jeff realized that was as close as he was ever going to get to acquiring a Harley. Ever the compassionate one, Shanny went and bought a chrome Harley Davidson emblem for the front of the stove, and that's how you make a one of a kind Harley stove—fastest stove in Austin.

LANGUAGES

DON'T FORGET YOUR HAT

Nobody said the restaurant business was an easy life. Bradley, fresh from the Culinary Institute of America, came on board as a prep cook. On his first day, he was met at the door by the infectiously funny chef Becky Barsch Fisher. As far as we could tell, all was well. He was just a slicin' and a dicin' and seemed to be a perfect fit for our lovely Hudson's family. About 3:00 p.m., he told Becky that he was going to go to his car and fetch his hat. That was the last we ever saw of him. The menu has frightened many a new arrival on the kitchen staff because it is lengthy and exotic. As previously mentioned, the restaurant life is not always an easy life, but, it is recommended that you give it at least a week before deciding it's not the life for you!

AN ODE TO JARED

Restaurants have their very own language. It is a universal language. This language is easy to learn for most, but not for all. "All day" means sum total on food orders, "86" means there is no more, "Two top" means a table that seats only two people, and so on.

A customer once gave a fledgling busser an order for a coffee with a side of Baileys. Struggling with the new world of words, he went to the kitchen, asked for it, and returned to the table with a cup of hot steaming coffee and a plate with two bay leaves on it. Jared took a little longer to train than most! But when he got it, he was "A" team.

GRINGO SPANISH

"Stock to a cook is voice to a singer." –Anonymous

The most important language in restaurants is Spanish. There is a variety of this that at we call Gringo Spanish. Gringo Spanish is a combination of words with the letter "o" added to the end, loudly spoken, and accompanied by wildly elaborate hand gestures. This language must be used with caution and supervision. Robert Rhoades, the executive chef, spent many hours preparing his veal stock. This stock is the base of all sauces and is truly a labor of love. Robert took his fifty-quart pot filled with water and steaming vegetables and bones to the dish washer and thought that he had clearly asked, in Gringo Spanish, for the dishwasher to remove the vegetables and bones out of the stock and return the flavorful juices. Happily and promptly, the dishwasher returned the stock pot to Robert, minus all juices, with only the veggies and bones remaining in the pot. In some cultures, the value is in the vegetables and the bones. Back to square one Robert—and maybe get your translator next time.

This Gringo Spanish has always produced comical results. The dishwasher was once asked to soak a wine bottle and remove the label so that the customer could take the label home with him as a souvenir. Happily and promptly, the bottle was returned to the server, with the label thoroughly scrubbed off.

COOKING SCHOOL

THE DOCTOR IS IN

The cooking schools at Hudson's are more of a stand-up comedy routine than anything else. Forty eyes upon a chef performing his culinary skills brings out the ham in all!

At one point, most of our private cooking schools were being held for the larger pharmaceutical companies who invited doctors and nurses to the classes. Jeff always tries to put a personal spin on the classes, and he suggested the possibility of prescribing habaneras as a replacement for Prozac. Jeff prescribed depressed patients keep a pepper in their pocket to ward off the blues. They can pull it out and take a big bite, and as the fire alarms are going off in their mouths, dopamines and serotonins are activated and surge through their entire bodies, acheiving a cheap high. Furthermore, for a bipolar patient, he recommends keeping a popsicle in the other hand. Switch them ... hot—cold—hot—cold! The result is perfect brain chemistry. Better living through "food science."

Then there was the cooking school for surgeons. As Jeff was butchering a piece of well-marbled meat, he realized the parallels in what he was doing with their job. He asked the audience of surgeons if a fat person is well marbled. The surgeons looked a little shocked and surprised by the question. After a long pause, one of the surgeons explained that when they operate, it is on a warm living specimen, and fat cannot be seen. Marbling can only be seen in a chilled cadaver. But to answer Jeff's question, a chubby cadaver is indeed well marbled!

SPIRITUALITY IN THE HOUSE

GRACIAS ABEL GARCIA

At Hudson's there is a phenomenon and that phenomenon has a name. It is Abel Garcia. Abel can accomplish anything using his hands, his mind, and his heart. He can build homes, wire for electricity, install plumbing, fix bread warmers, repair car engines, turn landscape into art, keep Jeff calm, father *muchas chicas y chicos,* on and on and on—all with a song in his heart. He has this deep well of knowledge that indicates that he has had many former lives in many different professions. Watching Abel create and solve is an incredibly spiritual process.

Jeff is an idea man. His ideas tend to be outrageous and nearly impossible. Abel has yet to encounter one of Jeff's ideas that he could not bring to fruition.

Every year during the Christmas holidays, Abel returns to central Mexico for a lengthy family visit. He is never specific about his return date. One year this visit lasted a very long three months. During Abel's absence, Jeff's staff noticed that he was becoming increasingly nervous and irritable. Shanny, noticing this same uneasiness, pointed out to Jeff that he was probably feeling vulnerable with the absence of Abel. She helped him to realize that he was half the man when Abel was not present. After all, what good is an idea by itself?

DIAMONDS ARE A GIRL'S BEST FRIEND

Once a year all restaurants in Austin can expect a surprise visit from the local food critic Dale Rice. He makes a visit to all of the fine dining restaurants throughout the year. In the fall, he does a final rating column of the eateries in the *Austin American Statesman.* He does not publish his picture along with his article so as to remain incognito. Many of these other restaurants in town had reported to Hudson's throughout the years that he had visited them, and they had recognized him at the door. With this recognition, they were able to seat him at the best table in the house, assign the best server to his table, and have the executive chef personally prepare his dinner. Everyone at Hudson's was envious. For the past twenty years, he has slipped past the host staff at Hudson's undetected. During Becky Barsch Fisher's reign in the kitchen, Hudson's was awarded the coveted number one spot on Dale's list. It was held on to for the next two years. Then there was the ill-fated visit of

2003. Dale likened this visit to Purgatory. He was seated in a plastic walled room at a table that had a downward slope, and his server was less than attentive. The fare at Hudson's saved the disaster—he did still rave about the quality of the food. On his visit of 2004, the same hostess that had seated him so poorly before was escorting him to his table. She was heading toward the same room that he had been seated in the previous year. Although, the room was completely remodeled as a result of his justifiably scathing comments from the 2003 review, there was a screaming toddler seated in that area. The hostess looked over her shoulder at Dale, and his diamond earring began twinkling at her. She likened the experience to an out of body moment. She reported that the earring had spoken to her and notified her of the identity of her customer. She quickly took a left turn and seated him at a table overlooking "Purgatory." Hudson's made it back up to the number two spot and was given their fifth star back. Diamonds are a girl's best friend.

How To Use This Book

Each recipe is broken down into categories and accompaniments. The flavor note tells you what tastes to look for as you take your first bite of the completed recipe.

 **TOOLS:** We like fancy tools as well as the next guy, but you don't need exotic knives and French pans. We use whatever does the job—from blow torches to duct tape. You can invest in a fancy smoker for your backyard, but we'll also show how to smoke meat on your stovetop. We have also found things in the hardware store (e.g., blow torches and needle nose pliers) to be invaluable kitchen tools!

 TIMING: We emphasize good planning. The French term is *mis en place,* which translates "everything in its place." We recommend reading the recipe from start to finish before you begin cooking. Many of the recipes in this book can be completely or partially prepared in advance.

For our cooking school, it is necessary for us to do all of the chopping and dicing of ingredients in advance. We recommend that you break up the cooking tasks into relaxing and manageable chunks. The meal will be more enjoyable for you, the cook, if you are not stressed out by the time everyone sits down for your culinary offerings.

The German that taught Jeff how to cook used to say "gosh darn, you have to have all of your ducks in a row and then it is smooth as a goose."

 PHILOSOPHY: The fired-up philosophy is about turning your kitchen into a trip around the world, a safari, an Alaskan fishing adventure— adventures great and small in your kitchen! A big part of our philosophy recognizes that there is no such thing as a mistake—we have turned many a culinary oops into a crowd pleasing fave! Getting fired up is challenge to one and all to get all of your taste buds squirting at the same time. We are born with approximately 9,000 taste buds in our mouth. It is traditionally taught that the sweet and sour taste buds live on the side of the tongue, salty mostly in the front, and bitter in the back. This classical taste map is oversimplified. Sensitivity to all tastes is distributed across the whole tongue and in other regions of the mouth. We like to use ingredients that will invite all of the taste buds to the party with a WOW! So get out your compass and make your own map to the world of "Fired Up"!

MUSICAL ACCOMPANIMENT: When we cook, we like to have music going in the kitchen, or at least in our heads. It adds to our enjoyment of the cooking process. Throughout the book, we recommend music that suggests the feeling that we have about the dishes. Let all the senses get into the game. So folks, download the songs on your iPod and start dancing while you cook. It is much like singing in the shower!

Salt and Seasoning

The jury is still out on salt. If your doctor has you on a restricted salt diet, then listen to your doctor. If not, listen to your own taste buds. Some people need more and can process more. As a rule of thumb, it is most likely the way your mother cooked that sets your standards. Cooks in Mexico they would, "sal al gusto"—salt as you like it. Salt is important because it brings out the natural flavors in the food. So don't be afraid of it. Use it well.

When we do cooking school, people always ask, "What kind of salt do you use?" Chefs use iodized table salt, kosher salt, or sea salt. Jeff has always had a preference for sea salt. Sea salt is an essential element in the diet, and the use of it is as old as human history. Sea salt is one of the most effective and most widely used of all food seasonings and natural preservatives. Nutritionists and dieticians say that sea salt is much better for you because of its pureness. The composition of the crystals of ocean salt is so complicated that no laboratory in the world can produce it from its basic eighty chemical elements. Nature is still a better chemist than people. Besides all of that, it has a saltier taste, so you get more bang for your buck. Here's a trick that Jeff learned from Jay Moore; mix 20% black Madagascar peppercorns (ground in spice mill) and 80% sea salt for an all purpose, around the kitchen mix. We call it "sabor." When our recipes say add or adjust salt and pepper levels, we use the mix. If you really need to watch your salt intake, use our Bronze Rub, in which salt is the least dominant ingredient.

When Jeff says salt, he really means sea salt!

ANCHO PUREE

6 ancho chilies, seeded

2 cups warm water

1. Soak the ancho chilies in water for 30 minutes or until soft.
2. Puree in blender. To encourage the puree add a little of the chile water.

BLACKENING SPICE

Yields 5 cups

1 cup paprika

1 cup ancho powder

1/4 cup granulated onion powder

1/4 cup granulated garlic powder

1/4 cup white pepper

2 tablespoons cayenne pepper

1/3 cup seasalt

1/4 cup black pepper

1/4 cup dried oregano

2 tablespoons dried thyme

1. Mix all ingredients.
2. Store in an airtight container.

BRONZE RUB

Our favorite on many things, low salt with a little spice.

1/2 cup of toasted and ground coriander seeds

1 tablespoon ground onion powder

3 tablespoons lemon pepper

1 tablespoon oregano, dried

1 teaspoon white pepper

1 teaspoon black pepper

1 teaspoon cayenne pepper

1 tablespoon salt

1. Mix together in a food processor.

CHILI POWDER MIX

We encourage you to customize this mix by using powders native to your area.

Equal parts:

Ancho chili powder

Chipotle chili powder

New Mexico chili powder

San Antonio chili powder

1. Mix all ingredients together.

ESPRESSO RUB

1/2 cup espresso coffee, ground fine

2 tablespoons sea salt

1 teaspoon ancho chili powder

1 teaspoon fresh ground black pepper

1. Combine all ingredients and mix well.
2. Rub the mixture on the meat 1 hour prior to smoking.

JERK SEASONING

No, jerk season is not the time of year when certain chefs get full of themselves. It's a highly potent, lip tingling rub for smoking or grilling.

1 cup sugar, granulated

1/4 cup garlic powder

4 tablespoons sea salt

1 tablespoon white pepper

1 teaspoon allspice

1 tablespoon dry mustard

1/4 cup onion powder

1/4 cup thyme, dried

1 tablespoon black pepper

1 tablespoon cayenne or 1 tablespoon habanero, ground

3 tablespoons curry

1/2 teaspoon clove, ground

1. Combine all ingredients.

SMOKE RUB

A little bit salty but goes great with anything smoked on the grill.

1 cup paprika

1/3 cup onion powder

1/8 teaspoon cayenne

1/2 teaspoon white pepper

2 teaspoons dark chili powder

3 tablespoons brown sugar

1/4 cup granulated garlic

1 teaspoon curry

1 teaspoon black pepper

1/4 cup kosher sea salt

1. Combine and use freely to coat meat.

Stocks

Most of our soups and sauces call for stocks. Technically a stock is a flavored liquid. If you use chicken bones to flavor that liquid, usually water, then you have chicken stock. If you use a rock, then you have stone stock, the base for stone soup.

Of course, you could substitute water for stock in these recipes, but in the end it would result in heartache. The use of stocks in cooking adds depth and intricacy to the taste. It is one of the layers of flavor. Try your next batch of rice with all chicken stock instead of water. You'll be thrilled at the depth of the flavor that is bestowed on the simple rice grain.

When we walk into the restaurant on Monday or Tuesday, when the chefs are making stock, we're immediately taken with the warm rich smells waltzing through the kitchen. It triggers the olfactory senses that fire up on Thanksgiving when the turkey stock is simmering away for giblet gravy.

Stocks may seem intimidating because you think you need to make the stock fresh before you start the recipe—not so! On a quarterly or semi annual basis, take time to make, reduce, and freeze your stocks. This way you'll always be ready to make some great food. You don't go to the mill when you need a cup of flour; you have it in your pantry. Think of stock in the same way.

If freezer space is limited, simmer more of the liquid/water out of the strained stock. You can easily make 1 gallon of stock into a 1/2 gallon and save the space. But we warn you, your stock will be so rich and intense you will never want to go back to the diluted kind. Guess what, you will be on your way to being a better cook.

If you are new to making stock, fear not. Just follow the steps, and you will do fine. Be sure to taste your stocks and refine your technique the next time around. If your brown veal stock isn't rich and brown, roast the bones longer next time. Chefs practice their craft, so keep practicing.

One more note: never salt your stocks. They're used as a flavor ingredient, and you may be required to reduce them (which in turn would make them saltier). Adjust your seasoning at the end of the process; that way you are fearlessly in control.

BROWN VEAL STOCK

Yields 1 gallon
1/2 cup vegetable oil
8 pounds veal bones, browned (we use lots of wild game bones, as well)
1 pound mirepoix, browned (50% chopped onion, 25% chopped celery, 25% chopped carrots)
6 ounces tomato paste
4 cloves garlic, whole
1 tablespoon whole black peppercorns
3 bay leaves
2 cups burgundy
6 quarts water

1. Preheat oven to 400 degrees.
2. Place bones in a single layer in a large preheated pan with 1/2 cup oil. Roast for 2 hours.
3. Add mirepoix and tomato paste in the last 20 minutes to caramelize.
4. Transfer all to stock pot and deglaze pan with burgundy.
5. Scrape fond (the brown bits stuck to the bottom) from roasting pan and add to stock pot.
6. Cover everything in stock pot with cold water and bring to a boil.
7. Reduce to a simmer.
8. Skim scum periodically.
9. Simmer six hours, adding more water to cover bones as needed.
10. Strain and refrigerate or cool liquid.

If you want deeper, richer stock, keep simmering, but do not reduce over 50% more.

POULTRY STOCK

Yields 1 gallon
8 pounds chicken or any game bird, bones and carcass
6 quarts water
1 pound mirepoix (50% chopped onion, 25% chopped carrot, 25% chopped celery)
12 black peppercorns
3 bay leaves
1 bunch parsley stems

1. Combine all ingredients in stock pot.
2. Bring to a boil and skim the scum.
3. Reduce to a simmer and cook for 3 hours.
4. Strain and refrigerate or freeze.

SEAFOOD STOCK

Seafood stock comes in handy for many recipes. You can use any inexpensive white fish scraps, bones, and trimmings (your seafood market or grocery store probably sells fish packaged for just this purpose). You can also use crab, shrimp, and lobster shells for adding flavor to seafood stocks.

4 to 5 pounds mild white fish (such as cod or halibut) bones and trimmings, and/or shellfish shells
2 tablespoons butter
2 large onions, chopped
4 or 5 garlic cloves, chopped
1 stalk celery
1 tablespoon lemon juice
1/2 cup chopped parsley
1 teaspoon whole black peppercorns
1 cup dry white wine (optional)
1 gallon of water

1. Melt butter in bottom of stock pot and sauté onion, garlic, and celery for about 5 minutes or until soft.
2. Add remaining ingredients and simmer for about an hour.
3. Periodically skim off foam that appears at the top of pot.
4. Cool and strain solid ingredients. Your stock is now ready for use or for the freezer.

LOBSTER STOCK

1 lobster body shell
1 large onion, roughly chopped
1 stalk celery, chopped
1 carrot, chopped
2 bay leaves
1 gallon water
1/2 cup tomato paste
1 cup white wine

1. Roast the lobster body shell in 400 degree oven, approximately 30 minutes, turning until a rough red brick color.
2. Add carrots, onion, celery, and tomato paste to the roasting pan and roast an additional 30 minutes.
3. Deglaze the pan with the white wine. This releases all the flavor nuggets from the pan.
4. Put the ingredients from the roasting pan into a large stock pot with water. Add the bay leaves and simmer 2 hours or until the stock has reduced by half of its volume.
5. Strain and reserve stock.

Grilling, Smoking and Holding Meats

Grilling has become the most popular method of cooking meat in America, both indoors and outdoors. This happens to be one of our specialties! Whether you choose to cook outside over a charcoal grill or to use a smoker and slow cook, we would like to share some of the lessons we have learned through our successes and mistakes....

GRILLING (aka Direct Cooking)

When direct cooking, the meat is grilled right over the hot coals. This is the preferred method for steaks, chops, and other small pieces of tender meat. It seals in the juices and gives the meat that light charred flavor, which excites the taste buds at the back of your mouth.

SMOKING (aka Indirect Cooking)

This is a popular way to cook meat in a covered barbecue and is ideal for large pieces that require longer cooking times, more than fifteen minutes or so. The meat is centered on the grill with a drip pan beneath, and the coals or wood are heaped up on either side of the pan. The meat actually roasts and takes on the aromas of smoke from the charcoal and from any hardwood added to the fire.

HERE'S HOW IT WORKS!

STEP 1: Place the wood chips in a small pile in the center of the smoker base.

STEP 2: Place drip tray on top of wood chips inside the smoker base. Spraying the tray with vegetable spray or placing a sheet of aluminum foil on it makes for an even easier cleanup.

STEP 3: Place the wire rack on top of the drip tray and arrange the food to be hot-smoked on the wire rack. Spraying the rack with vegetable spray makes for an easier cleanup.

STEP 4: Slide the lid closed and place the entire unit on the heat source. Medium heat settings generally yield the best results.

CAUTION — FLAT TOP STOVES: Before using the Cameron Stovetop Smoker on a flattop stove, refer to the manufacturer's instruction manual. Problems may occur if the cooking utensil is larger than the element(eye).

In many of our recipes we recommend that you use a stove top smoker. This is a more rapid smoking method. By smoking on the stovetop, you are allowed more time to concentrate on developing your culinary skills instead of tending the fire. We have sold hundreds of the stovetop smokers through our cooking school. Go to our Web sight, www.hudsonsonthebend. com, for more information on purchasing this smoker.

Tenderness and Temperature

Tenderness depends on the amount of work a particular muscle does. The areas along the back of the animal (the loin, ribs, and rump) don't get as much exercise as the neck, shoulders, brisket, and flanks. We almost always go with the loin! It isn't called "tender"loin for nothing.

If you visit a restaurant with an open kitchen, you'll see that as the cooks grill the meats, they seem to be touching them. This is not just an illusion. This is the secret to successful grilling. Touch your meat and know your meat, but do not cut into your meat to see if it is done. All meats have long protein strands, and as the meats cook the protein strands contract and become firmer. That makes the different textures, and at the same time that this is occurring the moisture that was in those protein strands exits the strands and moves around the meat as it is being cooked, so it is always important to let the meat rest before you slice into it. People who that have cooked with their mother remember her saying, "Let it rest before you cut in to it." There is actually scientific reasoning behind this statement. If you let the meat rest, the moisture will reenter into the protein strand and will relock into the strand. When you go to slice the meat all of that moisture remains in the meat and mouth and does not run out on the plate. Now you have a juicier piece of meat.

Face Testing Method

Experienced cooks punch the meat with their fingers to check the temperature and to know when it's ready to eat. Yes, it takes a little experience, but the secret is as plain as the nose on your face. Try this method of "face" testing as you cook your meats.

With a straight face (no smiling or you'll be overdone), touch your cheek—that will be "rare." The internal temperature of the steak will be between 110 degrees to 120 degrees and will have a cool red center. Still poker faced, touch your chin. This is "medium rare," with the internal temperature at 120 degrees to 130 degrees and a warm red center. Now touch the end of your nose. This will coincide with the texture of a "medium" steak, internal temperature of 140 degrees to 145 degrees with a hot pink center. The area just above the bridge of your nose on your forehead is the tactile equivalent to a "medium well" piece of meat—internal temperature of 155 degrees to 160 degrees with just a thin line of hot pinkness still left in the center. The bottom of your shoe is well done. The internal temperature is 180 degrees and there is no turning back. Visually there is no pink. However, even though a piece of meat is well done there should be some juices left. Remember, it is a well-done steak, not beef jerky. For the folks who don't want to use the face method, we recommend using a probe thermometer. If you are considering well done, stop and reconsider. Chefs all over the world would say that if you opt for well done, you should use this cookbook as fuel. But we are not going to say that! We understand that religion, politics, and meat temperature should not be discussed!

Hang Over Cooking

In telling temperatures, there is a thing called "carry over" cooking. Tom Perrini from Perrini Ranch in Buffalo Gap, Texas, coined this phrase. After you take your meat off the grill, the meat will continue to cook for another five minutes and another five degrees. Always remove the meat five degrees less than you want the finished meat to be.

Seasoning and Salting

Seasoning and salting prior to cooking your meat is always better. Contrary to popular belief, the meat will not dry out. It ain't beans.

Hudson's Best Kept Secret for Cooking Backstrap and Tenderloin

In my opinion, this cooking technique, when followed and practiced is worth the cost of this cookbook. If you enjoy your tenderloin medium rare, you will love this. We have used this method for groups of 2 to 400 with amazing results. It works well with both large beef tenders and with smaller leaner cuts like a back strap of venison, antelope, pork, or lamb. We have even used it on eighteen pound rib eye roasts. It works on virtually any cut of meat.

It all started with butter poached lobster from Thomas Keller's book and restaurant *The French Laundry*. In the process of explaining how to butter poach lobster, he mentions that it works well with smaller pieces of wild game as well. This was a game we were willing to try! We tried it and we liked it! With the help of Ron Brannon, one of our more creative chefs, we expanded on this technique.

To try this at home you will need only two extra pieces of equipment and you probably already have them: a small ice chest (the type that holds six to twelve canned drinks) and a meat probe thermometer.

To begin, you need to cook your loin or hunk of meat. You can slow grill it, roast it in the oven, smoke it in the stovetop smoker (see section on smoking), or smoke it in your favorite smoker. We always lean toward smoking because of the extra flavor dimension. Always season the outside of your meat very liberally with your favorite salt-based rub. We love the Espresso Rub in our Salt and Seasoning section. Choose the one that appeals to you.

When cooking your meat, the first hurdle is to learn not to cook your meat past rare or 125 degrees internal temperature. This is probably the most difficult step in this preparation. We are programmed to cook; I mean really cook that meat, but resist the urge. After achieving this perfect 125 degrees rare cut of meat a few times (using your meat thermometer), it will become second nature. Using a meat thermometer with a remote temperature gauge is helpful. We always check the meat during the cooking process in a hands-on method. It works well to pinch the meat between your thumb and forefinger and then pinch your cheek. They will have the same feel when the meat is approaching 125 degrees.

While your meat is smoking or cooking, warm two quarts of oil, or enough oil to fill your ice chest 1/3 way full. The oil temperature should be 140–145 degrees. Use your meat thermometer to ensure this.

As your meat is reaching its finished 125 degrees, pour your 140 degree oil into the ice chest. Place the meat in the oil and close the lid securely to avoid any heat loss. The meat will hold for three to four hours at a perfect medium rare (130 to 135 degrees internal temperature). As the meat lies in waiting, a couple of other things are occurring. The oil has a heavier viscosity than the juice in the meat. This ensures that none of the juice from the meat will escape. Hence, you will serve a juicier piece of meat. None of the oil will penetrate the meat, so it is not important to use expensive olive oil. You can use a common, inexpensive vegetable oil. There is also an enzyme reaction occurring when meat protein is held at 130 degrees. This reaction works to tenderize the meat! This may seem hard to believe, but you will have a juicer, tenderer piece of meat three hours later and the internal temperature will stay at 130–135 degrees medium rare.

You will need several layers of paper towels or cotton towels to absorb the oil from the meat prior to slicing.

You can now go on with the rest of your meal preparation.

We have done this in large thermal chests for hundreds of diners and had great results. This can take all the pressure off the cook when preparing for a large group. This also travels well as long as you have a tight-fitting lid.

Frying Secret—SHHHH

Fried vegetables are definitely a Southern phenomenon. Frying has gotten a bad rap by nutritionists, which is unfounded if the right methods and oils are used. To avoid the taboo term "fried," we call it deep sautéed.

If you get your oil up to 350 degrees and don't overcrowd the pan you will avoid the temperature dropping (325 degrees is too low). You will form a crust on the outside, and none of the oil will get absorbed into the food.

Come to find out, Gramma had a reason for saying, "Don't crowd the pan." Putting too much product in the pan causes the temperature of the oil to drop, and then the food sucks up the grease and you got a greasy meal. The same theory applies to every thing you "fry" (aka deep sauté).

An important part of successful frying is applying a proper breading in the correct manner. Please follow our standard breading procedure.

Standard Breading Procedure

1. In three similar sized pans, place
   a) 2 cups flour
   b) Egg wash (4 fresh eggs and 1 1/2 cups milk whisked together)
   c) Breading
2. Dredge the food item in the flour until well dusted.
3. Pat off excess flour.
4. Pass dusted food item through the egg wash, wetting the entire food item.
5. Place the food item in the breading mixture and cover.
6. Remove.
7. Set aside on a dry sheet pan or cookie sheet until all of the food items are breaded.

Good knives that hold a sharp edge are the most useful and important tool for any cook.

Jeff has run the gamut of countries and their knives from Germany to Switzerland to Japan. After traveling the world of knives, he has discovered that his love in the world of blades is Japanese knives—home of the Samurai: they know their stuff!

Historically, he has owned and enjoyed good German blades (.e. Henckels, Wusthof, and Forschne), using predominantly Forschner-Victornox (you know, the Swiss Army knife people) at the restaurant. They are fairly inexpensive but still hold a good edge. Knives in restaurant kitchens have always had a way of disappearing, so the goal in knife purchasing is to get the biggest bang for the buck. A professional knife sharpener makes a house call to the restaurant every two weeks to keep a well honed edge on the blades. We strongly recommend that you get your knives sharpened annually.

Several years ago, Jeff bought his first Japanese knife—a "Global" chef's knife. He fell in love with its razor sharpness and exceptional lightness. The stainless steel used in Global knives is harder than the steel used in traditional German cutlery, which gives Global knives a noticeably sharper edge and allows them to hold their edge longer than traditional forged cutlery. Their lightness, combined with their superb balance, makes them easy to control and a joy to use!

After collecting a dozen Globals, Jeff found Kyocera and Shun knives. These are both outstanding knives. The Kyocera is made from a space age ceramic and will hold an edge for the greatest length of time. The only draw back to the ceramic materials of these knives is if you drop them, they can crack. Shun knives have exceptionally sharp blades and are made of high carbon v-gold no.10 stainless steel: it's a very Zen metal in that it is hard but flexible at the same time. So it can be honed but rarely needs actual sharpening.

Go to www.japaneseknives.com where you will find a new world of knives. Be aware, some of these knives can cost up to $2,000 per and you run the risk of acquiring a costly new addiction!

Cooking School

"Noncooks think it's silly to invest two hours' work in two minutes' enjoyment; but if cooking is evanescent, so is the ballet." —Julia Child

Hudson's on the Bend cooking school was first held about ten years ago. Originally it was held at the restaurant in the kitchen on Sunday mornings. As with all things at Hudson's, we have changed at least three ingredients in this format and have one heck of a gig going. When serving the public in a restaurant, you must resign yourself to "you can't please all of the people all of the time," but this has not been the case at the cooking classes. To our knowledge, we have never had one person leave less than thoroughly entertained, somewhat educated, and sometimes a bit tipsy.

There have been benefits from these classes that we could not have imagined. Jeff and his staff of chefs brainstorm every three months and create three four-course menus that excite and entice the general public. These new recipes appear on the restaurant menu and are enthusiastically received. These classes fulfill our passion for creating and cooking and performing. It is hard to tell who is having the best time, the audience or the performing chefs!

We have a nucleus of regular students who come back time and again. Some are hunters who want to do something delicious and adventurous with their bounty. Others are already good cooks who want to expand their skills. And some come just to enjoy the camaraderie and good food. This has also become a very popular event for companies to use as an entertaining tool. Merrill Lynch, Vinson & Elkins, GlaxoWellcome, and JP Morgan are among a few of the companies that are regulars on our calendar.

When Jeff and Shanny built their new house they had their architect (Ryan Street, their oldest son) design a space for the cooking school, with both indoor and outdoor kitchens. Then the Caribbean-style pool entertainment area was added (always changing). When arriving at Jeff and Shanny's house, after you open the Old Mexico-style double doors you are greeted with an incredible view of glistening Lake Travis and Shanny's artistic touches all around the pool and patio. You know you are about to take a three hour vacation. Turn off your cell phones, grab a Prickly Pear Margarita from Oscar, and prepare to be wined and dined!

Gourmet Sauces

Our special line of sauces is gourmet sauces of restaurant quality. In fact, they appear on our world-renowned menu nightly. The sauces were designed to be added at the end of the cooking process, whether it is grilled, roasted, broiled, or smoked. We call them finishing sauces because, in most cases, they are not cooked or marinated with the food but are added just before serving to complement or finish the entrée. Here are a few serving ideas.

APPLE CIDER BRANDY

Warm and serve with any pork dish. Peel and dice fresh apple in the sauce just before topping a grilled pork chop or pork tenderloin—your guests think you've been cooking for hours. (Hide the bottle.) This one is also tasty with chicken, lamb, or turkey. It's great with roasted game birds, such as duck, dove, or quail.

BOURBON VANILLA PRALINE

This is our only dessert sauce. We serve it warm over cheesecake. It is also irresistible over ice cream, apple pie, waffles, brownies, and even holiday sweet potatoes.

CHAMPAGNE HERB VINEGAR

This vinegar is a blend of my favorite herbs and spices—sweet basil, lemon thyme, garlic, pink peppercorns, and a fresh hot pepper. It makes any salad dressing better and any recipe calling for vinegar more flavorful.

CHIPOTLE BBQ SAUCE

In this nontraditional barbeque sauce there are lots of garlic and onions with the chipotles to bring a hot, spicy barbeque to life. Enjoy this on all kinds of grilled or smoked meats or seafood.

GUAVA SOUR CHERRY

We serve this with grilled venison and other game dishes. It is also excellent with duck or ham. As with our other sauces, warm and serve atop any finished meat.

MADAGASCAR PEPPERCORN SAUCE

This is our red meat steak sauce. It has lots of garlic, shallots, and burgundy, along with the peppery green Madagascar peppercorn. Serve with any steak and instantly turn it into steak au poivre. This hearty sauce is fabulous with game. Just warm and serve with your entrée.

MANGO JALAPEÑO

Warm and serve with a grilled pork chop or tenderloin. It is excellent with lamb or chicken. After cooking your entrée, just warm and serve the Mango Jalapeño. We also serve it with egg rolls, or sate shrimp in the sauce. Try topping cream cheese and crackers with this chilled sauce. Garnish with fresh mangoes for that extra touch.

MEXICAN MARIGOLD MINT HONEY MUSTARD

This makes any sandwich a special treat—or mix with honey and vinegar for a honey mustard salad dressing. Serve warmed over spinach with bacon bits and chopped hard boiled egg for a tasty salad.

ORANGE GINGER BBQ SAUCE

Like the other barbeque, this is a nontraditional sauce that is both versatile and extremely flavorful. Use creatively on all meats and game birds.

STRAWBERRY/RASPBERRY SAUCE

We serve atop grilled pheasant with fresh berries sprinkled on top. There are lots of garlic, shallots, and chardonnay to give this sauce its special zing. This does wonders to baked, broiled, or grilled chicken, or to any game bird. Just warm and serve atop your favorite poultry—it's great with pork loins too.

TOMATILLO WHITE CHOCOLATE

We serve it warm over grilled, broiled, or baked fish and shrimp. It does wonders to grilled chicken, or use it to top off your favorite enchiladas or omelets. We like it chilled with tortilla chips. This is truly a versatile sauce—just use your imagination. Remember, it contains only a small amount of Belgium white chocolate. This is not a sweet sauce. Some call it mole.

**HUDSON'S ON THE BEND
GOURMET SAUCES**

1-800-996-7655

www.hudsonsonthebend.com

HUDSON'S FAVORITE 4 GIFT PACK

Tomatillo White Chocolate, Mango Jalapeño, Mexican Marigold Mint Mustard and Bourbon Vanilla Praline—all wrapped in an attractive wooden crate. An excellent idea for the gourmets in your life.

HUDSON'S GIFT PACK

Strawberry Raspberry, Chipotle BBQ, Mexican Marigold Mint Mustard and Mango Jalapeño, we recommend that you mix the Strawberry Raspberry and the Chipotle BBQ for an interesting BBQ!

ONE OF EVERYTHING

Apple Cider Brandy, Bourbon Vanilla Praline, Champagne Herb Vinegar, Chipotle BBQ, Guava Sour Cherry, Madagascar Peppercorn, Mango Jalapeño, Mexican Marigold Mint Honey Mustard, Orange Ginger BBQ, Strawberry/Raspberry, Tomatillo White Chocolate—a gift crate with every sauce we offer! This is the gift to give for the hard to shop for!

BBQ GIFT CRATE

Chipotle and Orange Ginger BBQ sauces packed in a wooden crate, perfect for gift giving.

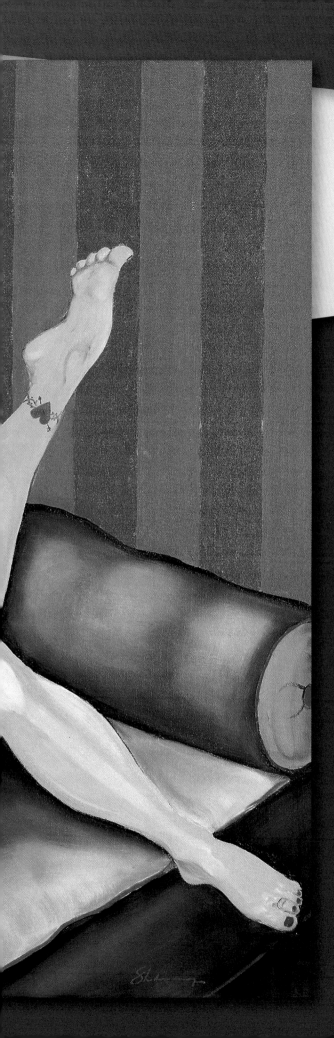

Appetizers

Buffalo Quail Riding Jalapeño Cheese Grits

Crisp Asparagus Wrapped in an Ancho Cured Salmon—Deep Sautéed in an Herb Crust atop an Ancho Ginger Aioli

Duck Pot Stickers with a Pair of Dipping Sauces

Hot and Crunchy Oysters on Sesame Crisps with a Mango Salsa and a Spicy Ancho Paint

Lobster Shooters aka Dirty Lobster Martinis

Mr. Pibb's Ribs with Sarsasparilla BBQ Sauce

Rain Forest and Tejano Ceviche

Seared Duck Liver atop Truffled Smashed Potatoes with a Red Onion Apple Jalapeño Marmalade

Smoked Duck Diablos

Succumb to the sauce and worry about laundry later.

Buffalo Quail
Riding Jalapeño
Cheese Grits

Serves 6

"Serve the dinner backward, do anything - but for goodness sake, do something weird." —Elsa Maxwell

All great recipes are born out of the love of food and a gnawing hunger. Every night at Hudson's on the Bend Restaurant, one of the cooks prepares a "family" meal. One crisp fall evening (wait, who are we kidding, we are in Austin, Texas), one warm and toasty fall evening, Becky Barsch Fisher was contemplating what to feed her Hudson's family. Becky had overheard Lisa yearning for chicken wings. Being the people pleaser that she is, Becky planned her meal accordingly. We never have chicken in the refrigerator at Hudson's, so Becky took the proverbial football and ran with it. She used smoked quail from the Diamond H Quail Farm* in Bandera Texas. Coincidentally, earlier that day she had made smoked tomato blue cheese grits as the veggie of the day. Shortly thereafter, the quail met the Cholula Hot Sauce; it saddled up and mounted the grits! Since then it has become one of the favorites at charity events. This was the birth of the Buffalo Quail!

*Without a doubt the fattest, plumpest quail in the world and you can mail order these quail @ www.texasgourmetquail.com.

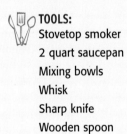 **VARIATIONS:** Dove, pheasant, or duck. Okay! If you must, you can go the chicken wing path. Cholula Hot Sauce is the hot sauce of choice in our kitchen. The Tabasco sauce of New Iberia, Louisiana works just fine.

TIMING: Grits can be pre-made, the same day please. Smoking should be done fresh!

TOOLS:
Stovetop smoker
2 quart saucepan
Mixing bowls
Whisk
Sharp knife
Wooden spoon

Smoked Tomato Bleu Cheese Grits

2 pints cherry tomatoes
6 slices bacon, 1/4" diced
1 small onion, 1/4" diced
1/4 cup garlic, minced
2 chipotle peppers en adobo sauce, 1/4" diced
6 cups whole milk
1 1/2 cups Quick Cook grits
1 cup bleu cheese, crumbled (the stronger the bleu cheese, the better)
1/2 cup Parmesan, grated
Salt and pepper (don't salt until the cheese has melted into the sauce, the cheese is salty)

1. Smoke tomatoes in your stovetop smoker for approximately 10 to 12 minutes. (Refer to your stovetop smoker page in the Grilling Section.) Reserve.
2. Cook the bacon in a heavy bottom sauce pot. Some folks drain the bacon.
3. When the bacon is crispy, add the onions, garlic, and chipotles.
4. Pour in the milk and bring to a simmer.
5. Add tomatoes.
6. Gradually pour in grits and stir well.
7. Reduce heat and stir occasionally.
8. Cook approximately 10 to 15 minutes, or until grits are no longer gritty.
9. Remove from heat and stir in the cheeses.
10. Adjust seasoning with salt and pepper.

 "How come ya'll don't serve cheese grits with thuh fish?" —Dixie Chicks

Cholula Buffalo Sauce

15-ounce bottle Cholula Hot Sauce (or your favorite hot sauce)
2 tablespoons rice wine vinegar
1 stick unsalted butter, diced 1/2" cubes
Salt and pepper

1. Combine all ingredients, except the butter, in a small saucepan.
2. Bring to a simmer.
3. Gradually incorporate half of the butter with a whisk, stirring continuously.
4. Remove from heat and whisk in the remaining half of the butter.
5. Sauce will emulsify and thicken with the butter.
6. Hold in a warm spot (120 degrees).

Smoked Quail

This should be done immediately prior to service.

Salt and pepper to taste
6 quail
1 each yellow, red and green bell pepper, 1/4" diced and held for garnish

1. Season 6 quail with salt and pepper.
2. Smoke in the stovetop smoker with your favorite wood chips. This week Jeff's favorite is apple wood chips, with cherry wood running a close second.
3. This process takes 12 to 15 minutes over high heat.*

*See our section on the stovetop smoker in the Grilling Section.

Assembly

1. Place an 8 ounce cup of grits on each plate.
2. Baptize or dip each quail in the Cholula Buffalo Sauce.
3. Mount it atop the grits.
4. Garnish with diced peppers.

Tart heat matched with cool bleu and creamy grits.

Crisp Asparagus Wrapped in an Ancho Cured Salmon

—Deep Sautéed in an Herb Crust Atop an Ancho Ginger Aioli

Serves 6

"You needn't tell me that a man who doesn't love salmon and asparagus and good wines has got a soul, or a stomach either. He's simply got the instinct for being unhappy."
—Anonymous

Fried vegetables are definitely a southern phenomenon. Frying has gotten a bad rap by nutritionists, which is unfounded if the right methods and oils are used. To avoid the taboo term fried, we call it deep sautéed. If you get your oil up to 350 degrees and don't overcrowd the pan, you will avoid the temperature dropping (325 degrees is too low). A crust will form on the outside and none of the oil will get absorbed into the food. Come to find out, Grama had a reason for saying "don't crowd the pan". Putting too much product in the pan causes the temperature of the oil to drop and then the chicken sucks up the grease and you got a greasy chicken. The same theory applies to everything you fry (aka deep sauté).

VARIATIONS: Substitute proscuitto, ham or bacon (bacon must be precooked) for salmon.

TIMING: The assembly and breading can be done 2 hours prior to cooking.

The ancho ginger aioli and salmon can be prepared 24 hours in advance.

GARNISH: Edible garden flowers, begonia buds pink and red sprinkled atop.

TOOLS:
2 -2 quart sauce pans
Mixing bowls
Whisks
Sharp knife
Food processor
Tongs
Tooth picks
Blender
3 – 9" casseroles for breading assembly
Squirt bottle
Cookie sheet

ANCHO GINGER AIOLI

6 anchos, seeded and soaked in 1/2 cup hot water
4 tablespoons pineapple juice
8 slices fresh ginger, coin size
1/4 cup brown sugar
4 shakes Tabasco
1 cup mayonnaise
Salt and pepper to taste

1. Drain chiles and reserve the liquid.
2. Puree the chiles with a little of the soaking water.
3. Add all other ingredients and puree until smooth.
4. Strain through wire sieve.
5. Store in a squirt bottle in the refrigerator.

ASPARAGUS

30 medium size asparagus spears, 5 per serving

1. Trim the woody ends off of the asparagus and cook in well salted boiling water for 2 minutes.
2. Shock the asparagus by plunging into ice water. This stops the cooking and sets the bright green color.
3. Drain and refrigerate.

ANCHO PUREE

6 ancho peppers, stems and seeds discarded

1. Soak the peppers in warm water for 30 minutes or more. Save the water.
2. Puree in a blender until smooth.
3. Use some of the soaking water to encourage the puree.

SALMON

2 to 3 pounds fresh salmon

1. Using fresh skinless salmon (we prefer Alaskan native king salmon) slice 30 thin strips of salmon (at least 6 inches long).
2. Rub the salmon with the ancho puree.
3. Refrigerate for 2 to 3 hours.

HERB PANKO CRUMB CRUST

4 tablespoons coriander seed (cilantro seed is one and the same)
4 tablespoons salt
2 tablespoons dried oregano
1 teaspoon cayenne pepper

New Age Vegetarian Song
"Peas would rule the planets, and love would clear the bars.
It was the dawning of the Age of Asparagus."

4 cups panko bread crumbs*
*Panko bread crumbs are Japanese bread crumbs. They can be found in the Asian aisle in your grocery store.

1. In a food processor, with the S-blade, process all ingredients, except the bread crumbs.
2. Add panko bread crumbs and pulse briefly.

DEEP SAUTEING ASPARAGUS/SALMON

2 quarts of canola oil

1. Heat 2 quarts of oil in a large, deep pan to 350 degrees
2. Wrap 1 salmon slice around a spear of asparagus. Secure with a toothpick. Repeat 30 times.
3. The standard breading procedure is flour to egg wash to herbed panko breading in three similar sized pans:
   a) 2 cups flour
   b) Egg wash (4 fresh eggs and 1 1/2 cups milk whisked together)
   c) Breading
4. Dredge the salmon wrapped asparagus in the flour, until well dusted.
5. Pat off excess flour.
6. Pass dusted asparagus through the egg wash, wetting the entire asparagus.
7. Place the asparagus in the breading mixture and cover.
8. Remove.
9. Set aside on a dry sheet pan or cookie sheet until all of the asparagus are breaded.
10. Deep sauté for 3 to 4 minutes or until golden brown.
11. Set on paper towel to drain.

ASSEMBLY

1. Place 5 asparagus on each plate in a bonfire formation.
2. Drizzle the asparagus with the ancho ginger aioli.

*Crunchy crust,
crisp asparagus,
paired with spicy, rich salmon*

Duck Pot Stickers with
a Pair of Dipping Sauces

Makes 25 stickers

"If it looks like a duck,
walks like a duck, talks
like a duck, it probably
needs a little more
time in the microwave."
—Lori Dowdy

Pot stickers can be a party in themselves. It takes a whole crew in an Asian kitchen to make them, therefore, it is recommended that you invite everyone over and get them involved in the chopping and mixing. The variations of pot stickers are endless! One of Jeff's favorite things to do is to go to the Asian market and peruse the aisles for things he has never tasted before,...the stranger the better. This recipe is more of a guideline. Use your own shopping excursion for your inspiration. The technique is the same regardless of what you choose to put in the pot stickers. The greatest thing about this kind of kitchen party is no one sits to eat; everyone eats the pot stickers as they are completed. A real picker's idea of a party!

"Cause I'm a picker
I'm a grinner
I'm a lover
And I'm a sinner
I play my music in the sun"
—Steve Miller Band

 VARIATIONS: Any protein can replace the duck.
Pot sticker wraps can be purchased in any grocery store.

 TIMING: Both sauces can be made a day in advance.
Pot stickers must be done no more than 6 hours prior, otherwise they will get gooey.

FILLING

2 cups Napa cabbage, minced
1 cup cilantro leaves, roughly chopped
1/2 pound skinless duck breast, 1/4" diced
2 tablespoons fresh ginger, minced
2 tablespoons garlic, minced
2 tablespoons soy sauce
2 tablespoons dark toasted sesame oil
1/2 cup soft goat cheese
1 1/2 tablespoons salt
2 limes, zest and juice
1 teaspoon red curry paste

1. Combine all of the above ingredients and mix well.
2. Hold in the refrigerator.

DOUGH FOR THE WRAPPERS

(The Asian grocer will have pot sticker wrappers that work perfectly,...really! So, if you don't have the time to make your own wrappers, go for it. It will not endanger the integrity of the dish.)

2 cups water
4 cups all-purpose flour
1 teaspoon salt

1. Combine flour and salt in a stainless bowl.
2. Bring water to a boil in a sauce pan.

GARNISH: None needed

TOOLS:
Sharp knife
Pasta machine
4 mixing bowls
Large Teflon skillet or wok
Large lid for skillet
Saucepan
Whisk
Food processor

3. Slowly whisk the boiling water into the flour and salt.
4. As a ball forms, dump the ball onto a floured surface and knead until it becomes smooth.
5. Return it to the bowl in ball form. Cover and let rest for 1 hour.
6. Roll into 1 inch logs and cut into 1/2 inch pieces.
7. Roll into flat 3 inch rounds, or using a pasta machine, run the dough through into 3 inch wide strips
8. Cut 25 - 3 inch rounds.

FILLING POT STICKERS

2 cups corn starch

1. Place 1/2 tablespoon of the filling into the center of the 3 inch round.
2. Fold the wrapper over.
3. Pinch the edges with your fingers. Keep your edges clean and clear of the filling to avoid the heartache of exploding pot stickers.
4. Dust the cookie sheet with corn starch. Place the pot stickers on the cookie sheet. Press each pot sticker gently to flatten the bottom. This will be the browned side. Dust the pot stickers with corn starch.
5. Place on the cookie sheet in the refrigerator, well wrapped in plastic. This can be done 6 hours prior to cooking.

Its like the 4th of July exploding in your mouth!

COOKING POT STICKERS

4 tablespoons peanut oil

1. Heat a 12 inch skillet or wok over high heat.
2. Add 3 to 4 tablespoons of peanut oil to the pan.
3. When it begins to shimmer (like a Texas blacktop highway in August), add the pot stickers—don't touch them for 4 minutes.
4. They should be brown on the bottom.
5. Add 1/2 cup water and cover immediately.
6. Let them steam for about 10 minutes. They should puff up—you may need to add a little more water. You don't want the pan to steam dry.
7. Pour off remaining water and return to high heat to re-crisp the bottoms. This takes approximately 3 minutes.
8. Serve hot with dipping sauce

SPICY LIME DIPPING SAUCE

1/2 cup lime juice, with the zest from the limes

1/2 cup fish sauce

1/2 cup hoisin sauce

1 tablespoon green curry sauce

1/2 cup ancho paste (see Salt and Season Section for paste recipe)

2 tablespoon rice wine vinegar

3/4 cup honey

1/2 cup cilantro leaves, chopped

1/4 cup garlic, minced

1. Mix all ingredients well and let stand for 1 hour before serving.

SPICY PEANUT SAUCE

2 tablespoons tamarind paste

1 tablespoon red curry paste (less for the wimpy)

2 tablespoons ginger, minced

2 tablespoons garlic, minced

2 tablespoons lemongrass, chopped (the lower tender part)

2 tablespoons peanut oil

3/4 cup shallots, minced

1 teaspoon turmeric

1 teaspoon cumin

1/2 cup cilantro, chopped

1/2 teaspoon black pepper

1 teaspoon cayenne pepper

1 1/2 cups unsweetened coconut milk

1/2 cup fish sauce

2 tablespoons soy sauce

1/4 cup brown sugar

1 1/2 cup unsalted and roasted peanuts, minced in food processor

1. In a food processor, add tamarind paste, red curry paste, lemongrass, and ginger and process until well mixed.
2. Add a little hot water if needed.
3. Set aside.
4. In a large skillet, heat peanut oil.
5. Sauté shallots until soft.
6. Add all of the other ingredients and bring to a simmer over medium heat.
7. Simmer for 5 minutes.
8. Adjust salt and heat levels and cool.

Hot and Crunchy Oysters
on Sesame Crisps
with a Mango Salsa and a Spicy Ancho Paint
Serves 4

"Do not meddle in the affairs of dragons for you are crunchy and good with salsa"
—unknown

Restaurant chefs are famous for stealing ideas...shhh! So many good ideas have come from stolen variations, and this recipe is no exception. Chefs with large egos, (yes it is true, there is a lot of artiste temperament and ego in kitchens all over the world), call recipe thievery menu research. Let it go on the record; we are giving credit to David Garrido of Jeffrey's Restaurant in Austin for this particular recipe. He has done a crispy oyster on a yucca chip at more food and wine festivals than he cares to remember. When a chef becomes enchanted with another's ideas, he usually likes to complicate the recipe so that it cannot be recognized as out and out thievery. We have convoluted his recipe to a satisfactorily unrecognizable "one of our own". This recipe also continues to affirm the idea that hot and crunchy is great on anything.

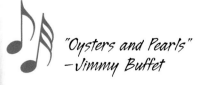

"Oysters and Pearls"
—Jimmy Buffet

 VARIATIONS: Hot and crunchy shrimp, snapper, avocado...anything you want to "hot & crunch".

TIMING: The mango salsa can be done 2 hours ahead of time. The spicy ancho paint can be done the day before. The hot and crunchy breading can be done the day before and stored in an air tight container. Make the crisps a couple of hours ahead.

GARNISH: Salsa is bright and colorful and does the job.

 TOOLS:
Cookie sheet
Mixing bowls
Sharp knife
Food processor
Whisks
3 quart pot for frying
3 – 9" casseroles for breading assembly
Spider (basket) for frying
Wire strainer
Squirt bottle
Airtight container

SESAME CRISPS
12 egg roll wrappers (frozen)
Dark sesame oil
Sesame seeds
Salt to taste

1. Preheat oven to 350 degrees.
2. Place the egg roll wrappers on a cookie sheet.
3. Dribble 4 to 5 drops of sesame oil on the wrappers and spread evenly with your fingers.
4. Dust with sesame seeds and salt.
5. Bake in oven 6 to 8 minutes or until light brown and crispy.
6. Cool and store in an airtight container to keep crisp.

MANGO SALSA
1 cup mango, 1/4" diced
1/2 cup pineapple, 1/4" diced
1/2 cup Granny Smith apple, 1/4" diced
1/4 cup red onion, minced
1/4 cup garlic, minced
1/4 cup red pepper, 1/4" diced
2 jalapeños, seeded and minced
1 bunch cilantro, roughly chopped
1/4 cup rice wine vinegar
1/4 cup lime juice
Salt

Mix all ingredients and refrigerate for 1 hour.

SPICY ANCHO PAINT
1 cup mayonnaise
1/2 cup ancho puree (see Salt & Seasoning Section)
3 cloves garlic
1/4 cup shallots
2 jalapeños
1/4 cup fresh lime juice
1/4 cup honey
Salt to taste

1. Place all of the above ingredients in the blender and puree until smooth.
2. Pass the paint through a wire strainer, making sure all lumps are removed.
3. Store in a squirt bottle and refrigerate.

HOT AND CRUNCHY MIX

1/4 cup almonds, sliced
1/4 cup sesame seeds
3 cups corn flakes
1/4 cup granulated white sugar
2 tablespoon red chili flakes
1 tablespoon salt
1 quart vegetable oil (reserve for frying)
4 eggs
1 1/2 cups milk
2 cups flour
12 oysters

1. Place all dry ingredients in a food processor and pulse until finely ground.
2. Set up standard breading station—flour, egg wash, breading—in three similar sized pans, place:
   a) 2 cups flour
   b) Egg wash (4 fresh eggs and 1 1/2 cups milk whisked together)
   c) Breading
3. Dredge the oyster in the flour, until well dusted.
4. Pat off excess flour.
5. Pass dusted oyster through the egg wash, wetting the entire oyster.
6. Place the oyster in the breading mixture and cover.
7. Remove.
8. Set aside on a dry sheet pan or cookie sheet until all of the oysters are breaded.
9. Heat oil to 350 degrees and fry oysters for 90 seconds.
10. Place oyster on a sesame crisp, top with the salsa, add a squirt of ancho paint and serve!

The crunchy experience of the spicy oyster paired against the sweet tropical fruit ...yummy fun!

Lobster Shooters
aka Dirty Lobster Martinis

Serves 10–12

"I like a cook who smiles out loud when he tastes his own work. Let God worry about your modesty; I want to see your enthusiasm."
—Robert Farrar Capon

Sometimes reliable becomes boring. After doing the same presentation at the March of Dimes Benefit for the past 4 years, Jeff and Robert wanted to shake it up. The March of Dimes Benefit is held in the most chic hotels in Austin; The Four Seasons and The Driskill have both hosted the affair. When inventing a new dish, chefs have to consider the elegance of the festival. Every year the event completely runs out of silverware. So Jeff and Robert's mission was to devise an elegant dish that required no silverware. While shopping for restaurant supplies, Jeff found some eye-catching martini glasses. Dirty Martinis, stirred—not shaken, was the end result. Everyone found this presentation unusual and delightful. This left the partygoers with one hand available for giving. The fundraiser was a success!

Develop a relationship with your fishmonger. He can save the lobster shell or crab shells, so you don't have to buy the whole lobster. Remember: A tip to your local fishmonger insures better products.

LOBSTER STOCK

1 lobster body shell
1 large onion, roughly chopped
1 stalk celery, chopped
1 carrot, chopped
2 bay leaves
1 gallon water
1/2 cup tomato paste
1 cup white wine

1. Roast the lobster body shell in 400 degree oven, approximately 30 minutes. Turning until a rough red brick color.
2. Add carrots, onion, celery, and tomato paste to the roasting pan 30 minutes after roasting begins. Roast for another 30 minutes.
3. Deglaze the pan with the white wine. This releases all the flavor nuggets from the pan.
4. Put all ingredients from the roasting pan into a large stock pot containing the gallon of water. Add the two bay leaves and simmer two hours or until the stock has reduced by half of its volume
5. Pour contents of the stock pot, including lobster shells, to a blender and puree. It will take several trips to the blender. Beware of steam expansion and potential explosion when blending.
6. Strain through a wire sieve and reserve stock.

SPICY LOBSTER BISQUE

12 ounces of cooked lobster for the final dish presentation.
12 ounces of peppered vodka
1 cup onion, chopped
1/2 cup carrot, chopped
1 cup red bell pepper, chopped
1 cup tomatoes, chopped
1 tablespoon garlic, minced
2 tablespoons chipotle peppers en adobo
1/2 cup tomato juice
1 cup white wine
1 cup heavy cream
Salt and pepper
Lobster stock

1. Sauté carrots, onions, peppers, garlic, tomatoes, and tomato juice in a heavy bottom sauce pot until browning begins.
2. Deglaze the pot with wine.
3. Add the stock.
4. Simmer approximately 50 to 60 minutes.
5. Puree in a blender until smooth.
6. Pass through a sieve or strainer.
7. Add the heavy cream.
8. Adjust salt levels.

ASSEMBLY

1. Pour spicy bisque into martini or shot glasses.
2. Add a shot of pepper vodka.
3. Garnish with diced lobster

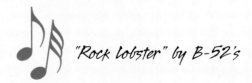

"Rock Lobster" by B-52's

VARIATIONS: Substitute shrimp shells or crab shells for lobster shells. Served in a large soup cup, this makes an entire soup course. Add enough lobster chunks and it makes an entire meal!

TIMING: The lobster stock and the bisque can be done up to 48 hours prior to serving.

GARNISH: Crème Fraiche and caviar with chopped chives. Serve in an exotic martini glass that is unusual and artistic

TOOLS:
Stock Pot or Roasting Pan – 2 gallon minimum
Strainer or wire sieve
Blender
Food processor
Sharp knife
Spoon
Tongs

The creamy richness of lobster bisque meets the peppery power of vodka!

Mr. Pibb's Ribs
with Sarsasparilla BBQ Sauce

Serves 10

 "Hot Smoke & Sassafras" by the Bubble Puppies

"In the days of the Old West, sarsaparilla was often said to cure everything except a gunshot wound." —Anonymous

Evolution in the kitchen never stops. In the spirit of Hudson's, we have added layer upon layer of changes to this recipe.

To tell the story of the conception of this recipe, we must first give you the family tree. In the beginning, there was Jay Moore, former chef of Hudson's. He went to school at the Culinary Institute of America. There he roomed with Jim Fisher. While at Hudson's, Jay hired Becky Barsch. Becky Barsch was introduced to Jim Fisher by Jay Moore. Becky Barsch became Becky Barsch-Fisher.

Out of this union was born the Coca-Cola Baby Back Ribs, a long-standing favorite on the menu at Hudson's on the Bend. We think this recipe was acquired through a little pillow talk in the Fisher house. Apparently, the love of a recipe trumps all loves.

Stephen Pyle handed down the knowledge of the hoya santas leaf and its many uses. It is an addition of biblical proportions! Then we took some twists and turns down the road of discovery and ended up with Mr. Pibb's Ribs with Sarsasparilla BBQ Sauce.

Here is a little known culinary fact that we are going to share, rhyming food is always tasty!

 VARIATIONS: Use St. Louis style ribs, you're still using pork ribs, they are just larger than the baby back ribs. They are commonly known as spare ribs. During the winter months in Austin, when hoya santas is not growing, we make this recipe without the leaves and it still has a wonderful root beer flavor.

 TIMING: BBQ sauce can be made in advance. It has a long shelf life. Marinate ribs 48 hours in advance.

GARNISH: hoya santas leaf

TOOLS:
Smoker or BBQ pit
Large Ziploc bag (1 gal)
Whisks
Sharp knife
2 quart saucepan

BABY BACK RIB MARINADE

4 quarts Mr. Pibb (or Dr. Pepper)
1 cup of hoya santas, minced
1/4 cup salt
3 cups dark, dark, dark brown sugar (use a little black strap molasses if you can't get real dark sugar)
3 to 4 racks of babyback pork ribs

1. Place all ingredients, except the ribs, in a large pot and simmer until the sugar and salt go into solution.
2. Cool mixture.
3. Submerge the ribs in the marinade and hold in refrigerator for 48 hours. (Extra large Ziploc bags work great.)
4. Salt the ribs and slow cook over low smoky embers until the ribs are tender and falling off the bone.

SARSASPARILLA BBQ SAUCE

1/4 cup garlic, minced
1/4 cup onion, minced
1 stick butter
1/4 cup fresh ginger, minced
2 cups root beer
1/2 cup hoya santas, minced
1/4 cup molasses
1/4 cup dark brown sugar
1 cup ketchup
1/4 cup Worcestershire sauce
1/4 cup lime juice
1/4 cup orange juice
2 teaspoons salt
2 tablespoons Tabasco sauce

1. Simmer the butter, garlic, and onion in a saucepan until they sweat.
2. Add the other ingredients and simmer for 30 minutes.
3. Serve with the slow cooked ribs.

The rich tender pork ribs are offset by the gooey sweet ginger lime BBQ sauce

Rain Forest
and Tejano Ceviche

6–8 servings

 VARIATIONS: The world of seafood is open to you. Use anything that is raw and fresh.

TIMING: The seafoods can be marinated no more than 2 hours prior to serving or they will over cook. All good ceviches are mixed at the last minute.

GARNISH: Rain forest pineapple & coconut or pepper curls

TOOLS:
Sharp knife
Bowls, stainless steel or glass
Juicer
Blender

Growing up in Texas, Jeff thought the only approach to ceviche was lime juice, tomatoes, jalapeños and cilantro. Then he saw the light. His first alien ceviche encounter was with the acquaintance of Gary Cartwright who introduced Jeff to Tejano Ceviche. This is a complicated and involved recipe!

Then Jeff found himself in Douglas Rodriguez's Ceviche Bar in New York City. Here you can get 20 different kinds of ceviche. Wow, this Texas boy had an eye opening culinary experience!

We have put two distinct kinds of ceviche recipes in this book that are as contrasting to each other as Texas is to New York City. One has a sweet coconut and spicy flavor and the other has a peppery sharp limyness to it. This is where the creative juices need to be released. After seeing 20 different kinds of ceviche, Jeff had the realization that almost anything goes!

"Rainforest Rain"
–Clarelynn Rose

RAIN FOREST CEVICHE

MARINADE

1 cup coconut milk (unsweetened if from a can)

2 tablespoons fresh ginger root

1 tablespoons scotch bonnet peppers or habanero peppers

1 cup Coco Lopez (found in the bar supply section at your grocer… used to make piña coladas)

1/4 cup fish sauce (found on the Asian aisle in your grocery store)

1/2 cup pineapple

3/4 cup lime juice, fresh

1. Place all ingredients in blender and purée until smooth.
2. Refrigerate.

SALAD/TOSSING STUFF

1/2 cup shaved coconut, toasted

1/2 cup pineapple, 1/4" diced

1/2 cup red onion, 1/4" diced

1/4 cup green onion, minced

1/2 cup cilantro, leaves chopped roughly

2 pounds top quality fresh tuna, 1/4" diced

1. In a large bowl, mix tuna or fresh seafood with marinade.
2. Add coconut shavings, pineapple, red onion, green onion, and cilantro.

3. Lightly toss and serve in your most outrageous martini glasses.
4. This ceviche is a raw tuna ceviche. You do *not* need to allow for marinade time in order for the lime juice to cook the tuna.

TEJANO CEVICHE

2 pounds shrimp, 21 to 25 per pound*

3 cups lime juice (use 1 1/2 cups to marinate and the remaining 1 1/2 cups to cook)

1/4 cup garlic, minced

1/2 cup red onion, minced

2 cups Roma/Mexican tomatoes, 1/4" diced

1 red bell pepper, 1/4" diced

2 bunches cilantro, mince leaf only

1 poblano pepper, 1/4" diced

4 jalapeños, seeded and minced

1/4 cup mixed chili powder**

1 1/2 cup Kalamatta olives, pitted and halved

1. Peel shrimp.
2. Marinate in 1 1/2 cups lime juice for 1 hour.
3. Drain and discard lime juice
4. Mix shrimp together will all other ingredients, cover and refrigerate for 2 hours before serving.

Damn near everything fresh from the ocean tastes sweet, fresh and mild.

A repeated theme in this book is stealing, borrowing, and what have you. This recipe is Gary Cartwright's recipe. Jeff had the fortune of meeting Gary Cartwright, a senior editor of *Texas Monthly Magazine*. They cooked together at the St. David's Foundation Cooking School Fundraiser. Gary used a combination of 4 different chili powders, Kalamatta olives, and items that had not seen ceviche before. It was a wonderful taste explosion, much like his writing and stories!

Our recommendation for this recipe is to let go of your previous parameters while shopping. Try combinations of seafood, veggies, fruits, and chili powders that are unexpected. Put your signature on this dish! This is the attitude that has kept Hudson's all fired up for the last 20 years!

♪♪ *"Down on the Riverbed"* —Los Lobos

*Shrimp is traditionally classified in the following sizes: U-10, 10-15, 16-20, 21-25. This indicates how many shrimp are packed per pound.

**CHILI POWDER MIX

(Equal parts)
Ancho chili powder
Chipotle chili powder
New Mexico chili powder
San Antonio chili powder

Upper scale or ethnic markets have the best selection of chili powders. We advise buying as many as possible and making your own custom blend. Just remember some are quite hot. Jalapeño and chipotle powders pack a wallop.

Seared Duck Liver atop
Truffled Smashed Potatoes
with a Red Onion Apple Jalapeño Marmalade

Serves 8 (with a few mashers left over for breakfast)

> *"Once a man next to me found the handle of a radiator in his mashed potato; he said nothing, merely moving it to the side of his plate after sucking the mashed potato off it first. Nobody else said anything either. If the truth was known several of us were probably jealous." —Tom Baker, on army food, in his autobiography*

"If it makes you happy It can't be that bad If it makes you happy Then why the hell are you so sad"
—Sheryl Crow

You may have noticed by the title of this recipe that we do not say foie gras. It is politically incorrect because the animal rights activists are concerned that the ducks and geese are being mistreated by overfeeding them, when in reality, if you visit any of the farms that raise the fowl during feeding time, you will never see happier ducks. The activists like to tell stories about funnel feeding and nails. If you haven't already heard their rantings, we are not going to be the ones to impart this morbid myth.

The ducks and geese run freely to the farmer with their jaws dropped in delighted anticipation of the rich feed they are treated to. The true fact of the matter is that the ducks and geese overfeed naturally at the end of every summer to enlarge their livers in anticipation of making the long flight to their winter home down south, and this is their energy source! We are saving them airfare, but, they do lose out on sky miles. That's where the injustice comes into play!

VARIATIONS: In the event that you have environmentally pc guests, omit the liver and the taters are sure to please!

TIMING: Marmalade can be made several weeks in advance. Keep well refrigerated of course. The foie gras must be seared at the last moment. The potatoes can be made several hours in advance as long as you keep them warm.

GARNISH: Foie gras is its own garnish. Maybe just toss an edible flower or chopped chives atop.

TOOLS:
Food mill or potato ricer
Sauce pan
Spoons
Mandolin or sharp knife
Skillet
Heavy wire whisk
Pastry bag

TRUFFLED SMASHED POTATOES

3 pounds peeled potatoes (russet Idaho bakers)
3 tablespoons white truffle oil
3 tablespoons black truffle pieces (fresh is best, frozen is okay, canned if you must)
1/3 pound butter at room temperature
1/2 cup heavy cream at room temperature
Salt and pepper

1. Boil potatoes until they are tender to the fork. Don't overcook—they will become watery.
2. Drain potatoes well.
3. Mash with a potato ricer.
4. Mix in the remaining ingredients.
5. Salt and pepper to taste.
6. Reserve in a warm spot.

SEARING THE LIVER

8–2 ounce portions of liver (16 ounces total)

1. While your skillet is heating over high heat, take the chilled liver and cut it into medallions.
2. Sear the liver in the dry pan for 60–90 seconds on each side, until a brown caramelized crust is formed on each side.

Earthy, rich, aromatic, sweet, and spicy all at once!

RED ONION APPLE JALAPEÑO MARMALADE

3 pounds red onions, julienned (Maui, Vidalia, or 10–15 onions are good as well)

3 tart Granny Smith apples, julienned (use a mandolin)

5 large jalapeños, seeded and julienned

1/2 cup mirin (sweet rice wine found in Asian markets)

1 cup apple juice concentrate (no water added)

2 cups white sugar

1 teaspoon salt to taste

2–3 tablespoons cornstarch and water, to thicken

1. In a large saucepan, add everything except the cornstarch and water.
2. Simmer for 20 minutes or until the liquid has been reduced by half.
3. Mix cornstarch and water into a slurry.
4. Add half the cornstarch slurry to the saucepan, stir and continue simmering.
5. If additional thickening is desired, add more cornstarch. (Note, when cool, it will be thicker.)
6. Adjust the salt and simmer approximately another 5 minutes.

ASSEMBLY

1. Put potatoes into a pastry bag with a star tip. This pastry bag is optional. You can build a mountain of spuds with spoons.
2. Place the foie gras on top of the mountain.
3. Top with marmalade.
4. Serve!

63

Smoked Duck Diablos

Makes 16 Diablos...how many will each guest eat?

"The only real stumbling block is fear of failure. In cooking you've got to have a what-the-hell attitude." —Julia Child (1912-2004)

This was created as a finger food for the Share Our Strength Benefit, which refills the food banks for the homeless in the Hill Country. The inspiration came from a Hill Country wild game finger food staple: dove and jalapeño wrapped in bacon. Hudson's, not being able to leave well enough alone, and always changing three ingredients, fired it up with fierier jalapeños, jicama, balsamic vinegar, and mission figs. We made it our own! We left the bacon as it was in the beginning. Now the bite sized hors d'oeurve has become more than a mouth full. When we are unable to locate mission figs, we often times sneak in the dark of the night out to the fig tree in our neighbor's yard and pluck the under appreciated morsels from their tree. You are welcome to come and join us!

"El Diablo"
—ZZ Top
...recommended volume, full blast!

 VARIATIONS: Smoked quail, pheasant, or dove. Faint of heart can use smoked chicken thighs. But, wait, you shouldn't even be reading this cookbook if you are not ready to get fired up. You can substitute the Hudson's Mango Jalapeño sauce for the Red Chile Glaze.

TIMING: Duck Diablos can be preassembled the morning of service and held in the refrigerator under plastic wrap. The sauce can be made 24 hours in advance.

RED CHILI GLAZE

1 cup champagne vinegar
1 to 1 1/2 tablespoons red chili flakes (if you like it hot, use 1 1/2 to 2 tablespoons of flakes)
1 tablespoon garlic, minced
2 tablespoons onions, minced
2 cups light brown sugar, packed
1/4 cup tomato paste
1/2 cup soy sauce
1 teaspoon salt
1 stick sweet butter, cut into 8 to 10 chunks

1. Simmer champagne vinegar, chili flakes, garlic, and onion in a heavy saucepan until reduced by half.
2. Add brown sugar, tomato paste, soy sauce, and salt and bring back to a simmer for 3 minutes.
3. Remove from heat and whisk in butter chunks.

Smoked Duck

3 duck breasts, skinless
4 dried figs (mission figs are our favorite)
1 small jicama
8 slices of smoked bacon (apple wood smoked is best)
4 jalapeños

GARNISH: Cut a jicama or potato in half to be used as a skewer holder.

TOOLS:
Stovetop smoker
Toothpicks or skewers
Apple wood chips
Saucepan
Cookie sheet or sheet tray
Mandolin or sharp knife

4 ounces balsamic vinegar
Red Chili Glaze
Salt and pepper

1. Quarter the figs from stem to nose.
2. Marinate figs in the balsamic vinegar for 1 hour or more.
3. Salt and pepper the duck breast and smoke in a stovetop smoker over high heat for 10 minutes. (Refer to the stovetop smoker information in the Grilling Section.)
4. Cool and slice the duck into 1/4 inch slices.
5. Quarter the jalapeños and remove the seeds. Leave the seeds if you like the fire.
6. Peel and cut the jicama into 16 French fry shapes. (A mandolin is helpful.)
7. Cut bacon strips in half and cook until halfway done or medium rare.
8. Place bacon strips flat on a cookie sheet. Stack a fig slice, jicama slice, jalapeño slice, and duck slice at one end of each piece of bacon. Roll and secure with a skewer. Repeat 15 times.
9. Bake in the oven for 15 to 20 minutes at 350 degrees.
10. Drizzle with Red Chili Glaze.
11. Serve!

A Texas firecracker with protein!

不 怕 的

Sometimes the things that are meant to be together are hiding at the back of your refrigerator.

Soups & Salads

Apricot and Butternut Squash Soup Spiked with Thai Green Curry Topped with a Tea-Smoked Lobster

Caesar Atun atop Hearts of Romaine with a Mango Vinaigrette With Parmesan Crisps

Coconut Curry Soup with Smoked Duck

Creamy Mussel Soup with a Spicy Jalapeño and Cilantro Pesto

Fire-Roasted Green Chile Corn and Cabrito Stew

Gewürztraminer Poached Pear with an Herbed Goat Cheese atop Arugula in a Sherry Vinaigrette

Hearts and Hearts Salad with Key Lime Vinaigrette

Hill Country Peach Salad with Spicy Candied Pecans, Pure Luck Dairy Goat Cheese and a Balsamic Apple Reduction

Hot and Crunchy Avocado atop a Mango Jalapeño Aioli with Ancho Paint

Iced Passion Fruit and Raspberry Soup Topped with a Rain Forest Ceviche

Apricot and Butternut
Squash Soup Spiked with
Thai Green Curry
Topped with a Tea-Smoked Lobster

Yields 8 bowls

 VARIATIONS: Smoked scallops or smoked shrimp or oysters

TIMING: Soup can be made the day before; the seafood should be smoked the day of.

 GARNISH: Julienned apples and lobster

 TOOLS:
4 quart saucepan
Blender
Smoker
Sharp knife
Mandolin

"Vegetables are a must on a diet. I suggest carrot cake, zucchini bread, pumpkin pie and butternut squash soup!"
—Jim Davis, Garfield

This soup screams "warm fuzzy". It is Hudson's Hill Country stand-in for chicken noodle soup. It has been a traditional offering on the Thanksgiving menu due to its wonderful fall flavors of the squash and the Granny Smith apples. But it actually originated in the Hudson's kitchen for the first Aids Services of Austin (ASA) dinner that we participated in. The initial recipe with julienned apples and seasoned, toasted pumpkin seeds has morphed to lobster medallions and claws, apricots, and spicy curry. This soup welcomes in the fall nights with friends and family by your side and a roaring fire! Acorn or other winter squash can be used in this recipe, but the butternut has the best meat to seed ratio. You'll find as you roast these winter squash that they'll brown on the pan side. As you're removing the meat from that side, taste it and see how naturally rich and sweet the squash is.

"Song for a Winter's Night" —Sarah Maclachlin

SQUASH SOUP

1 large butternut squash, roasted
2 cups dried apricots
5 Granny Smith apples, peeled and cored (4 for recipe, 1 for garnish)
3 cups rich poultry stock (refer to stock section)
1/4 teaspoon nutmeg
1/4 teaspoon cinnamon
1 tablespoon green curry Thai paste (this is very spicy)
1 cup heavy cream
Salt and pepper to taste

1. Cut the squash in half lengthwise, stem to blossom.
2. Roast with the cut side down at 375 degrees for approximately 1 hour or until the meat is tender to the fork.
3. Discard the seeds and skin.
4. Combine squash and all of the other remaining ingredients and simmer for 20 minutes over medium-high heat in a large saucepan.
5. Puree the hot soup in a blender. Caution: because of the steam, the blending will cause expansion and can overflow.
6. Return the soup to the saucepan and reheat over medium heat.
7. Adjust seasoning.

TEA-SMOKED LOBSTER

1 lobster tail and claws
4 envelopes orange pekoe tea for smoking in stovetop smoker (refer to stovetop smoker information in the Grilling Section)

1. Smoke the lobster tail and claws for 8 minutes, using the tea as smoke.
2. Let lobster cool enough to touch.
3. Cut lobster tail in 1/4" thick medallions. Reserve the claws for garnish.

ASSEMBLY

1. Pour hot soup in serving bowls.
2. Top soup with the lobster medallions or claws.
3. Lay julienned Granny Smith Apples atop lobster.

Sweet, tart, rich, smoky, just add a roaring fire!

不怕的

Ceasar Atun
atop Hearts of Romaine
with a Mango Vinaigrette with Parmesan Crisps

Serves 6

> *"Life is like a tin of sardines and we are all looking for the key"*
> —Allen Bennett

We would like to clarify the history of the Caesar salad, once and for all. The original version was created in 1924 by Caesar Cardini, an Italian restauranteur in Tijuana, Mexico. That's right, the salad is named after its creator, a chef, not Julius Caesar of the famed Roman Empire.

We can trace sushi's origin back to the 4th century BC in Southeast Asia. In the 1980's, in the wake of increased health consciousness, sushi, one of the healthiest meals around, has gotten much more attention. Consequently, we have witnessed the birth of sushi bars. Who would have guessed that some day we would evolve to eating raw fish, medium rare pork, or swimming immediately after that picnic? Never say never.

"I could be as happy as a sardine in a can long as I got my woman"
"Aw Heck"
—by John Prine

VARIATIONS: If rare tuna is not your thing, use smoked salmon.

TIMING: Smoke the tuna at least 4 hours ahead and refrigerate.

GARNISH: Parmesan crisps and herb flowers

TOOLS:
Cookie sheet with a silpat
Iron skillet
Blender
Zester
Sharp knife
Juicer
Saucepan
Mixing bowls

MANGO VINAIGRETTE

1 cup Hudson's on the Bend Mango Jalapeño Sauce
2 ounces sardines, canned is a-okay
1/2 cup rice wine vinegar
1/4 cup sesame oil
1/2 cup lime juice
1 teaspoon red curry paste
2 limes, zest
2 lemons, zest and juice
1/2 cup orange juice and zest
Salt and pepper to taste
1 mango, peeled, seeded, and diced (reserved for garnish)
1. Put all ingredients except the mango in a blender and puree.
2. Place in refrigerator to chill.

MANGO JALAPEÑO SAUCE

(Shortcut: purchase sauce online @ www.hudsonsonthebend.com)
1 pound mangoes, diced
1 1/2 cups granulated sugar
3 ounces champagne vinegar
2 tablespoons garlic, minced
3 tablespoons red onion, diced
4 jalapeños, seeded and sliced
1/2 teaspoon salt
1. Combine mangoes, sugar, vinegar, garlic and red onion in a saucepan. Bring to a boil.
2. Reduce to a simmer and cook 10 minutes.
3. Add jalapeños and salt.
4. Serve the sauce hot or cold.

BLACKENING SPICE

1 cup paprika
1 cup ancho powder
1/2 cup granulated onion powder
1/2 cup granulated garlic powder
1/4 cup white pepper, ground
1/3 cup salt
1/4 cup black pepper, ground
1/4 cup dried oregano
2 tablespoons dried thyme
1. Put all ingredients in a mixing bowl and blend well.

BLACKENING TUNA

1 1/2 pounds fresh Ahi tuna #1 grade

3 ounces oil, macadamia nut or
   grape seed

1. Cut the tuna into logs measuring
   2" x 2" x 2". You can ask your
   fish market to cut it for you upon
   purchasing.
2. Coat the tuna with Blackening Spice.
3. Turn on the vent hood.
4. Heat skillet on high heat.
5. Add 3 ounces oil. Use oil that has a
   high smoking point, such as grape
   seed or macadamia.
6. Sear the tuna 30 seconds on
   each side.
7. Refrigerate for at least 1 hour. Tuna
   should be served cold.

PARMESAN CRISPS

1 1/2 cups fresh parmesan cheese
1. Grate parmesan.
2. Place a Silpat* on a cookie sheet.
   *(a reusable non-stick baking sheet
   found at gourmet cooking stores or
   surletab.com)
3. Evenly spaced, place six 1/4 cup
   mounds of parmesan cheese on
   silpat.
4. Bake at 325 degrees for 20 minutes.
   The cheese will form pancakes.
5. Cool and store in an airtight
   container.

ASSEMBLY

6 heads of Romaine lettuce
1. Using 6 heads of Romaine lettuce,
   remove large outer leaves, exposing
   the 7" heart leaves. (Do not use the
   large leaves. Save for tomorrows
   sandwiches or salads.)
2. Separate the small heart leaves
   and toss in the Mango Vinaigrette
   dressing.
3. Place 5 to 7 leaves of lettuce on the
   serving plate. Fan them out.
4. Place 4 slices of tuna atop the
   lettuce. Fan them out.
5. Garnish with the parmesan crisps
   and diced mango.

This salad is a cool main course for a hot summer day!

Coconut Curry Soup
with Smoked Duck

Serves 10

> "Do you have a kinder friend in the food world than soup? Who comforts you when you are ill? Who stays with you when you are impoverished and stretches the dollar for you? Who warms you in the winter and cools you in the summer? Yet, who can impress your most demanding guests? You don't catch steak hanging around when you're poor and sick!" —Miss Manners

Malaysia is the motherland of the coconut palm, which now grows in parts of South America, India, Hawaii and throughout the Pacific Islands. Curry is a leaf from a plant native to southern Asia. Its flavor is essential in a substantial percentage of East Indian fare. Today's domestic ducks are all direct descendents of the three ducks and a drake brought from Peking on a clipper ship in 1873.

This recipe has taken flavors from a wide range of faraway, exotic countries. This too, is the Hudson's way. Exotic people have come and gone and have left their mark at Hudson's. Front of the house, we have seen the influences of Hawaii, Bolivia, England, India, and Switzerland. The heart of the restaurant, the kitchen, has been enhanced by visits, some longer than others, from folks from Germany, Mexico, West Texas, New York, and Italy. We are a hodge podge—with Texas deep in our hearts!

 VARIATIONS: Smoked quail or pheasant or for vegheads no bird at all.

 TIMING: Smoke the meat a day ahead of time, and you can prepare the soup that day as well.

GARNISH: toasted and shredded coconut on top.

TOOLS:
Large stock pot
Sharp knife
Smoker
Stovetop smoker

SMOKED DUCK

Salt and pepper
3 duck breasts

1. Remove the skin from the duck breasts, using a boning knife.
2. Salt and pepper the duck breasts well.
3. Smoke or grill the duck to a medium rare, internal temperature of 130 degrees. (We like to use the stovetop smoker.)
4. Set aside to cool.
5. Slice the breasts against the grain in 1" thick medallions.

COCONUT CURRY SOUP

1 quart duck or chicken stock (refer to Stock Section)
1/2 cup shallots, minced
1/4 cup garlic, minced
2 ribs celery, 1/4" diced
1 red bell pepper, 1/4" diced
1 poblano pepper, 1/4" diced
1 bunch cilantro, chopped roughly
1 cup coconut milk

2 cups Coco Lopez (found in the bar supply section at your grocery store...used to make Piña Coladas)
1 tablespoon green curry paste
1 tablespoon salt
2 tablespoons brown sugar
2 tablespoons fish sauce (found in the Asian aisle in your grocery store)
1/2 cup lime juice
1 cup toasted, shredded coconut (reserve for garnish)

1. In a large stock pot, add all the ingredients except for the Coco Lopez, coconut milk, and the cilantro. Let simmer for 30 minutes
2. Add the Coco Lopez, coconut milk, and the cilantro. Return to a simmer for 5 minutes.
3. Put the soup in soup bowls. Place the sliced duck breast in the soup.
4. Garnish with the toasted, shredded coconut. Serve!

"Gonna follow my nose to where the coconut grows"
—Widespread Panic

With all these exotic flavors your taste buds will be squirting!

Creamy Mussel Soup
with a Spicy Jalapeño and Cilantro Pesto

Serves 8–10

"Muscle, mussle, muesel... hmm...how would Dan Quayle spell this?" —Fanny Courington

This soup is a cleverly disguised health food.

The mussels are a rich source of omega-3 polyunsaturated fatty acids (PUFA's). They also provide naturally occurring glucosamine and chondroitin, which help keep joints supple and mobile.

Cilantro is a member of the carrot family and is also referred to as coriander. Cilantro has a very pungent odor and is widely used in Mexican, Caribbean, and Asian cooking. It aids in the secretion of gastric juices, and is therefore a valuable friend of the digestive system. The other reported health benefits are relief for painful joints, hangover remedy, fungicide (when mixed with violets), and lowers cholesterol. It can also be used as a heavy metal detox. I wonder if it helps after a wild night with Black Sabbath, Judas Priest, Motorhead, or Iron Maiden?

Are you wondering if this is the superhero of soups? Sounds too good to be true. We guarantee that it is too good!

VARIATIONS: Oysters can be used and if you don't like cilantro you probably should try a different book because cilantro pops up in a whole lot of our recipes. Cilantro seems to be a full out thing...you love it or you hate it. Please do not try to substitute the cream...no soy, no skim

TIMING: With any seafood soup, the fresher the better, but it reheats gently the second day and still tastes wonderful.

GARNISH: Whole leaf cilantro

TOOLS:
Blender
4 quart saucepan
Sharp knife

 "They're getting noisy in Boise
They're getting loud in Wainright
They're getting lost in Austin
They know who's boss in Boston
They go soul in the Hole
Down in Mussel Shoals
They know what it means
Down in New Orleans...."
"The Git Down Towns"
—John Boydston

CILANTRO PESTO

2 ounces pine nuts
2 to 3 jalapeños, seeded
6 cloves garlic
4 ounces olive oil
4 large bunches cilantro
2 tablespoons Parmesan cheese
Salt to taste

1. Combine jalapeños, pine nuts, garlic and oil in blender.
2. Puree.
3. Add cilantro and cheese and blend into a paste.
4. Add salt to taste.
5. Set aside until stew is assembled.

MUSSEL SOUP

2 quarts heavy cream
1 cup chardonnay
1/2 cup shallots, minced
4 dozen mussels, rinsed clean--shells and all
1/4 pounds butter
1/2 cup fresh lemon juice
Salt and cayenne pepper to taste
All of the Cilantro Pesto

1. In a large, heavy bottomed saucepan, reduce chardonnay wine until it is almost dry.
2. Add the butter and lightly sauté the shallots for 3 minutes.
3. Add the heavy cream and lemon juice and bring up to a simmer.
4. Add the mussels.
5. Bring back to a simmer and gently stir in all of the Cilantro Pesto.
6. Once it begins to simmer, adjust the salt and cayenne pepper levels to your liking.
7. Serve with the whole leaf cilantro garnish on top.

Hardcore!
Cilantro lover's
soup with 'head banging'
fusion of jalapeño!

不怕的

Fire-Roasted Green Chile
Corn and Cabrito Stew

Yields 10 to 12 Texas-sized bowls

 **VARIATIONS:** Game birds or chicken, if you must.

TIMING: Better the second day. If you are going to smoke your cabrito, this can be done several days in advance.

GARNISH: Diced confetti of a variety of colored peppers (green, yellow, red, orange). Juliennes of corn tortilla chips, grated jalapeño Jack cheese.

TOOLS:
Smoker
Large stock pot
Sharp knife
Boning knife

"Next to jazz music, there is nothing that lifts the spirit and strengthens the soul more than a good bowl of stew."
—Harry James

 "Keeps your belly and backbone from bumping"—Guy Clark (one of Texas finest song writers)

There are many ways to cook cabrito. In Old Mexico, the method is very similar to a Hawaiian pig roast. First you dig a pit about 3 feet deep, line the bottom with large rocks, and build a roaring bonfire in the pit. After that burns down (approximately 4 hours), clean out the ash and place the seasoned cabrito on the rocks. Cover the goat with leaves from the century plant, also known as the agave plant—the same one they make tequila from. Next, cover the cactus leaves with burlap and then cover that with more rocks and dirt. Then build another large fire on top. You might want to let your neighbors in on what you are doing, as it might appear like a pagan ritual of sorts. Now, go to sleep for at least 12 hours. We have found that if you are going to this much trouble to cook your cabrito, you should cook more than one. You can pull the meat off the bone and freeze it for other meals. The following morning, uncover your pit-roasted goat and pull the tender, juicy meat off of the bones and reserve for your soup. This method is not recommended for 21st century urban dwellers. If you are not comfortable digging a 3 foot pit in your landscaping, read on for alternatives.

In Monterrey, Mexico, they slow roast cabrito over coals, much like the famous BBQ at Coopers in Llano. Cabrito in Monterrey is like BBQ in Austin. Beware, you can stir up a fury of emotion when discussing "who cooks BBQ best and which method is choice"!

We have our own secret way. We place the goat (very well seasoned) on the second rack in our smokehouse. Next, we grind 5 pounds of bacon end and pieces and place the bacon on the screen racks above the cabrito and let the bacon fat drip slowly over the cabrito. Just remember to get a small cabrito, no more than 20 pounds. The mayor of Lajitas, Clay Henry, inspired this dish. You should all go to his beautiful home in the magnificent Big Bend country and look him up.

CABRITO STEW

1 yellow onion, 1/4" diced
2 ribs celery, chopped roughly
1 to 2 fresh jalapeños, sliced into wheels
3 tablespoons butter
1/2 gallon chicken stock (see our stock section, pg. 34)
1 cup green chiles, roasted, peeled, and seeded, (Hatch is preferable, Ortega is okay)
1 1/2 cups kernel corn (fresh is best)
16 ounces cream style corn
2 cups heavy cream
1 1/2 tablespoons brown sugar
2 teaspoons ground black pepper
3 teaspoons Tabasco sauce
2 tablespoons salt
1 pound cabrito, smoked
Crushed corn tortilla chips, grated jalapeño jack cheese, and diced peppers for garnish

1. Sauté onion, celery, and jalapeños in butter until the onions soften.
2. Add stock, chiles, and kernel corn. Bring to a simmer.
3. Add cream style corn, cream, sugar, pepper, and Tabasco and bring to a boil.
4. Add cooked cabrito and salt.
5. Garnish with fried julienned corn tortilla chips, grated jalapeño Jack cheese, cabrito, and diced pepper confetti.

The flavors from New Mexico, Old Mexico,
and Texas will warm your heart!

Gewürztraminer Poached Pear
with an Herbed Goat Cheese
atop Arugula in a Sherry Vinaigrette

Serves 8

"**G**ewurz" is the German word for spicy. It is a white wine grape that produces highly fragrant wines known for their crisp, spicy characteristics with aromas of rose petals, peaches, nutmeg, allspice, and sometimes tropical fruit. This is the drink of choice for all pears! Add a delicious Dripping Springs, Texas goat cheese on top of the perfect flavor of arugula. Now all we need is some aged sherry vinegar to finish this dish! True sherry vinegar is produced only in the Jerez region of Spain and is treasured by connoisseurs!

The balsamic vinegars have gotten all of the praise and attention from most chefs. The neglected sherry vinegar has been the red-headed step child in the kitchen. Sherry vinegar was originally produced by accident. Winemakers gave the fouled up sherry to their families and friends for cooking because they were ashamed to admit that some of their wines were unfit for sherry. We would like to take a stand and recognize the power of a mistake...hence the delicious sherry vinegar!

AGED SHERRY VINEGAR SHALLOT VINAIGRETTE

1/2 cup shallots, minced
1/2 cup extra virgin olive oil
1/2 cup aged sherry vinegar
1 cup light olive oil
Salt and pepper to taste

1. Combine shallots, salt, pepper, extra virgin olive oil, and aged sherry vinegar in a blender.
2. Add in the light olive oil in a thin stream as the blender is running.
3. Adjust seasonings.

POACHED PEARS

1 bottle Gewürztraminer wine
1 cup sugar
1 cinnamon stick
4 strips orange zest
4 firm Bosc pears, peeled, halved, and cored

1. Combine the Gewürztraminer, sugar, cinnamon, and orange zest in a 3-quart pot.
2. Bring to a gentle boil over medium heat, stirring until the sugar dissolves.
3. Drop in the pear halves, cut side down.

4. Cook until the pear halves are tender when pierced with a knife, turning once to cook evenly, about 15 to 20 minutes total (watch that they do not overcook, or they will fall apart).

HERBED GOAT CHEESE

16 ounces goat cheese
1 tablespoon garlic, minced
2 tablespoons herbs, minced (basil, thyme, and oregano)

1. Let goat cheese sit out at room temperature for 1 hour so that it will soften.
2. Blend the cheese, garlic and herbs together with a fork.

ASSEMBLY

8 handfuls of arugula

1. Toss arugula in vinaigrette.
2. Place the arugula on a serving plate.
3. Nestle 1/2 pear on the arugula.
4. Place goat cheese in a pastry bag with a star tip. Squeeze a dollop of the goat cheese in the indention of the pear.

"Sweet pear, sweet pear
Those who say they love you would never dare
I'll watch out for you
I'll always be there
In the hour of distress you need not fear"
Sweet Pear–Elvis Costello

VARIATIONS: Some people just hate arugula, so, a mixed garden green salad will be fine. The reason we picked arugula for this is because of the sharp bitterness that wakes up the taste buds at the back of your mouth where mixed greens do not do this.

 TIMING: The pears can be poached, goat cheese prepared and the vinaigrette can be made a day ahead of time.
Assembly must be done just before service.

TOOLS:

Pastry bag

Blender

Peeler

3 quart pot

Spicy pear with creamy herbed goat cheese and a sharp vinaigrette caboom!

不怕的

Hearts and Hearts Salad
with Key Lime Vinaigrette

Serves 4

"Some people ask the secret of our long marriage, we take time to go to a restaurant two times a week. A little candlelight dinner, soft music and dancing. She goes Tuesdays, I go Fridays." —Henny Youngman

*J*e t'aime (French), *ich liebe ddich* (German), *ti amo* (Italian), *te amo* (Spanish), *Hearts and Hearts Salad with Key Lime Vinaigrette* (Hudson's on the Bend). Those are a small sampling of the languages overheard on the most romantic night of the year at Hudson's on the Bend. They are all saying "I love you" on Valentine's Day.

Hudson's is known as the "Most Romantic" Restaurant in Austin. We have seen many, many happy couples leave sparkling with tears of joy and diamonds. (Note to the Fellas, we have a 99.9% success rate at Hudson's with proposals. In the past 20 years, we have only witnessed one refusal.) The pastry chef has buried carats in more ways than you can imagine. A nervous proposer is known to have the most unusual imagination! Ladies, if you are in love, find yourself at a romantic corner table at Hudson's with the man of your dreams, be careful with every bite you take. Be especially careful with the dessert!

"Cupid" —Jack Johnson

VARIATIONS: Canned or frozen artichokes and hearts of palm can be substituted if you can't get them fresh.

TIMING: Vinaigrette can be made the day before.

GARNISH: Fresh flowers; begonias go well due to the citrusy flavor.

TOOLS:
Blender
4 quart sauce pot
Sharp knife
Sauté pan 10 inch
Pastry bag

KEY LIME VINAIGRETTE

1/4 cup key lime juice
2 tablespoons honey
2 teaspoons garlic, minced
1/2 cup fresh basil
3/4 cup pistachio olive oil*
Salt and pepper to taste

1. Combine all ingredients except pistachio oil in blender.
2. Pulse to combine.
3. Slowly incorporate the oil while the blender is running.

*Note: Pistachio oil—place pistachios in sauté pan and season liberally with salt and pepper. Pour 3/4 cup of olive oil over the pistachios and toast over low to medium heat, approximately 5 to 7 minutes or until crunchy. Cool the oil and reserve for the vinaigrette. Chop the nuts for salad garnish.

SALAD

12 hearts of palm
4 artichoke hearts
3 cups mixed greens
6 ounces Boursin cheese
3/4 cup toasted pistachios, chopped (see above)
Key Lime Vinaigrette

1. To prepare fresh hearts of palm, place in a sauce pot with salted water.
2. Bring to a simmer and cook approximately 25 to 30 minutes.
3. Check for doneness. The hearts of palm should still retain some of their crispness. If additional time is needed, allow to steep in hot liquid.
4. After cooked, plunge into ice water to stop the cooking process.

5. If all hearts of palm are not needed, they may be stored in the cooled cooking liquid and refrigerated.

6. To cook whole artichokes and remove the hearts is a real labor of love. This is reserved for artichoke fanatics! There are good artichoke hearts in the frozen food section of better stores. The ones in cans taste like where they last came from. Okay, now we have our artichoke hearts. Let's continue with the recipe.

7. To stuff the hearts of palm, push out the centers and reserve. Stuff hollowed out hearts of palm with softened Boursin cheese. You can use a pastry bag for this step. (Homemade pastry bag can be made with a Ziploc bag by simply snipping a corner off.)

8. Slice the centers of the hearts of palm and save for salad. (Hearts of Palm in glass jars will be okay to use. Try not to use canned, because they will taste of tin.)

ASSEMBLY

1. Toss the mixed greens and sliced hearts of palm centers with the Key Lime Vinaigrette.

2. Place on a serving plate.

3. Top with artichoke hearts, hearts of palm, and chopped nuts.

The rich Boursin cheese and the crisp hearts of palm and artichokes are offset by the tart key lime vinaigrette

Hill Country Peach Salad
with Spicy Candied Pecans, Pure Luck Dairy Goat Cheese
and a Balsamic Apple Reduction

Serves 4

> "The ripest peach is
> the highest on the tree."
> —James Whitcomb Riley

Want to treat your out of state guests to a real taste of the Texas Hill Country? This recipe comes with lots of down home love, labor, and lore. First stop is the Annual Stonewall Peach Jamboree. Don't forget to pick up a basket of the famous Fredericksburg peaches from the farmers.

For your next ingredient, go to Dripping Springs to the Pure Luck Goat Farm. While shopping for your goat cheese, you will catch the scent of sweet peas and peppermint wafting on the prevailing southeasterly breeze. Their goats have a natural diet...no expense is spared. At the Pure Luck, the billy goats are kept separate from the does. As you have probably already guessed, this has resulted in a stress-free, milder cheese!

You have one last stop in Dripping Springs. The Navidad Pecan Farm has the best pecans in the Hill Country, (we think). While you are there, ask the folks, "Why are Texas native pecans so great?!?"

After a cold winter and a wet spring, you are guaranteed to be blown away by the flavors of this salad! Also, you can be proud, Hill Country proud, 'cause you have shopped locally!

VARIATIONS: For that generation, and you know who you are, poppy seed dressing can replace the balsamic reduction. Gorgonzola for those of you who like really strong cheese makes a great replacement for goat cheese. The toasted pecan recipe originally came from Becky Barsch Fisher's grandmother. The cayenne pepper was Jeff's addition to the recipe. If you are not fired up about hot pecans, leave out the cayenne pepper.

TIMING: Apple reduction can be made days in advance as can the toasted pecans.
Assembly must be done immediately before service.

GARNISH: The salad is so colorful, it requires nothing more.

TOOLS:
Silpat
Parchment paper
Baking sheet
Saucepan
Squirt bottle (see glossary)
Sharp knife
Whisk

"Fruits of My Labor"
—Lucinda Williams

BB FISCHER'S TOASTED PECANS

2 egg whites
1 1/2 cups powdered sugar
1 tablespoon Gran Marnier
2 tablespoons cayenne pepper
1/2 teaspoon salt
4 cups pecan halves

1. Whisk the egg whites until foamy.
2. Add the Gran Marnier and whisk again.
3. Add the salt, sugar, and cayenne pepper and whisk until the sugar is blended.
4. Mix in the pecans and spread on a cookie sheet topped with parchment paper.
5. Bake at 350 degrees for 15 minutes.
6. Remove and stir.
7. Return to the oven and bake 15 more minutes.
8. Remove and cool.

BALSAMIC REDUCTION

4 cups balsamic vinegar
1 tablespoon apple juice concentrate

1. Reduce balsamic to 1/2 cup.
2. Stir in 1 tablespoon of apple juice concentrate.
3. Transfer to squirt bottle and hold at room temperature.

ASSEMBLY

12 ounces goat cheese
4 tree ripened Hill Country peaches

1. Slice and remove the pit from the peaches.
2. Place sliced peaches in a pinwheel around the serving plate.
3. Place toasted pecans between the peaches.
4. Dollop goat cheese around the pinwheel.
5. Find your inner Jackson Pollock and drizzle the Balsamic Reduction on the peach salad.

The sweet juicy peaches, The spicy pecans, and The mellowness of goat cheese screams Austin summer.

不怕的

Hot and Crunchy Avocado
atop a Mango Jalapeño Aioli with Ancho Paint

Serves 8

> "An onion makes people cry, the avocado makes people laugh!"
> —Fanny Courington

 VARIATIONS: Anything that will stand still

TIMING: Breading can be done hours prior. Aioli can be made prior as well.

 GARNISH: Diced mangos.

 TOOLS:
Fryer
Blender
4 quart saucepan
Food processor
Squirt bottle
Sharp knife
3-9" casseroles for breading station
Sieve
Whisk

Austin City Limits Festival is held every September in Zilker Park and is not to be missed! If you've ever bought an album from Waterloo Records, listened to KGSR, watched Austin City Limits, or wanted to get a taste of the offerings from Hudson's on the Bend Restaurant, there's something out at Zilker Park for you at this yearly music festival. We have been in attendance since 2003, serving our version of gastronomic enchantment, the Hot and Crunchy Chicken Cones. This hot and crunchy thing we do to food is like potato chips, in fact in 2004 it was so popular, we sold 11,000 of them, but who's counting? The cones are always a resounding hit! We will be back next year with the chicken, but we are having pity on the veg heads and serving Hot and Crunchy Avocado Cones. Bet you can't just have one! Jeff will apply "hot and crunchy" to anything that will stand still. So, if you find yourself standing in line for a H&C cone, keep wiggling!

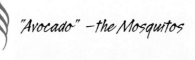

"Avocado" –the Mosquitos

HOT AND CRUNCHY AVOCADO

1/4 cup almonds
1/4 cup sesame seeds
2 cups corn flakes
1/4 cup granulated sugar
1 1/2 tablespoons red chili flakes
1 tablespoon salt
6 avocados, peeled, pitted, and quartered
1 quart vegetable oil for frying

1. Put all the above ingredients, except the avocado and cooking oil, in a food processor with an "S" blade and pulse lightly, until combined, making it coarse and not overly processed.
2. Set up standard breading procedure station—flour to egg wash to breading—in three similar sized pans, place:
   a) 2 cups flour
   b) Egg wash (4 fresh eggs and 1 1/2 cups milk whisked together)
   c) Hot and crunchy mixture
3. Dredge the avocado in the flour, until well dusted.
4. Pat off excess flour.
5. Pass dusted avocado through the egg wash, wetting the entire avocado.
6. Place the avocado in the hot and crunchy mixture and cover, lightly pressing the mixture on the avocado with the palm of your hand. Caution! Do not crush the avocado.
7. Remove and shake off excess.
8. Set aside on a dry sheet pan or cookie sheet until all of the avocados are breaded.
9. In a large, heavy sauté pan, heat 1 quart of vegetable oil to 350 degrees.
10. Lay the avocados in the hot oil and deep sauté for about 3 minutes. They will cook to a golden, crunchy brown if the pan is at the right temperature.
11. Place on a cookie sheet or pan in a 150 degree oven until you have completed this process for all of the avocados.

*MANGO JALAPEÑO SAUCE

(Shortcut: purchase sauce online @ www.cookingfearlessly.com)

1 pound mangoes, diced

1 1/2 cups granulated sugar

3 ounces champagne vinegar

2 tablespoons garlic, minced

3 tablespoons red onion, diced

4 jalapeños, seeded and sliced

1/2 teaspoon salt

1. Combine mangoes, sugar, vinegar, garlic, and red onion. Bring to a boil.
2. Reduce to a simmer and cook 10 minutes.
3. Add jalapeños and salt.
4. Refrigerate.

MANGO JALAPEÑO AIOLI

2 lemons

1 bunch cilantro

1/2 cup Hudson's Mango Jalapeño Sauce*

1 cup mayonnaise

2 cloves garlic

1 tablespoon salt and pepper

1. Combine all ingredients.

SPICY ANCHO PAINT

1 cup mayonnaise

1/2 cup ancho puree (see Salt & Seasoning section)

3 cloves garlic

1/4 cup shallots

2 jalapeños

1/4 cup lime juice

1/4 cup honey

Salt

1. Place all of the above ingredients in the blender and puree until smooth.
2. Pass the paint through a wire sieve, making sure all lumps are removed.
3. Store in a squirt bottle and refrigerate.

ASSEMBLY

1. Put 3 ounces of aioli on a serving plate.
2. Place 3 avocado quarters on top of the aioli.
3. Drizzle the ancho paint lightly and decoratively on the avocados.

Iced Passion Fruit and Raspberry Soup

Topped with a Rain Forest Ceviche

Serves 6

"Find something you're passionate about and keep tremendously interested in it." —Julia Child

 VARIATIONS: Add some rum and leave out the ceviche for an outstanding daiquiri. It looks great in martini glasses as a soup or a cocktail.

TIMING: Soup and ceviche should be made no earlier than the morning of the event. Make them at least 4 hours prior to be well chilled.

GARNISH: needs none, ceviche garnishes the colorful soup

TOOLS:
Blender
Strainer
Squirt bottle

We did this soup for Jeff and Shanny's son's wedding rehearsal dinner. We chose a very special dish for very, very special people; Ryan and Dinah Street. On that occasion, we served it in beautiful, flower-filled ice bowls. If you are interested in duplicating this, check for the directions in our first cookbook, *Cooking Fearlessly* (www. hudsonsonthebend.com). We think that the oversized martini glasses are a great presentation! The sweetness of the Chambord Liqueur and the raspberry fruit is offset by the tartness of the raspberry vinegar and the extreme tartness of the passion fruit. This soup will make you pucker...but, it's sweet too! The combination of the fruits and the ceviche will take you on a tropical vacation.

"Tarantula"
—Bob Schneider

ICY RASPBERRY CHAMBORD SOUP

7 pints raspberries
1/2 cup Chambord Liqueur
1/2 cup lemon juice
1 cup sugar
1/4 cup raspberry vinegar
Pinch of salt
1/4 cup heavy cream

1. Combine all ingredients in a blender and puree until smooth. Strain through a sieve to remove seeds.
2. Chill for 4 hours.
3. Prepare Rain Forest Ceviche (refer to ceviche recipe in Appetizer section of this book)

PASSION FRUIT SAUCE*

8 to 10 passion fruits
1/2 to 1 cup sugar

1. Cut fruit in half and strain through a sieve or wire strainer.
2. Push all of the liquid and moisture through, using a spoon or your hand.
3. Mix the liquid with sugar in a saucepan over low heat until sugar has mixed into the solution.

4. Pour into a squirt bottle and refrigerate.

*Or do what we do and go to www. perfectpuree.com

ASSEMBLY

1. Place Raspberry soup in a bowl.
2. Paint with Passion Fruit Sauce.
3. Top with Rain Forest Ceviche.

PASSION FRUIT DESIGN

1. It is best to have your soup and passion fruit well chilled before you paint. The Passion Fruit Sauce floats and paints better when chilled. This will prevent the colors from bleeding into each other.
2. Practice your designs before service. You can mix the passion fruit into the soup and start the art process over and over again until your artistry is perfected.
3. Put your chilled passion fruit mix in an old fashioned mustard squirt bottle with a tapered point.
4. Squirt out a zig zag or whirlpool design on top of the soup.
5. With a toothpick, pull the passion fruit sauce back and forth through the soup. Voila! You are an artiste!

Fresh seafood with clean crisp flavors atop the cool flavors of the luscious raspberry fruit for a hot summer night

Brunch & Holiday Feasts

American Bison Stuffed with a Blackened Turkey Tenderloin Served with a Peppered Cranberry Relish

Game and Wild Mushrooms Rolled in a Spicy Jalapeño Cilantro Crepe Topped with a Holy Mole Sauce

Holiday Hill Country Eggs with Smoked Wild Pig and a Basil Lime-Daise

Huevos Verde Broncos Topped with Rio Bravo Grapefruit Hollandaise

Malassadas with an Onolicious Sauce

Shrimp and Lobster in Saffron Crepes with a Brandied Lobster Sauce

Smoked Duck Potato Frittata

Tamale Cheese Pie with Smoked Quail Topped with Chipotle Mexican Crème

"When I choose between two evils, I always like to try the one I haven't tried before." —Mae West

American Bison Stuffed with a Blackened Turkey Tenderloin

Served with a Peppered Cranberry Relish

Serves 6

Paul Prudhomme has "Turduckin" (turkey-duck-chicken) as his holiday feast, which is a nice alternative to the traditional turkey. Paul's recipe requires the skills of a Samurai with a knife and approximately two day's time to prepare.

We think that the American bison stuffed with the American turkey really rings of Southwest Americana. It also takes less time and can be accomplished with your everyday run-of-the-mill knife skills.

The Peppered Cranberry Relish is served on all of our plates at Thanksgiving. It comes highly recommended as a salsa for fresh-shucked oysters. It also makes an exceptional spread for a leftover turkey sandwich! Heaven to Jeff is a leftover turkey sandwich spread with some cranberry relish atop a Laz-y Boy with a side of remote control for a Saturday filled with football.

"Go Your Own Way"
—the Cranberries

 VARIATIONS: Beef tenderloin if bison is not readily available

TIMING: Turkey tenderloin can be peppered, blackened, and stuffed into the bison early in the day. Relish can be made a couple of days in advance.

 GARNISH: the relish

 TOOLS:
Iron skillet
Grill
Boning knife
2 quart saucepan
Food processor
Sharp knife

BISON

1 bison tenderloin (8" long)
1 turkey tender
3 tablespoons vegetable oil
Blackening seasoning*
*We have a blackening spice recipe in our Salt & Seasoning section (pg. 33). There are several good ones on the spice aisle in your grocery store.

1. Preheat a cast iron skillet on high.
2. Coat the outside of the turkey tender with the blackening spice.
3. Turn on your vent hood.
4. Add oil to the skillet.
5. Blacken the turkey tender for 6 to 8 minutes, making sure it is cooked all the way through.
6. Refrigerate the turkey tender.
7. Using a boning knife, bore a hole in your bison tenderloin, from end to end.
8. Carefully and gently, enlarge the hole by pushing the boning knife toward the sides. Be careful not to cut open the sides.
9. Gently push the cooled and blackened turkey tender into the bison tenderloin. Enlarge the pocket if the turkey tender does not fit. Vegetable oil can be helpful.
10. Season the bison tenderloin with salt and pepper.

11. Grill the bison over an open fire. The hotter the fire, the better. This will take 4 to 5 minutes on each side. Remember, the turkey is cooked fully.
12. Remove from heat and let meat rest for 5 minutes before slicing.
13. Slice the tenderloin in 1/2 " wheels.

PEPPERED CRANBERRY RELISH

24 ounces fresh cranberries
1 cup lime juice, fresh
2 tablespoons shallots, roughly chopped
1 teaspoon salt
2 bunches cilantro
3 jalapeños, seeded (optional for you chili-heads)
3 cloves garlic
2 1/2 cups brown sugar

1. Combine all ingredients in a food processor and blend until well blended yet coarse. Avoid overpureeing. Texture makes a better relish!
2. Refrigerate.

ASSEMBLY

1. Spoon 3 ounces of cranberry relish on your plates.
2. Place 3 slices on the relish.

American Indians would approve of this one.

Game and Wild Mushrooms
Rolled in a Spicy Jalapeño Cilantro Crepe
Topped with a Holy Mole Sauce

Serves 8 to 10

*"What you see before you,
my friend, is the result of a
lifetime of chocolate."*
—Katherine Hepburn

Blas Gonzales brought the world's greatest mole recipes to Hudson's on the Bend from his mama's kitchen in San Luis Potosi. In Mexico, moles are made for celebrations. Therefore, we celebrated with Blas every day! Blas came to work at Hudson's on the Bend as a very young man: *como se dice en Ingles* "teenager". One beautiful bride, three healthy and smart children, and 15 years later Blas has moved on to the Ocotillo Restaurant in Lajitas as a grown man. With Blas's departure, we have lost our daily praise to the powers above for the beauty of life. Every day when we arrived at Hudson's, he would greet each and every one of us with a hug, and then he would raise his hands to the sky and say, "Thank you, my God". We realized that Blas had much to teach. The lesson that he shared with all of us is to appreciate the beautiful skies, the rainy days, the chilly days, the hot days of August, the friendships, the health we enjoy…in a nutshell, appreciate being ALIVE! Thank you, Blas, for being our daily reminder of how lucky we all are at Hudson's on the Bend. We refer to the mole sauces that we serve at Hudson's as "Blas's Holy Mole Sauce". We dearly miss our smiling saint! *"Buenos suerte a amado Blas! Vaya con dios!"*

 VARIATIONS: Any game such as wild boar, pheasant, or quail. Clean out the wild game freezer folks. Wild mushrooms can be substituted with domesticated and tamed mushrooms if you're afeard.

 TIMING: As with all crepes, these can be made a day in advance, but, don't pre-fill them because they will get gooey. Mole can be made several days in advance.

GARNISH: Sesame seeds

TOOLS:
Crepe pan
Blender
Sharp knife
Large sauté pan
2-2 qt saucepans
Parchment paper
Spatula
2 ounce ladle
Spice grinder
Food processor

WILD GAME CREPES

7 eggs
1 cup chicken stock
1 1/2 cups milk
1 1/2 cups flour
1/3 cup cornmeal
3 cloves garlic
2 teaspoons red onion, roughly chopped
2 jalapeños
1 bunch cilantro
1/2 teaspoon vegetable oil for crepe making
Salt and pepper to taste

1. Combine all ingredients except oil in blender.
2. Blend until smooth.
3. For best results, allow batter to rest 1 to 2 hours before making.
4. Heat 1/2 teaspoon of vegetable oil in 8" Teflon pan over medium heat.
5. Using a 2 ounce ladle, pour in one ladle of the crepe mixture.
6. Roll the mixture in the pan, evenly coating the bottom.
7. Loosen the crepe with a spatula and flip over to cook the opposite side.
8. Slide off onto a plate.
9. Layer each crepe with a piece of parchment paper.
10. Repeat until you have made 20 crepes.

WILD GAME FILLING

1/2 cup olive oil
1 1/2 pounds venison, 1/4" diced
1/2 pound rabbit tenderloin, 1/4" diced
1/2 red onion, 1/4" diced
4 garlic cloves, minced
2 red bell peppers, 1/4" diced
1/2 pound mushrooms, sliced
12 ounces spinach, trimmed and washed
2 quarts veal stock, reduced to 2 cups (see Stock Section for recipe, pg. 34)
2 ounces Lea & Perrins Worcestershire sauce
1/2 ounce Tabasco sauce
Brandy to taste, 3 ounces recommended
Salt and pepper to taste

> "I can change the world, with my own two hands. Make a better place, with my own two hands. Make a kinder place, with my own two hands." – Ben Harper

1. Heat olive oil until almost smoking in a 14" sauté pan.
2. Sear venison and rabbit in small batches.
3. Remove from pan and reserve on the side.
4. Pour off most of the oil. Discard all but 2 tablespoons of the oil.
5. Sauté onions, garlic, peppers and mushrooms until onions soften.
6. Deglaze with Lea & Perrins, brandy, and Tabasco sauce.
7. Add veal stock and simmer for 10 minutes or until the sauce thickens.
8. Add the spinach and wild game.
9. Simmer until the spinach has wilted.
10. Remove from the heat and cool.

HOLY MOLE SAUCE

1 cup celery, 1/4" diced

1/2 cup carrot, roughly chopped

1/2 cup yellow onion, roughly chopped

6 cloves garlic, minced

2 jalapeños, seeds and all, roughly chopped

1/2 cup olive oil

2 tablespoons Mexican oregano (regular will work)

1/2 cup chili powder (we prefer to use a blend of chipotle, ancho, and New Mexico chili powders www.mexgrocer.com)

1/2 cup ancho paste (see recipe in Salt and Seasoning Section, pg. 33)

1/2 cup tomato paste

1/4 cup ground cumin

1 cup almonds, sliced

1/2 cup sesame seeds

5 cups chicken stock (see Stock Section for recipe, pg. 34)

1/2 cup Worcestershire sauce

1/2 cup brown sugar

8 ounces dark semisweet chocolate, 1/4" diced

2 bunches cilantro, chopped roughly

2 teaspoons salt, al gusto (as you like it)

1. Toast sesame seeds in a dry skillet until lightly browned. Set aside to cool. Toast almonds the same way. Grind separately in spice grinder.
2. Mince celery finely by hand before adding to carrots, onions, garlic, and jalapeño in the food processor. Puree until well blended.
3. Sauté veggies in very hot olive oil until they begin to turn a light brown.
4. Add oregano, chili powder, ancho paste, tomato paste, cumin, almonds, and sesame seeds and cook over medium, high heat for another 10 to 12 minutes.
5. In a large saucepan, bring chicken stock, Worcestershire sauce, and brown sugar to a boil.
6. Add sautéed ingredients and simmer for 10 minutes.
7. Add cilantro and chocolate.
8. Remove from heat and stir until chocolate melts into the sauce.
9. Salt to taste.

Note: When reheating sauce, bring to a simmer (180 degrees). Do not boil.

ASSEMBLY

1. Place approximately 3 ounces (2 large tablespoons) of filling evenly across the center of the crepe.
2. Roll.
3. Fill all of the crepes.
4. Heat in oven until warm at 325 degrees for 7 to 8 minutes.
5. Place 2 crepes on each plate and top with 2 to 3 ounces of mole sauce.

Holiday Hill Country Eggs with Smoked Wild Pig and a Basil Lime-Daise

Serves 10

> "A gourmet who thinks of calories is like a tart, who looks at her watch."
> —James Beard
> (1903-1985)

This sounds and looks like Eggs Benedict with a German/Fredericksburg accent. It is! Jeff cooks this Hill Country version of Eggs Benedict every Christmas morning for his beloved family. It has become a favorite and guarantees that all of his relatives will show up on Christmas morning. In this day and age of blended families, off-spring usually have a litany of parents, step-parents, in-laws, and step-in-laws to visit during the holidays. Ryan, Kristen, and Andrew (the Blank and Lott children) have all grown up and acquired better halves (i.e. spouses). They each face the arduous journey of celebrating with all their families on Christmas Day, but all of their hosts understand that they will be saving their appetites for Jeff's house. Even though they are all nearing or have recently entered their third decade of life, they still hang eagerly onto the traditional dish. Or could it be that Santa still fills their stockings! Some things are never outgrown.

"Happy Xmas"
—John Lennon

VARIATIONS: Pork tenderloin or venison backstrap

TIMING: The pancakes are truly sturdy and can be done hours before final assembly.
The Unbreakable Hollandaise can be prepared 3 to 4 hours ahead of time and held in a thermal pitcher.

GARNISH: We always serve with a variety of fresh fruits.

TOOLS:
Blender
Stovetop smoker
Sharp knife
Box grater or grater attachment in food processor
Saucepan
Large skillet
Cookie sheet
2 ounce ladle

HILL COUNTRY POTATO PANCAKES

4 medium russet potatoes (approx. 1 1/2 quarts), scrubbed and grated with peel
1 1/2 cups smoked bacon, drained and minced
4 garlic cloves, minced
1 cup red onions, minced
1/4 cup flour
3 whole eggs
2 teaspoons salt, or to taste (potatoes really suck up the salt)
1/2 teaspoon cayenne pepper
1/4 cup vegetable oil for sauteing

1. Blend all of the ingredients together in a bowl with both hands. Squeeze out the liquid and shape into English-muffin-size pancakes.
2. In a large skillet, heat the vegetable oil and sauté potato pancakes over medium heat until golden brown and crunchy. This will take approximately 10 minutes on each side. Make 2 small potato cakes per person.
3. Set aside on a baking sheet.

UNBREAKABLE HOLLANDAISE

8 extra large egg yolks
2 tablespoons Hudson's Champagne Herb Vinegar
3 dashes Tabasco
Juice of 2 limes
1 teaspoon salt, or to taste
1 pound butter
1 cup basil leaves

1. Blend all ingredients, except for the butter and basil, for 3 to 4 minutes at high speed.
2. Heat butter to rolling boil.
3. Take boiling butter and very slowly add to the blender (still on high), using a ladle, 1 ounce at a time. Remember to add the butter very slowly or the heat from the butter will cook the eggs.
4. If it becomes too stiff and will not blend, add 1 to 2 tablespoons of water to thin.
5. Add basil and blend.
6. Store in a thermal pitcher.

POACHED EGG

1/2 cup white vinegar

20 eggs

We don't use fancy poachers. We use a large pot with 1/2 cup vinegar (white) to hold the eggs together while they are poaching.

1. Fill an 8 quart saucepan 2/3 full with water.
2. Add 1/2 cup of white vinegar.
3. Bring the water to a very light simmer and with a large slotted spoon, spin the water in a gentle "whirlpool" motion.
4. Crack the eggs and drop the raw egg into the swirling water.
5. Maintain this motion by gently stirring along the side of the pot.
6. After 4 minutes, your eggs should be poached in a teardrop shape.
7. Remove them from the water with a slotted spoon and begin assembly.

Note: Practice poaching one or two eggs if you have not done this technique before. If you are serving a large number of people, divide the final assembly into 2 or 3 shifts. Unless you are a pro at this procedure, poach no more than 8 eggs at a time.

SMOKED BOAR TENDERLOIN

Salt and pepper

2 wild boar tenderloins, approximately 16 ounces each

1. Season tenderloin with salt and pepper.
2. Smoke in stovetop smoker for 8 to 10 minutes. (Refer to our stovetop information in the Grilling Section, pg. 36)
3. Boar tenderloin will be medium rare after leaving the stovetop smoker but, it will finish cooking in the oven

ASSEMBLY

1. Place 1 to 2 pancakes per person on a baking sheet.
2. Cut the boar into 1/4" slices and place 2 to 3 slices on top of the pancakes.
3. Warm these in the oven at 375 degrees for 7 minutes.
4. Remove from the oven and place 2 potato cakes on each plate.
5. Place the poached eggs on top of the boar.
6. Using a large spoon, top the dish with the hollandaise.
7. Garnish with fresh fruit and serve.

This will start a culinary tradition at your house!

Huevos Verde Broncos
Topped with Rio Bravo Grapefruit Hollandaise

Serves 8

> "If you poach an egg while singing two verses and chorus of the hymn, 'Onward Christian Soldiers,' it will be cooked perfectly when you come to Amen." —Letter to the Editor, London's 'Daily Telegraph'

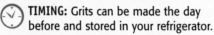

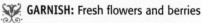

This is a traditional Deep South recipe taken to a whole new cuisine region by our chefs from San Luis Potosi. It starts out with a jalapeño cheese grit recipe made sturdy enough to look more like polenta than the classic Deep South breakfast starch. The grits are cut into circles and are about the size of an English muffin. Our wild game green chili is next, followed by a poached egg and topped with Rio Bravo Grapefruit Hollandaise. The green chili recipe is one folks will think you spent hours cooking. But, in reality, you didn't.

VARIATIONS: Variations of the hollandaise can go any direction. You can add basil, tomatoes, etc. Pork tenderloin or chicken can replace the wild game.

TIMING: Grits can be made the day before and stored in your refrigerator.

GARNISH: Fresh flowers and berries

TOOLS:
Blender
Poaching pan for eggs
Mandolin
Slotted spoon
Saucepan
Whisk
Skillet
Sharp knife
Thermal pitcher
12" x 12" casserole dish
Cookie cutter
Cookie sheet
Grill or smoker
Food processor

JALAPEÑO CHEESE GRITS

1 1/2 quarts water
1 stick butter
1 cup red onion, 1/4" diced
1/4 cup garlic, minced
1 cup heavy cream
2 jalapenos, minced (seeds removed if you can't take the heat)
1 yellow bell pepper, 1/4" diced
1 1/2 tablespoons salt
3 cups quick grits
8 eggs, beaten
8 ounces cheddar cheese, grated
8 ounces Monterey Jack cheese, grated

1. Bring water, butter, onion, garlic, cream, yellow peppers, jalapeños, and salt to a simmer.
2. Add the grits and, stirring constantly, cook at a simmer for 3 minutes until soft and creamy.
3. Set aside to cool.
4. Whisk in beaten eggs, cheddar cheese, and Monterey Jack cheese. Mix well.
5. Grease a casserole and dust with grits.
6. Pour in grit mixture and bake at 350 degrees for 30 to 35 minutes or until firm.
7. Remove and cool.
8. Cut into 3" circles, using a cookie cutter or a glass. You will get 16 grit cakes.

WILD GAME GREEN CHILI

2 pounds wild game (what's in your freezer?)
12 ounces of your favorite green salsa (we like to use Hudson's on the Bend Tomatillo White Chocolate Sauce for an extra flavorful option)

1. Grill or smoke any combination of game from boar to venison, elk to pheasant.
2. After you have grilled or smoked the meat, cut into thin julienne strips and mix with verde salsa or Tomatillo White Chocolate Sauce.
3. Simmer the green chili for 15 to 20 minutes on medium-low heat.
4. You may need to add a little water to thin before service.

con't on page 98.

"Some trails are happy ones, Others are blue. It's the way you ride the trail that counts, Here's a happy one for you." –Roy Rogers Show Theme Song

This will make them sing "Happy Trails"!

TOMATILLO WHITE CHOCOLATE SAUCE

(You can go to our website and order at www.hudsonsonthebend.com)

1/2 cup chicken stock
1 tablespoon garlic, minced
1 tablespoon red onion, 1/4" diced
2 cups tomatillos, husks removed and quartered
1 jalapeño, roughly chopped
1/4 cup almonds
2 tablespoons sesame seeds
2 limes, juice and zest
2/3 cup white chocolate chips
1/2 tablespoon cornstar ch
1 tablespoon water
1 1/2 bunches cilantro, leaves only
1/2 tablespoon salt and pepper blend

1. Separately toast almonds and sesame seeds in a dry skillet until lightly browned.
2. Puree stock, garlic, onion, tomatillos, jalapeño, almonds, sesame seeds, lime juice, and zest in a food processor.
3. Transfer to a sauce pot, and bring to a simmer over medium heat. Incorporate chocolate, stirring until smooth.
4. Combine cornstarch and water until smooth and stir into sauce. Bring to a boil and remove from heat.
5. Puree cilantro in blender with 1/2 the hot sauce. Careful now!
6. Return to pot and mix together.
7. Adjust seasoning with salt and pepper blend.

RIO BRAVO GRAPEFRUIT HOLLANDAISE

8 extra large egg yolks
2 tablespoons Hudson's on the Bend Herb Vinegar
3 dashes Tabasco sauce
1 1/2 lemons, juice only
1 teaspoon salt, or to taste
1 pound butter, melted
2 cups grapefruit meat at room temperature

1. Peel rind and white pith off of the grapefruit. With a paring knife, cut between each section of the grapefruit removing the meat of the grapefruit.
2. Blend all ingredients (except for the butter and grapefruit meat) for 3 to 4 minutes at high speed.
3. Heat the butter to a rolling boil.
4. Add the butter to the egg white mixture. The heat from the butter will cook the eggs, so it is important to add the butter to the blender 1 ounce at a time. After half the butter has been added, the remaining butter may be added quickly.
5. If the mixture becomes too stiff, add 1 to 2 tablespoons of warm water to thin.
6. Whisk in the grapefruit meat.
7. Hold in a thermal pitcher until service.

POACHED EGG

1/2 cup white vinegar
18 eggs
1 gallon of water
We don't use fancy poachers. We use a large pot of water with 1/2 cup white vinegar. The acid in the vinegar hydrolizes the proteins in the eggs, holding them together.

1. Fill an 8 quart saucepan 2/3 full with water.
2. Add 1/2 cup of white vinegar.
3. Bring the water to a very light boil and with a large slotted spoon, spin the water in a gentle "whirlpool" motion.
4. Crack the eggs and drop the raw egg into the swirling water.
5. Maintain this motion by gently stirring along the side of the pot.
6. After 4 minutes, your eggs should be poached in a teardrop shape.
7. Remove them from the water with a slotted spoon.
8. This should be the very last step in your recipe before assembling.

Note: Practice poaching one or two eggs if you have not done this technique before. If you are serving a large number of people, divide the final assembly into 2 or 3 shifts. Unless you are a pro at this procedure, poach no more than 8 eggs at a time.

ASSEMBLY:

1. Place two grit cakes on each plate.
2. Top with the meat and salsa mixture.
3. Place poached eggs on top.
4. Add Hollandaise as the final layer.

Malassadas with an Onolicious Sauce

"Blue Hawaii"
—Elvis Presley

Serves 10

> "Don't eat until you're full, eat until you're tired!"
> —Hawaiian luau saying

While Jeff and Shanny were staying with their dear friend, Roger Joseph, at his house in Hawaii, they were introduced to the Hawaiian version of Krispy Kreme donuts—Malassadas. Every morning Jeff would head to the gym to hit the treadmill. The gym was on the second floor, just above the bakery. As he was jogging upstairs, the morning shift would come in on the first floor to prepare the malassadas for breakfast. By the time Jeff finished his daily workout, he was completely overcome by the wafting malassada aroma. Guess where he went immediately after an invigorating six-miler? Jeff came back to the states with an added five pounds. He nearly gave up running as exercise, insisting that it only caused him to gain weight!

The onolicious sauce came from a nearby breakfast spot called Boots & Kemo, where they would top macadamia nut pancakes with a heart-stopping sauce that tasted liked a blend of cream and coconut milk. Jeff and Shanny returned to Texas with a serious addiction to both these new treats. Fortunately, they shared their new found love. So we are topping the beloved malassadas with the more beloved Onolicious sauce. This may taste like dessert—we like to call it Hawaiian KEMO-THERAPY. Aloha!

 VARIATIONS:
You shouldn't mess with the Hawaiian volcano gods.

TIMING:
Onolicious sauce can be made a day ahead.

GARNISH:
Passion flowers or other tropical flowers

TOOLS:
Large pot for frying
Mixing bowls
Whisk
Table top mixer
Dough hook
Cookie sheets
2 quart saucepan
Plastic wrap
Sieve

MALASSADAS

1/4 ounce active dry yeast
3 cups and 1 teaspoon sugar
1/4 cup warm water
8 eggs
1/2 stick soft butter
2 cups half & half
1/2 teaspoon salt
8 cups all-purpose flour
1 quart canola oil for frying
Sugar for topping

1. Mix the yeast, teaspoon of sugar, and warm water together to activate the yeast. If it's not foaming, buy new yeast.
2. Beat the eggs, sugar, and butter in an electric mixer, (using the wire whisk attachment), until it turns a pale yellow. This should take approximately 8 minutes.
3. Remove the wire whisk and attach the dough hook
4. While on low speed, add the yeast, half & half, and salt.
5. Add the flour gradually.
6. A soft ball will form and begin to climb the hook.
7. Place the dough into an oiled bowl (slippery sides allow the dough to rise) and cover with plastic wrap.
8. Place in a warm spot, draft free, for about 2 hours.
9. Roll out the dough on a flour dusted table until it is about 1/2" thick.
10. Cut into 2" squares.
11. Place the squares back on an oiled cookie sheet and let them rise again. This should take about an hour.
12. Heat your canola oil to 350 degrees.
13. Fry the squares until golden brown, approximately 2 minutes on each side.
14. Remove and roll them in sugar.
15. Top with Onolicious Sauce.

CRÈME ANGLAISE

15 egg yolks
16 ounces heavy cream
1 quart milk
2 vanilla beans, split
4 cups sugar

1. Place egg yolks into a mixing bowl and set aside.
2. Combine cream, milk, vanilla beans, and sugar in a large heavy bottomed pot.
3. Bring to a boil.
4. Slowly add hot mixture to egg yolks while whisking vigorously until you have added approximately 2/3 of the mixture to the yolks.
5. Return the egg yolk and cream mixture to the remaining mix in the original pot and cook until you see the first bubble break the surface.
6. Remove, strain through wire sieve, and cool.
7. Refrigerate.

ONOLICIOUS SAUCE

Crème Anglaise
Coco Lopez

1. Mix equal parts Crème Anglaise and Coco Lopez (found in the bar section at your grocery store).

ASSEMBLY

1. Place 3 ounces of Onolicious Sauce on the plate.
2. Set the Malassadas on top of the sauce and serve.

Shrimp and Lobster in Saffron Crepes

with a Brandied Lobster Sauce

Serves 8–10

 TOOLS:
Stock pot
2 Saucepans
Blender
Mixing bowl
8" Teflon skillet
Whisk
Sharp Knife
Small roasting pan or sheet pan for roasting lobster
Strainer
Parchment paper

 VARIATIONS: Any shellfish would taste great.

TIMING: Stock, sauce and filling can be prepared one day in advance. The crepes are best when made one hour before serving.

GARNISH: Chopped chives and garden flowers

"Hospitality is making your guests feel at home even if you wish they were." —unknown

This wonderfully rich seafood dish is just what the doctor ordered. As mentioned in our previous book, *Cooking Fearlessly*, "cooks are gypsies in white coats." We have had a chef travel through Hudson's kitchen and then go on to become a doctor. On the other end of the traveling spectrum, we have our executive chef; the former could have been Dr. Robert Rhoades. After initially pursuing a career in the science of the body, Robert transferred his cut-up talents to the science of the kitchen. He graduated in the number one spot from the CIA. From there, he was the executive chef at the famous Watergate Hotel. I think we have it on a tape somewhere...mum's the word. He then went to work at Mar's Restaurant in Austin. From there he worked at Jeffrey's Restaurant with David Garrido. Through his chef travels, he worked with Becky Barsch and Jim Fisher. Now if you refer to our family tree, you will see that Becky Barsch Fisher worked at Hudson's a couple of times as a line cook and then as the executive chef. When Becky decided to leave Hudson's, she was loving and kind enough to locate Robert to fill her shoes. Thanks "Earl the Girl"! You found a replacement with quite a bedside manner!

"Doctor, Doctor gimme the news" –Robert Palmer

FILLING

1/2 pound lobster, 1/2" diced
1/2 pound shrimp, 21-25 count, cut in half
2 lemons, juice only
1/4 cups shallots, 1/4" diced
2 cups shitake mushrooms, sliced
2 tablespoons garlic, minced
1 cup of lobster brandy sauce
1 cup dry Sauvignon Blanc wine
1/2 stick butter
1 tablespoon fresh basil and thyme, chopped and mixed
Salt and pepper to taste

1. In a medium sauté pan, reduce the cup of wine to about 1 tablespoon.
2. Add the butter.
3. Put the garlic, shallots and mushrooms in the pan. Cook until the shallots are tender.
4. When cooked to almost dry, add the lobster sauce, lemon juice, herbs and salt and pepper to taste.
5. Add the seafood and cook for 2 minutes.
6. Cool the mixture in the refrigerator, stirring often to cool evenly.

LOBSTER STOCK

1 lobster body shell
1 large onion, roughly chopped
1 stalk celery, chopped
1 carrot, chopped
2 bay leaves
1 gallon water
1/2 cup tomato paste
1 cup white wine

1. Roast the lobster body shell in 400 degree oven, approximately 30 minutes. Turning until a rough red brick color.
2. Add carrots, onion, celery, and tomato paste to the roasting pan. Roast another 30 minutes.
3. Deglaze the pan with the white wine. This releases all the flavor nuggets from the pan.
4. Add all ingredients to a large stock pot filled with a gallon of water. Add the bay leaves and simmer for two hours or until the stock has reduced by half of its volume
5. Pour contents of stock pot, including lobster shells to a blender and puree. It will take several trips to the blender. Beware of steam expansion and potential explosion when blending.
6. Strain through a wire sieve and reserve stock.

Rich flavors of the sea with delicate hints of saffron!

LOBSTER BRANDY SAUCE

(This is same as sauce used in Dirty Lobster Martinis, leftovers can be served as a bisque.)

1 cup onion, 1/4" diced

1/2 cup carrot, roughly chopped

1 cup red bell pepper, 1/4" diced

1 cup tomatoes, 1/4" diced

1 tablespoon garlic, minced

2 tablespoons chipotle en adobo sauce

1/2 cup tomato juice

1 cup white wine

1 cup heavy cream

4 cups lobster stock

Salt and pepper to taste

4 ounces quality brandy

1. Sauté all vegetables in heavy bottom sauce pot until soft and tender.
2. Deglaze with wine.
3. Add chipotles, tomato juice and lobster stock.
4. Simmer sauce approximately 30 to 40 minutes.
5. Pour into blender and puree until smooth.
6. Stir in brandy and heavy cream.

SAFFRON CREPES

1/2 teaspoon vegetable oil

7 eggs

2 1/2 cups milk

2 tablespoons shallots

3 cloves garlic

6 leaves fresh basil

1/2 teaspoon salt

1/2 teaspoon white pepper

1/2 teaspoon saffron threads, crushed

1. Combine all ingredients, except oil, in blender.
2. Blend until smooth.
3. For best results, allow batter to rest in the refrigerator for 1 to 2 hours before making crepes.
4. Heat 1/2 teaspoon of vegetable oil in 8" Teflon skillet over medium heat.
5. Using a 2 ounce ladle, pour in one ladle of crepe mixture.
6. Roll the mixture in the pan, evenly coating the bottom.
7. Loosen the crepe with a spatula and flip to cook opposite side.
8. Slide off onto a plate.
9. Layer each crepe with a piece of parchment paper.
10. Repeat until you have made enough crepes. You will need 2 per person. For this recipe, you would need 20 crepes.

ASSEMBLY

1. Put 2 to 3 ounces of the mixture on the center of the crepe.
2. Roll the crepes no more than an hour before heating. Heat for 5 to 7 minutes at 325 degrees.
3. Top with hot Lobster Brandy Sauce.

Smoked Duck
Potato Frittata

Serves 6–8

"What is my loftiest ambition, I've always wanted to throw an egg at an electric fan."
—Oliver Herford

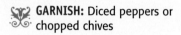

VARIATIONS: Leave the duck out for vegetarians…if there are no veg-heads in the vicinity, go ahead you and use smoked bacon or pork as a substitute for duck.

TIMING: The frittata is fairly sturdy and can be held for an hour before serving on a warm spot on the stove. We have also found that they re-heat in the microwave for a great snack.

GARNISH: Diced peppers or chopped chives

TOOLS:
12" sauté pan
Mandolin
Whisk
Stovetop smoker
Sharp knife
14" platter for service
Plastic wrap

When the holiday season has ended, after the last bit of turkey, goose, or duck has been eaten and the last crumbs of cookies and pies are cleaned up, our attention is often drawn to our expanding waistlines. Drive by the health club in December and the parking lot is empty, but by the first week in January you have to be a cousin of the doorman to get entry. Whether you make resolutions at New Year's or not, we all try to lighten up at this time of year. Those fresh, healthy veggies and fruits have not yet come to season. Enter the incredible edible egg, perhaps the most versatile ingredient in the kitchen. It is inexpensive, comes in its own neat package, keeps very well under refrigeration and is highly nutritious. The frittata is cousin to the omelet of France by way of ingredients, but the cooking method and final result are quite different. The result should be an airy, tender dish barely brown on the outside and just set on the inside.

SMOKED DUCK

3 duck breasts

1. Remove the skin from the duck breasts, using a boning knife.
2. Salt and pepper the duck breasts well.
3. Smoke or grill the duck to a medium rare, internal temperature of 130 degrees. (We like to use the stovetop smoker.)
4. Set aside to cool.
5. Dice into 1/4" cubes.

FRITTATA

3/4 cup olive oil
1 large yellow onion, 1/4" diced
1 large red bell pepper, 1/4" diced
8 large eggs
2 large Idaho potatoes, peeled and sliced into 1/4" rounds, (We recommend using a mandolin for slicing)
4 chipotle peppers en adobo sauce, minced
2 tablespoons salt and pepper mix
1 bunch cilantro, chopped
3 duck breasts, 1/4" diced

1. Heat oil in a 10" to 12" sauté pan until very hot. (Teflon pan makes this foolproof).

2. Add potato slices, one at a time, so that they brown evenly.
3. Season with salt and flip the potatoes over to brown the other side.
4. Remove potatoes from pan and set aside, leaving the oil in the pan.
5. Add the onion and red bell pepper to the pan and cook until tender over medium high heat, stirring occasionally.
6. As onions and peppers are cooking, beat the eggs in a bowl with the salt and pepper mixture, cilantro, duck, and chipotle peppers.
7. Add the egg mixture to the onions and peppers in the sauté pan and reduce to medium low heat.
8. As the eggs begin to firm, place the potatoes on the egg mixture in a shingle pattern to cover the eggs completely and evenly. The potatoes will perform as your pie crust when the frittata is inverted.
9. Place in 325 degree preheated oven for 20 minutes.
10. When firm, invert frittata on a plate and let sit for 5 minutes.
11. Slice in 8 wedges.

"Must a Not a Got a lot a"
—Joe Ely

MEXICAN CRÈME

1/2 cup ancho puree (see Salt & Seasoning Section, pg. 33)

2 cups heavy cream

1/2 cup buttermilk (active buttermilk, not ultrapasteurized buttermilk)

1. Mix the heavy cream and buttermilk together.
2. Let the mixture sit out overnight in a glass (nonreactive) bowl, covered with Saran Wrap. This is much like making yogurt.
3. Whisk in 1/2 cup ancho puree.

*Active buttermilk is sold in the dairy section as "buttermilk for baking". Modern dairies kill the bacteria in buttermilk. Bacteria is a must for most baking. With this active buttermilk, the French create a topping called crème fraische, Mexicans call it Mexican Crema.

ASSEMBLY

1. Place one serving of the frittata on plate.
2. Top with a dollop of Mexican Creme.

The incredible, edible egg!

Tamale Cheese Pie
with Double Smoked Quail

Topped with Chipotle Mexican Crème

Serves 6

> "Butter vs. Margarine?
> I trust cows over scientists."
> —Anonymous

Chef Jeff, Big Homey, Chief Jolly, Butter Boy, and Cheese Head are all names that Jeff will answer to! There is an accompanying story for each label. Sometimes he has to pinch himself to see if his life has been a dream.

One day in 1995ish, as a spokesperson for the Dairy Council, he found himself executing the Tamale Cheese Pie with Double-Smoked Quail Topped with Chipotle Mexican Crème in front of 500 of the finest women of the Junior League in Minnesota. "Somebody wake me up. All of my dreams have been fulfilled," he said.

Prior to that, he was a spokesperson for the Butter Council. This deemed him the title of Butter Boy. His friends and enemies had a deliciously malicious time with that one. But, being the ultimate Butter Boy, he rolled with it. In fact, he fell into the role so beautifully, he was quickly promoted to Head Cheese!

You may have already recognized this dish as a Mexican Quiche. We have never found the translation for "quiche" in Spanish. If you don't want to make the masa crust, then you can buy a store-bought crust. But, then you have gone gringo. Now, that's something Jeff has never been accused of!

 VARIATIONS: Use smoked tenderloin or duck breast, or, as we have learned, you can put anything in a quiche. If you add bacon, you have Quiche Lorraine.

TIMING: Always best when served fresh and eaten immediately, but we all have re-heated quiche in the microwave.

GARNISH: Salsa

 TOOLS:
9" pie tin
Box grater
Food processor
Whisk
Plastic wrap

"Voodoo Chile Fiddle Jam"
—String Cheese Incident

CRUST

1 cup masa (Maseca or Quaker Oat Brand)
2 tablespoons butter, cubed and cold
1 tablespoon chili powder (we always prefer a blend of ancho, chipotle, and New Mexico chili powders)
1 teaspoon salt
1 cup water

1. Mix the chili powder, masa, and salt.
2. Cut cold butter into masa with a fork or pulse in a food processor until the cold butter is pea size.
3. Add the water and blend until dough is formed.
4. Press into a 9" pie tin and bake for 15 minutes at 325 degrees. (just like prebaking pie crust).
5. Set aside to cool.

FILLING

1/2 cup jalapeño Jack cheese, grated
1/2 cup cheddar cheese, grated
1 cup red onion, 1/4" diced
1 tablespoon garlic, minced
1 poblano pepper, 1/4" diced
2 tablespoons chili powder mix
4 eggs
1 cup heavy cream
2 smoked quail, 1/4" diced (approximately 8 ounces)
1 1/2 teaspoons salt

1. Whisk heavy cream and eggs together.
2. Add garlic, onion, pepper, quail, chili powder, and salt to egg mix.
3. Sprinkle cheese into tamale shell.
4. Pour egg mixture into the tamale shell.
5. Bake for 50 minutes at 350 degrees.
6. Let the pie rest 10 minutes before serving.

*CHILI POWDER MIX

Equal parts
Ancho chili powder
Chipotle chili powder
New Mexico chili powder
San Antonio chili powder

Upscale or ethnic markets have the best selection of chili powders. We advise buying as many as possible and making your own custom blend. Just remember some are quite hot. Jalapeño and chipotle powders pack a wallop.

MEXICAN CRÈME

1/2 cup ancho puree (see Salt & Seasoning Section, pg. 33)

2 cups heavy cream

1/2 cup buttermilk (active buttermilk, not ultrapasteurized buttermilk*)

1. Mix the heavy cream and buttermilk together.
2. Let the mixture sit out overnight in a glass (nonreactive) bowl covered with Saran Wrap. This is much like making yogurt.
3. Mix in ancho puree.
4. Dollop on pie.

*Active buttermilk is sold in the dairy section as "buttermilk for baking". Modern dairies kill the bacteria in buttermilk. Bacteria is a must for most baking. With this active buttermilk, the French create a topping called crème fraische, Mexicans call it Mexican Creme.

Smoky, rustic, South of the Border brunch.

105

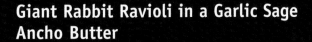

Meats

Giant Rabbit Ravioli in a Garlic Sage
Ancho Butter

Chicken Fried Antelope with a Red Eye Gravy

Chuy's Hill Country Surf 'n Turf

Dos Gringos Tamales with Strawberry
Raspberry Sauce

Espresso Rubbed Venison Backstrap with
Jumbo Lump Crab in Chipotle Bock Beer
Blanc Butter

Grilled Achiote Marinated Pork Chops Topped
with a Watermelon Rind Chutney

Grilled Duck Breast Shingled with Seared
Scallops in a Cranberry Chipotle Port Sauce

Texas Hill Country Wild Game Paella

Wild Lolli-Chop Salad atop a Macadamia
Lemon Honey Dressing

*We love
animals,
they're
delicious.*

Giant Rabbit Ravioli
in a Garlic Sage Ancho Butter

 "Lucky One"
—Allison Krauss

Serves 8–10

> *"My mother's menu consisted of two choices: Take it or leave it."*
> *—Buddy Hackett, comedian*

"Location, location, location" is the supposed secret for success in the restaurant business. Hudson's has been blessed with much success. But if you have ever driven out to Lake Travis down RR620, you know that this success does not support the "location" law of success. We are considered a destination.

Jeff (nicknamed Lucky Boy by many), has always been very blessed with pure dee luck! One very lucky day, Becky Barsch Fisher, nicknamed Earl the Girl because she was the lonely, only female in a male dominated kitchen, walked into Hudson's seeking employment. She was the sunshine for many years in the kitchen at Hudson's on the Bend.

As you can probably tell from the many "Earl" stories in this book, she left her footprints on our hearts when she left. She also left one of hers' and our favorite dishes with us, the wabbit wavioli. This dish is one that will impress your family and guests, with the "made from scratch" pasta. It is simple, yet, impressive and sooo delicious.

We recommend this one for a cool weather dinner. You will leave your pawprints on their hearts!

VARIATIONS: Pheasant or duck raviolis would be just ducky. Okay, even chicken for the less wild.

TIMING: Raviolis can be made prior to the day of serving, but they must be sprinkled liberally with cornstarch, well wrapped, and frozen.

GARNISH: Gingersnap cookie crumbs.

TOOLS:
Pasta machine
Food processor
4 Mixing bowls
Sharp knife
Cheese grater
Large sauté pan
Whisk
Thermal pitcher
Strainer
Slotted spoon

PASTA

3 1/2 cups durum flour
3 eggs
1/2 cup chicken stock
1 teaspoon olive oil
1/4 cup assorted fresh herbs (thyme, chives, basil, mint, etc.), minced

1. Place the flour in a large bowl and make a well in the center of the flour. (Think of making a swimming pool for the egg mixture.)
2. In another bowl, combine eggs, herbs, stock, and oil. Mix well.
3. Pour this mixture into the center of the flour well.
4. Working in a circular motion, gradually incorporate flour into the wet mix.
5. Knead dough approximately 5 minutes or until the dough is glossy, smooth, and elastic.
6. Allow the dough to rest at least half an hour before rolling.
7. The dough can also be refrigerated at this point. It can be refrigerated for 1 week. Obviously, this can be done days in advance. FYI, you can also buy sheets of pasta at the better grocery stores.

FILLING

2 pounds rabbit meat, diced 1/2" cubes
1 onion, roughly chopped
1/4 cup bacon
1 cup crimini mushrooms, chopped roughly
1 tablespoon garlic, minced
1 teaspoon black pepper
1 tablespoon salt
1 tablespoon balsamic vinegar
1 tablespoon red wine
3 tablespoons whole grain mustard (we prefer to use Hudson's on the Bend Mexican Marigold Mustard for extra flavors)
1 cup Parmesan cheese, grated

1. Mix rabbit, onion, bacon, mushrooms, garlic, salt, and black pepper in food processor.
2. All ingredients should be well chopped.
3. Put ingredients in a large sauté pan and cook until meat is done.
4. After meat is done, add vinegar and wine.
5. Heat and simmer approximately 5 minutes, or until almost all of the liquid is reduced.
6. Remove from heat and allow to cool.
7. Add mustard and cheese and combine well.
8. Allow filling to cool before making ravioli.

RAVIOLI

You can hand roll your pasta with a rolling pin or use a machine. We prefer the speed and consistency of the hand crank machines. These machines can be found at most culinary shops. The following instructions apply to the hand cranking machine.

1. With the pasta machine on the medium setting, begin feeding the dough into the machine. Continue reducing the thickness on each pass through the machine. The pasta should be rolled through the machine until you have thin sheets. You can roll out multiple sheets and layer them between baking paper.
2. Dust your work surface with flour and lay sheets of pasta out, one at a time.
3. With a fluted pastry wheel, cut 5" squares.
4. After all the squares are cut, begin filling them.

5. Place 2 to 3 tablespoons of filling on the center of each square.
6. Brush the edges with an egg wash (1 egg and 1 tablespoon of water whisked together). This is your glue.
7. Place another square on top of the filled square.
8. Press the edges firmly to secure filling and ready the ravioli for cooking.

SAUCE

1 ancho pepper (soften in water 30 minutes and remove seeds and stems)
2 cups sauvignon blanc
8 sage leaves, minced
4 garlic cloves, minced
1 lemon, juiced
1/2 cup heavy cream
1/2 pound butter, room temperature cut into 1" cubes
Salt to taste

1. Over medium high heat, reduce the wine to about 3 tablespoons.
2. Add garlic, lemon, ancho pepper, and heavy cream and reduce by half.
3. Pour the hot mixture into a blender. Puree and carefully add the butter, a couple of chunks at a time until it is completely added and blended into the mixture.
4. Add the sage leaves and salt to taste.
5. Hold the warm sauce in a thermal pitcher.

ASSEMBLY

Gingersnap cookies

1. Cook the raviolis in boiling water for 3 minutes.
2. Remove the raviolis from the water with a slotted spoon. (This step should be done immediately before serving.)
3. Top each ravioli with 1 ounce of sauce.
4. Garnish with gingersnap cookie crumbs.

109

Chicken Fried Antelope
with a Red Eye Gravy

Serves 4

"Only a fool argues with a skunk, a mule or a cook."
—*cowboy saying*

Home on the range, where the deer and the antelope play; we're talking gas range and maybe this is not the game the deer and antelope had in mind.

When creating a desert cuisine menu for Ocotillo, our off shoot restaurant in Lajitas (next to Big Bend National Park in the Chihuahua Desert), we just had to have a chicken fried steak for our upscale cowboy cuisine. We also wanted to make it with something that appears in the backyard of Lajitas…the antelope.

This cowboy dish can only be smothered in red-eye gravy. Cookie, chef of the old Salty Texas chuck wagon, was more than likely looking for something to season with, and coffee was something they never ran out of. Cookie seasoned the gravy with coffee, or maybe he just spilled the coffee grounds.

This antelope fried steak breaks what some would call the traditional chicken fried steak laws. But we are ruled by the search for flavor well above abiding by traditional culinary laws. In fact, we are the culinary outlaws.

 VARIATIONS: Venison, elk, wild boar, or even beef.

TIMING: Gravy is best made fresh. The breading can be prepared earlier that day.

 GARNISH: Chili peppers

TOOLS:
12" to 14" cast iron skillet for frying
3 medium casseroles for breading station
Plastic wrap
Meat hammer
Chef's knife
Boning knife
Tongs
4 quart saucepan
Whisk
Stovetop smoker
Cookie sheet

"But I like it,
I love it,
I want some
more of it!"
—*Tim McGraw*

Chicken Fried Antelope

4 6 ounce filets of antelope backstrap
2 tablespoons smoke rub (see Salt and Seasoning Section, pg. 33)
2 cups all-purpose flour
Salt and pepper to taste
1 cup egg wash (3 eggs and 1 cup milk whisked together)
1 quart vegetable oil for frying

1. Several hours before mealtime, season the meat with the dry rub and smoke the meat in your stovetop smoker for 3 to 4 minutes. (This is optional, but it really gives it that extra chuck wagon flavor.)
2. Cut each filet in half and then cool the filets of meat in your refrigerator.
3. On a flat surface lined with plastic wrap, pound the meat medallions into flat 1/4" –1/3" thin steaks. Before pounding, place another layer of plastic wrap on top of the meat to avoid it sticking to your pounding instrument. You can use a variety of pounding instruments, from the palm of your hand to a meat hammer to a small skillet.
4. Salt and pepper the flour to taste.
5. Dust each steak in the seasoned flour. Shake off excess flour.
6. Put the steaks into the egg wash and then back into the seasoned flour. Set aside on a cookie sheet while you heat your oil for frying.
7. Heat your skillet and oil to 335 to 350 degrees. Use a thermometer to insure the correct temperature. If you don't have a thermometer, wait until the oil begins to shimmer like Texas blacktop in August. Reduce the heat just before the oil begins smoking. You don't want the temperature to drop below 325 degrees. If the oil is not hot enough, the oil will absorb into the crust and you will have a greasy product…not good! The reason we ramble about the temperature is because achieving the right oil temperature is the key to a crispy, healthy, and tasty crust.
8. Cook the steaks, two at a time. Turn up the heat a couple of notches to make sure the oil temperature does not drop below 325 degrees.

DID YOU KNOW?

Charles Goodnight is said to have designed the first 'chuck wagon', which he devised from an Army wagon in the 1850s or 1860s. It was fitted with various shelves and compartments for storing food, cooking equipment, eating utensils, etc. It also had room for medical supplies (very limited), scissors and a shovel, for the 'coosie', 'cookie' or 'gut robber's' duties included acting as doctor, barber and burying the dead. Cooks were also paid double the dollar a day the cowhands earned.

9. In 4 to 5 minutes you will have a crisp, golden brown exterior with no oil absorption.
10. Place the cooked steaks on a paper towel to absorb exterior oil.
11. Hold the finished steaks in a warm spot while you cook all of the steaks.

RED EYE GRAVY

2 tablespoons light roux (1/2 stick of butter, 3 tablespoons all-purpose flour whisked together in a skillet over medium high heat, until light brown)

1 cup chicken stock (see Stock Section, pg. 34)

1 tablespoon Worcestershire sauce

1 tablespoon ground coffee

2 cups half and half cream

Several dashes Tabasco sauce

Salt and pepper to taste

1. In a 10" to 12" skillet, simmer the chicken stock down to 2 to 3 tablespoons.
2. Add the half and half, Worcestershire sauce, ground coffee, and Tabasco sauce.
3. Bring to a simmer.
4. Whisk in the roux, 1 tablespoon at a time. Stir until the gravy is smooth. If the gravy is too thick, add a little more half and half.
5. Adjust flavor with the salt and pepper.
6. Hold warm until chicken fried antelope is ready.

ASSEMBLY

1. Place the steak next to your smashed potatoes. You must serve smashed potatoes with anything chicken fried. We are partial to our green chili smashers or our ancho bock beer smashers from our first cookbook, "Cooking Fearlessly" (www.hudsonsonthebend.com).
2. Ladle 3 ounces of gravy on the potatoes and steak…followed by some Lipitor.

The German Wienerschnitzel moves in to the Texas Hill Country.

111

Chuy's Hill Country
Surf 'n Turf

Serves 4

"When we lose, I eat. When we win, I eat. I also eat when we're rained out."
—Tommy Lasorda

We thank goodness for Jesus (aka Chuy Caballero). He is *the man* on the grill at Hudson's. He has a magic touch with the meats! On the busiest of nights, Chuy gets no returns from the dining room. That is the sign of a master!

We have always found that our best cooks come from central Mexico. Once you have one cook from San Luis Potosi, the rest of the family will follow. Blas was our first transplant, and now we have the entire lineage in Hudson's kitchen.

Jeff's great, great, great, great, great uncle settled in San Luis Potosi in 1860. We are pretty sure that he is related to the Caballero clan from many generations.

This entree was created in Jeff's own backyard. The great thing about this dish is that it all happens at the same time, from your kitchen to the grill and on to the plate! Caramba! It is simple and virtually mess free!

SURF 'N TURF

4 beef tenderloins, 6 ounces each

3 tomatillos

4 U-10 shrimp (means this is huge shrimp and yields 10 shrimp to a pound)

4 jalapeños

8 slices jalapeño Monterey Jack cheese

Hudson's on the Bend Madagascar Peppercorn Sauce*

Salt and pepper

1. Build a hot fire on your grill.
2. Slice the tomatillos into 8 slices. You will need two slices per tenderloin.
3. Cut the jalapeños in half, lengthwise from blossom to stem. You can deseed if you can't take the heat.
4. Salt and pepper the tenderloins, tomatillo slices, and shrimp.
5. Put the tenderloins, tomatillo slices, shrimp, and jalapeños on the grill. The tenderloins should be placed on the hottest spot on the grill.
6. As the tenderloins reach your desired temperature, start placing your layers atop the tenderloins. Begin by placing the jalapeños atop the tenderloin, second layer is the grill marked tomatillo wheel (2 per tenderloin), third layer is the shrimp and top off with the cheese.
7. Leave on the grill until the cheese is melted.

*The sauce can be purchased at www.hudsonsonthebend.com or you can prepare your own.

MADAGASCAR PEPPERCORN SAUCE

2 cups burgundy wine

2 tablespoons garlic, minced

1/4 red onion, 1/4" diced

1/2 cup green peppercorn (in brine)

2 cups veal stock (see stock section, pg. 34)

1/4 cup dark brown sugar

1 teaspoon Tabasco sauce

1/2 cup Worcestershire sauce

1 cup heavy cream

1/4 cup balsamic vinaigrette

1 1/2 tablespoons sea salt

1. Over medium high heat, simmer the wine. Reduce to 1/4 cup.
2. Add onions, garlic, and veal stock to the wine and simmer. Reduce the liquid by half.
3. Add the peppercorns, sugar, balsamic vinaigrette, Worcestershire sauce, Tabasco sauce and cream. Simmer for 15 minutes.
4. Hold warm while steaks are prepared.

ASSEMBLY

1. Place the surf 'n turf on the dinner plate.
2. Drizzle the sauce generously over the meat.

"The Big Wheels"
—Jimmy LaFave

VARIATIONS: Use longhorn tenderloins or buffalo tenderloins. Lobster can be used in place of shrimp. Green tomatoes can replace tomatillos. You can use any variety of cheese.

TIMING: Grill a la minute. (French for "the very last minute.")

GARNISH: Needs none, already has so much garnish it might get top heavy

TOOLS:
Grill
Long tongs
Sharp knife
Sauce pan for the peppercorn
    sauce
Whisk

The grilled smoky flavor does a balancing act with the limey tomatillo and the spicy sauce.

Dos Gringos
Tamales
with Strawberry Raspberry Sauce

Yields 36 tamales

"It takes a village to make tamale."—unknown

Thanksgiving is one of our treasured holidays at Hudson's on the Bend. Every year we do something wild and crazy to our dressing. Turkey Day 2004, we added smoked brisket tamales to the dressing. It imparted a South of the Border zing to the flavor of the meal! We garnished the plate with our zesty Peppered Cranberry Relish and the crowd was crowing with pleasure at the results. If you are reading this book simply for the pictures and stories, and not at all inclined to step into the kitchen on Turkey Day, call for reservations and experience Thanksgiving in Hill Country Heaven!

These famous tamales are prepared by John Bleker and Cate Fox, owners of Dos Gringos Tamales. Chuy (aka Jesus) swears that Mexicans made these tamales. He said, "No way Jose" did two gringos make these tamales. You can access and order their fabulous tamales online at www.dosgringostamales@yahoo. com or make them yourself. Here is the recipe.

"Hot Tamale Baby"
—Marcia Ball

VARIATIONS: Smoked wild anything that is in your wild game freezer. Smoke it and grind it. Make Sloppy Joes for a great meal with the left over brisket.

TIMING: Tamales are always the very best when just out of the steamer. But they are still really good when reheated. They are labor intensive, so people usually make large amounts and freeze them. This works, too. Note of importance, prepare the brisket one day in advance! This cannot all be accomplished in one day. If you would rather, you can visit your favorite BBQ joint and pick up some prepared brisket.

GARNISH: Hudson's on the Bend Strawberry Raspberry Chipotle BBQ Sauce

 TOOLS:
Steamer
Sharp knife
Smoker
Food processor
Saucepan
Mixing bowls

BRISKET

(Must be prepared the day before!)

2 cups BBQ sauce
1 brisket, 5/6 pounds, untrimmed
Salt
Pepper
Mesquite wood
2 cups barbecue sauce, of course we use Hudson's Chipotle BBQ Sauce but you may use your favorite barbecue sauce. You might even want to use the recipe from Mr. Pibb's Ribs for the Sasparilla barbecue sauce.

1. Build fire in a smoker with mesquite wood.
2. Rub brisket with salt and pepper. Generous amounts on both sides.
3. Place brisket on the fire with the fatty side up.
4. Cook brisket with heavy smoke, adding wood as needed for 8 hours or until done. (170 degrees internal temperature taken with a probe thermometer)
5. Place cooked brisket in refrigerator overnight.
6. Grind the brisket with a food processor or chop by hand into small pieces.
7. Mix the brisket thoroughly with barbecue sauce until the meat and sauce are well mixed.

MASA

5 cups dry masa mix
3 1/2 cups warm water
3/4 cup vegetable shortening
1/4 cup vegetable oil
1/8 cup salt
1/8 cup paprika
1/4 cup fresh garlic, minced
1 tablespoon baking powder
2 tablespoons coarse black pepper
36 cornhusks

1. Soak cornhusks in warm water until soft.
2. Blend all ingredients for masa in electric mixer until mixture is the consistency of peanut butter.

3. Spread masa evenly over cornhusks approximately 1/4" thick.

4. Spread 2 ounces of the brisket mixture on top of masa.

5. Fold bottom of cornhusks upward and wrap both sides.

6. Place in steamer and steam for 45 minutes. Our preference for steaming the tamales is as follows: Place 3 tamales on a sheet of aluminum foil. Stack 3 more on top, making a package of 6 tamales. Fold the foil over to create a tight fit, and then fold the pieces together to make a tight seam on top. Then fold the ends under. You are making an airtight package. This ensures the tamales are evenly cooked and you can wrap what you don't eat—if that is possible!

7. The tamale has finished cooking when it separates easily from the cornhusk, approximately 45 minutes.

ASSEMBLY

Hudson's on the Bend Strawberry Raspberry Sauce

Hudson's on the Bend Chipotle BBQ Sauce

1. To prepare sauce, mix 50% Hudson's on the Bend Strawberry Raspberry Sauce and 50% Hudson's on the Bend Chipotle BBQ Sauce in a saucepan and heat. (Sauces can be purchased on line www.hudsonsonthebend. com)

2. Remove the tamales from the cornhusks.

3. Place tamales on dinner plates.

4. Top tamales with the sauce.

Sweet, hot, smoky, fruity South of the Border zing!

Espresso Rubbed Venison
with Jumbo Lump Crab
in Chipotle Bock Beer Blanc Butter

Serves 6–8

"You can't be a real country unless you have a beer and an airline - it helps if you have some kind of a football team, or some nuclear weapons, but at the very least you need a beer."
—Frank Zappa

This dish was partly created by Robert Del Grande of Café Annie in Houston, Texas. This is not only another example of chef thievery, but also more importantly, an example of how accidents can create great culinary creations!

As the story goes, Robert was cooking pork tenders for a Christmas Day brunch. He spilled the coffee grinder, which was full of coffee on top of the cleaned tenders. His next thought was, "This might be good". (Was Robert a chuck wagon cook in a former life?)

We have taken this to our own unique level by mixing a chili powder blend with the espresso coffee for an extra punch. We add the smoky flavor with the stove top smoker. Check out our resource page to mail order the smoker.

ESPRESSO RUB

1/2 cup espresso coffee, ground fine
2 tablespoons salt
1 teaspoon ancho chili powder
1 teaspoon fresh ground black pepper
2 pound venison backstrap

1. Combine all ingredients except the venison and mix well.
2. Rub the mixture on the venison 1 hour prior to smoking.

SMOKING AND HOLDING

(This is one of the most valuable techniques in the cookbook. Please refer back to the Grilling section under the "Best Kept Secret" Article for further information on preparing backstrap and making it the best that it can be!)

2 quarts vegetable oil
Small 4 quart cooler/small ice chest that holds a 6-pack of sodas (Igloo Playmate)
Probe meat thermometer
Stovetop smoker

1. Smoke the venison over high heat in the stovetop smoker until the internal temperature reaches 130 degrees. This will take approximately 15 to 18 minutes.
2. In a saucepan, warm the oil to 140 degrees.
3. Pour the warm oil into the 4 quart cooler.
4. Submerge the venison into the oil. This will hold the backstrap at a perfect medium rare for hours.

SHINER BOCH BEER BLANC WITH LIME CHIPOTLE PEPPERS AND BLUE LUMP CRAB

This is our favorite sauce to top the espresso rubbed venison backstrap. It is very similar to the French buerre blanc. But it has a Texas Southwest twist. We use Shiner beer instead of wine and chipotle peppers with fresh squeezed lime so we call it Beer Blanc, y'all.

12 ounces jumbo lump crab (held for final assembly)
1 Shiner Bock beer (all bock beers work)
2 shallots, 1/4" diced
2 cloves garlic, 1/4" diced
2 chipotle peppers in adobe sauce
1/4 cup fresh lime juice (3 limes)
1/4 cup heavy cream
2 sticks of butter, room temperature cut into 1" cubes
Salt and pepper to taste

1. Simmer and reduce 12 ounces of bock beer to 1/4 cup in a 4 quart saucepan over medium high heat
2. Add shallots, garlic, chipotle peppers, and heavy cream. Simmer until it has reduced in volume by half.
3. Add lime juice and return to a simmer.
4. Pour mixture into blender while very hot and puree.
5. While pureeing, add the butter cubes, one at a time.
6. Add salt to taste
7. Hold in a thermal pitcher.

ASSEMBLY

1. Warm the crab in a small saucepan with a little beer.
2. Remove the venison from the warm oil.
3. With paper towel, pat off excess oil from the tenderloin.
4. Slice the tender into 1/2" pieces.
5. Fan 3 pieces across each plate.
6. Top with sauce and crab meat.

"Yeah I like Texas, Ain't it fine here, Like to pick my guitar down in Luckenbach, and drink that Shiner Bock beer, Yeah I like Texas, man there ain't no doubt, just listen to me 'cause I know what I'm talkin' about" —Pat Green

 VARIATIONS: Elk, antelope, or beef back straps

TIMING: All must be done the day of service. The chipotle bock beer blanc can be done an hour prior to cooking of backstrap.

GARNISH: Rosemary and begonias

 TOOLS:
Blender
Smoker/stovetop smoker
Igloo Playmate cooler
5 quart saucepan
Mixing bowls
Chef's knife
Boning knife
Probe thermometer
Thermal pitcher
Saucepan

Smoky espresso flavor on the venison dances with the limey chipotle sauce.

117

Grilled Achiote
Marinated Pork Chops
Topped with a Watermelon Rind Chutney

Serves 4

"When one has tasted it, he knows what Angels eat. It was not a Southern watermelon that Eve took; we know it because she repented." —Mark Twain

While doing a cooking school down in the Yucatan of Mexico, Jeff was taken on an ecological hike through the jungle. This turned out to be a tropical high-humidity death march! Among other wild sightings, he saw wild vanilla bean vines, and he observed the annatto seeds growing in the annatto tree, which is where the achiote comes from. At the end of this death trek, the native Mayans were waiting with a treat. They had marinated jungle chicken in achiote and lime juice and then threw it on the fire to feed the survivors. Jeff developed a deep appreciation for achiote and what it suffers to reach civilization. Achiote adds just the right amount of zing to the luscious taste of this sweet watermelon-y dish.

Our Watermelon Rind Chutney is the perfect relish for the watermelon marinated pork chop! This is the most Southern treatment you can ever dream of to give to your pork chop. Marinate your pork chops in watermelon and stand back; the chops will develop the loveliest Southern manners. On a hot summer day, what can be more refreshing than watermelon? And down here in Texas, we specialize in hot summer days! Slip a watermelon juice marinated grilled pork chop underneath the chutney and your speech slows to a drawl and you start saying things like, "Mama, let's go to the Luling Watermelon Thump!"

VARIATIONS: Wild boar chops or a pork tenderloin or even chicken

TIMING: The marinating process should begin the day before; marinade overnight. Chutney can be made days in advance.

GARNISH: The chutney is a colorful garnish in itself. Add a nice slice of watermelon.

TOOLS:
5 quart sauce pot
Mixing bowls
Paring knife
Food grater
Blender
Ziploc bags
Mandolin
Wood fire grill
Vegetable peeler

"Watermelon Crawl"
—Tracy Byrd

WATERMELON PREPARATION

1 seedless watermelon

1. Cut the watermelon into smaller pieces.
2. Cut the red meat off the rind. Hold for marinade.
3. Remove the skin from the rind. Hold rind for chutney. The skin can be thrown away.

MARINADE

(We always use seedless watermelons and a few jalapeños for a little spice. We use a gallon Ziploc bag for easy marinating procedures. It is best to squeeze the excess air out before sealing the bag.)

1 quart watermelon meat
1 cup white sugar
4 ounces achiote paste
2 jalapeños, (remove the seed for a milder marinade)
1 tablespoon sea salt
4   8-ounce pork chops

1. Put all of the ingredients except the pork chops in a blender.
2. Puree well to make marinade.
3. Put the marinade and pork chops in a 1 gallon Ziploc bag.
4. Press air out of bag before sealing.
5. Place the bag in the refrigerator for 8 to 12 hours to let chops marinate.

WATERMELON RIND CHUTNEY

This chutney recipe will make more than you will need for four. It will store in your refrigerator for weeks. It is great on grilled birds and fish!

4 cups watermelon rind, peeled and 1/2" diced

2 cups Granny Smith apples, peeled and 1/2" diced

1 cup white sugar

1 cup rice wine vinegar

2 tablespoons ginger, minced

2 tablespoons garlic, minced

1/2 cup apple juice concentrate (no water added)

1/2 cup golden raisins

1/4 cup shallots, minced

2 tablespoons red chili flakes

1 tablespoon sea salt

1. Combine all the ingredients in a heavy bottom saucepan.
2. Simmer over medium heat for 30 to 40 minutes or until the rind is tender.
3. Adjust the salt to taste.
4. Refrigerate.

ASSEMBLY

1. Over a very hot outside grill, cook the chops to 150 degrees internal temperature (medium). This should take about 7 to 8 minutes on each side. Be careful over very hot spots. The marinated chops have sugar in them and can overchar if not watched.
2. Spoon 2 to 3 ounces of chutney on a serving platter.
3. Place the grilled chop on top of the chutney.
4. Begin counting barefoot children and fireflies!

The smell of the charcoal grill cooking, barefoot children and watermelon...all is right with the world.

Grilled Duck Breast
Shingled with Seared Scallops
in a Cranberry Chipotle Port Sauce

Serves 8

> *"If there hadn't been women we'd still be squatting in a cave eating raw meat, because we made civilization in order to impress our girl friends. And they tolerated it and let us go ahead and play with our toys."*
> —Orson Welles, actor, director, producer, writer (1915-1985)

Because Hudson's is located smack dab in the middle of the hunting grounds of the Hill Country, hunters often stop by the restaurant and ask us to smoke their kill of the day. The USDA does not allow restaurants to touch unapproved wild game, this is illegal. Jeff has been known to smoke a lot of this and that at his home in his personal smoker. For his troubles, the hunters pay him with limbs and loins. Jeff has discovered that wild duck is especially good with this cranberry sauce, which is a French gastrique. It's the berries with the wild duck! The scallops were added because we just cannot leave well enough alone!

"Perfect Combination"
—Jimmy LaFave

SAUCE

2 tablespoons butter
1 cup shallots, minced
1 cup ginger, minced
1 cup raspberry vinegar
1 cup dark brown sugar
3 cups port wine
3 oranges, juice and zest
3 cups veal stock, reduced (see Stock Section, pg. 34)
2 cups fresh cranberries (frozen is acceptable if fresh is not in season)
2 chipotle peppers en adobo sauce
Salt and pepper to taste
1 cup dried cranberries (craisins)

1. Sauté shallots and ginger in butter until they are soft.
2. Deglaze the shallots and ginger with the raspberry vinegar.
3. Add the brown sugar and over a high heat, reduce the liquid to a syrupy consistency.
4. Add the port wine and over medium high heat, reduce the liquid by half.
5. Add the remaining ingredients, except the dried cranberries, and cook and reduce over medium high heat until you have a sauce consistency.
6. Strain through a sieve.
7. Add the dried cranberries and adjust seasoning with salt and pepper.

DUCK

1 dead duck, deboned and defeathered, unless you prefer the roughage of bones and the fluffy taste of feathers (or go to your butcher counter and buy duck breasts).
Salt and pepper

1. Season the duck breasts liberally with salt and pepper.
2. Place on the grill. Over a hot, hardwood fire, grill with the skin side facing down first.
3. We like our duck medium to medium rare, internal degrees about 135.
4. Hold the duck breasts in a warm spot while you are preparing the scallops.

SCALLOPS

16 U-10 sea scallops (U-10 means less than 10 scallops per pound)
1/4 cup extra virgin olive oil
Salt

1. Liberally salt the sea scallops.
2. Heat a large sauté pan with the extra virgin olive oil.
3. Cook the scallops for approximately 3 minutes on each side. You should have a nice brown caramelization on both sides. We like ours a little underdone in the center.

ASSEMBLY

1. Slice the duck breasts with your chef's knife, leaning on a 45 degree angle. Slice the breasts into 6 even slices.
2. Lay the scallops on their side and slice them into 3 equal size slices.
3. Layer or shingle the scallops between each slice of duck.
4. Finish with a ladle of 2 to 3 ounces of the chipotle port sauce.

VARIATIONS: The duck breast could be replaced with pork tenders if you are unable to get your hands on duck breasts.

TIMING: The sauce can be made 24 hours in advance. The duck and scallops must be prepared just prior to serving.

GARNISH: Dried cranberries

TOOLS:
Grill
Sieve
Tongs
Ladle
Saucepan
Whisk
Sharp knife
Zester
12" skillet

Tart & sweet matched with the wildly rich ocean spray!

Texas Hill Country
Wild Game Paella

Serves 6

*"I'm just mad about Saffron
Saffron's mad about me
I'm just mad about Saffron
She's just mad about me"*
—Donovan

> *"A man who is stingy with saffron is capable of seducing his own grandmother." —Norman Douglas, English Writer (1868-1952)*

In search of the perfect paella? Jeff's foray into wild game paella started because Mike Reese was cooking paella during a male-bonding hunting weekend in the Hill Country. They were discussing the difficulty in finding good paella. Jeff has never been known to run away from a challenge. He was inspired to attempt to blow Mike away. Jeff is wild about this paella creation, but to date Mike still takes the number one spot.

People have their own recipe that was taught to them by their mother or grandmother. They all have family cooking rules that cannot be broken. Well, we may break a few. We stay true to the basic concepts that have made the dish a classic, the right short-grained rice and the best saffron threads we can find. We use the proper cooking procedures, but we use game meats or whatever we kill at the Reese River Ranch.

Paella is to Spain what gumbo is to New Orleans. It is a typical picnic dish for the Spanish spring and summer, often cooked by the family male adults. Paella was originally prepared by the field hands in Spain—cooking in the open range for their lunch.

If you can't find a local grocer with short-grain rice, good saffron, and Spanish paprika; go to www.spanishtable.com. They have the best of everything from a variety of paella pans to all of the spices.

 VARIATIONS: Any game or chicken for the wimps. In Spain, you will find paella offered with a variety of seafoods.

TIMING: Chicken or duck stock can be done 2 days in advance. Paella must be done at the last minute.

GARNISH: Needs no garnish

TOOLS
Paella pan with lid (aluminum foil will work as a lid)
(I have found my cast iron lodge skillet makes a great paella pan)
Stovetop smoker
5 quart saucepan
Sharp knife

Paella

4 1/2 cups rich chicken or duck stock (see Stock section)
1/2 cup dry white wine
1 teaspoon crushed saffron
3 ripe tomatoes, crushed and drained
1 pound venison backstrap
1 duck, bone out
8 ounces rabbit tender
6 ounces olive oil
3 teaspoons sweet paprika
10 cloves garlic
1 1/2 cup pearl onions
2 cups scallions, chopped
1/2 cup red and green peppers, 1/4" diced
2 cups artichoke hearts, quartered
1/2 cup peas
1/2 cup lima beans
Salt to taste
4 sprigs rosemary
3 cups short-grained rice

1. Season the meats with salt or smoke rub.
2. Smoke the meats to a medium rare in the stovetop smoker.
3. Remove meats and hold in a warm spot. After the meats have cooled, they will need to be deboned, quartered, and cut into 1/2" strips.
4. Heat the stock, wine, and saffron in a saucepan.
5. Hold on a low simmer.
6. Heat your paella pan over high heat.
7. Add the olive oil to the paella pan.
8. Add the garlic, pepper, scallions, and onions to the paella pan.
9. Cook over high heat for 5 minutes.
10. Reduce to medium high heat and add the paprika, rosemary, tomatoes, peas, lima beans, and artichokes hearts. Cook another 2 minutes.
11. Stir the rice into the paella pan.
12. Add the simmering stock and cook until it is no longer soupy or until the stock has been absorbed into the rice but still is very, very moist
13. Add the diced meats to the paella pan.
14. Remove from heat and cover.
15. Leave the paella pan on your stove another 10 to 15 minutes, covered, but, with no direct heat before serving. Everyone's oven and stove cook at different temperatures. You want all the liquid to be absorbed into the rice before you cover it.

Delicate perfume of saffron is hiding
behind the wild game!

Wild Lolli-Chop Salad
atop a Macadamia Lemon Honey Dressing

Serves 6

"She was so wild that when she made French toast she got her tongue caught in the toaster."
—Rodney Dangerfield

Generally speaking, when people come to Hudson's, they enter with wild abandon! They are fully prepared to throw their diets aside for the occasion. People are always surprised that they can eat a gourmet meal and still please their Atkins' conscience at our restaurant. The Lolli-Chops are our contribution to the craze!

This is our favorite wild game salad. We think it will probably replace your fave. Oh, you don't already have one? Take ours, please! You can use any combination of venison, wild boar, elk, or lamb chops. This is where you can put our resource page to work. The Broken Arrow Ranch is a great resource for a tasty variety of wild game chops (www.brokenarrowranch.com) For those who want a tamer salad, you can grill lamb or pork chops and have an equally great dish!

 VARIATIONS: A variety of all game chops, from antelope to wild boar to venison, anything you can hunt down. Lamb chops are perfect for a springtime Sunday brunch.

 TIMING: Oriental shellac can be made the day before. The dressing can be prepared 24 hours in advance.

GARNISH: Nuts 'n apples

TOOLS:
Wood fired grill
Blender
5 quart sauce pot
Chef's knife
Paring knife
Whisk

SPICY ORIENTAL SHELLAC

Like many of our sauces, you will have some left over. It is great on anything you might be grilling, including fish, shrimp, or poultry. You can refrigerate any extra sauce for two weeks.

1 cup rice wine
2 tablespoons red chili flakes
1/2 cup soy sauce
1/2 cup hoisin sauce*
1 cup tomato paste
1/4 cup fish sauce*
1/4 cup shallots, minced
1/4 cup garlic, minced
2 cups dark brown sugar
Sea salt to taste
1 stick butter, 1/2" cubes
*these are found in the Asian aisle of your grocery store

1. Simmer rice wine with the garlic, shallots, and chili flakes for 10 minutes over medium heat.
2. Add all remaining ingredients except the butter.
3. Simmer over medium heat for 15 minutes.
4. Remove from the heat and whisk in the butter.
5. Hold warm while you grill the chops.

LEMON HONEY MACADAMIA NUT OIL VINAIGRETTE

This is a simple, zesty, and healthy dressing that is made in the blender. Macadamia nut oil has a mild nutty flavor and is high in monosaturates, which is very heart healthy. It can be found in health minded grocery stores or on the web at www.macnutoil.com. This oil is great for frying! Its smoking point is 410 degrees.

1/2 cup fresh lemon juice
Zest from 3 lemons
1/2 cup honey
1/2 cup rice wine vinegar
1 tablespoon shallots, rough chop
1 whole egg
1 cup macadamia nut oil
Salt to taste (1/2 tablespoon)

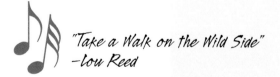
"Take a Walk on the Wild Side"
—Lou Reed

1. Set the nut oil aside.
2. Combine all the other ingredients in a blender and puree.
3. In a slow and steady stream, add the macadamia nut oil.
4. Hold in refrigerator until the final assembly.

SALAD

3 heads Boston lettuce

1 pint cherry tomatoes

1 Granny Smith apple, julienned and reserved for garnish

1 cup toasted macadamia nuts, reserved for garnish

1 cucumber, sliced in wheels

1 red onion, sliced in rings

1. Wash the lettuce and tear into bite size pieces.
2. Add the tomatoes, cucumber, and onion.
3. Toss together in a large bowl.
4. Add the vinaigrette dressing.
5. Toss.
6. Refrigerate while you grill chops.

GRILLING

6 wild boar chops

6 lamb chops

6 venison chops

Sea salt and pepper

(Any combination of chops will work. If you prefer to stick with one type of meat, that is okay)

1. Season each chop with sea salt and pepper before grilling.
2. Grill over a hot wood fire. We like to serve 3 chops (whatever variety you choose) per person.
3. The chop needs only 3 minutes on each side over the hot fire to cook.

ASSEMBLY

1. Place salad on a plate.
2. Dip the chops in the spicy Oriental Shellac.
3. Place the chops on the salad.
4. Garnish with apple juliennes and macadamia nuts.

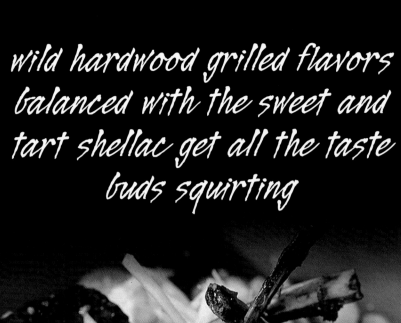

wild hardwood grilled flavors balanced with the sweet and tart shellac get all the taste buds squirting

Seafood

Giant Shrimp in a Masa Herb Crust Topped with a Cilantro Lime Butter

Grilled Salmon in a Gingered Corn and Herb Broth atop Baby Bok Choy with Shrimp Dumplings

Macadamia Nut Crusted Red Snapper with a Mango Butter Sauce

Mahi Steamed in a Banana Leaf with Herbed Lemon Wine

Really Expensive King Crab Legs and Lobster Salad

Sea Scallops Sautéed with a Saffron Cream in a Pumpkin Squash Cup

Spicy and Crispy Fried Oysters on a Bed of Spinach in a Bacon, Mustard, and Honey Vinaigrette

Tea Smoked Tuna in a Chipotle Gingered Shellac

Texas Jumbo Lump Crab Au gratin

Some people march to the beat of a different drummer, other people tango.

Giant Shrimp in a
Masa Herb Crust Topped
with a Cilantro Lime Butter

"Shrimp Song"
—Townes Van Zandt

Serves 4

Bubba : Anyway, like I was sayin', shrimp is the fruit of the sea. You can barbecue it, boil it, broil it, bake it, and saute it. Dey's uh, shrimp-kabobs, shrimp creole, shrimp gumbo. Pan fried, deep fried, stir-fried. There's pineapple shrimp, lemon shrimp, coconut shrimp, pepper shrimp, shrimp soup, shrimp stew, shrimp salad, shrimp and potatoes, shrimp burger, shrimp sandwich. That- that's about it. —from the movie Forest Gump

This recipe came to us from one of our cooks from south of the border. *Masa* is the Mexican word for dough. It refers to the corn dough used to make tortillas and tamales, as well as other traditional Mexican dishes. *Masa Harina* —Is dough flour. "A gift of the gods" is how corn was regarded by the Indians of Mexico. This a-maizing crop has been a staple food for the Mexican culture. The European settlers did not know what corn was until they received gifts of corn from the local Indians. In the traditional Navajo Indian wedding ceremony, the bride's grandmother presents the couple with a basket of cornmeal and the couple exchanges a small handful with each other. This is considered sweet—not corny! "Love means never having to say '*lo siento*.'"

VARIATIONS: This would be darn good on oysters, but, do not tell Bubba! It is also first-rate on veggies. We can also see adding other spices to the mix, such as spicy chili powders, garlic powder, onion powder, and celery powder. If you are up north and can't get masa, use white or yellow corn flour. The 1/2 cup of cornstarch in the recipe makes the crust extra crunchy, a Colonel Sanders trick.

TIMING: Breading can be made far in advance. Cilantro butter should be made no more than 1 hour prior to dinner. Fry at very last minute.

GARNISH: Cilantro leaves and edible flowers

TOOLS:
Sifter
Medium saucepan
Blender
Thermal pitcher
3 baking pans for breading
Whisk
Cookie sheet
Frying thermometer
Large frying pan
Tongs

20 U-10 shrimp
(means under 10 per pound, bigger is better)

MASA HERB CRUST

1 1/2 cups masa harina (white corn flour— found with the Mexican foods in your grocery store)
1/2 cup cornstarch
1 teaspoon cumin seeds, toasted and ground
1/2 teaspoon cayenne pepper
1 tablespoon salt

1. Sift all ingredients together.
2. Hold until ready to bread.

CILANTRO LIME BUTTER

2 sticks sweet butter, cubed in 1" squares at room temperature
1 cup chardonnay wine
1 medium shallot, rough chopped
3 cloves garlic, crushed
1 cup heavy cream
4 medium limes, zested and juiced
2 jalapeños (depending upon your love of the heat)
2 bunches cilantro
1 tablespoon salt

1. In a medium saucepan, reduce the chardonnay by half over medium high heat.
2. Add the shallots, garlic, heavy cream, lime juice, and zest.
3. Reduce in volume again by half.
4. Take the simmering liquid to the blender and blend on high. Be sure to vent the steam before turning the blender on.
5. Add the jalapeño to the blender and blend.
6. Add the butter a couple of squares at a time and blend until all of the butter is used.
7. Add the salt and cilantro and blend until the cilantro is well minced.
8. Hold the sauce in a thermal pitcher until service. This is a delicate butter sauce that needs to be held warm—not hot!

STANDARD BREADING PROCECDURE

2 cups all-purpose flour

3 eggs

1 cup milk

1. You will need 3 casserole dishes or baking pans.
2. Put 2 cups of all-purpose flour in one baking pan.
3. Make your egg wash with 3 eggs and 1 cup of milk whisked together and put the mixture in the second baking pan.
4. The third container will hold the masa herb crust.
5. Bread one piece of shrimp at a time. Begin by dragging the shrimp, holding by the tail, through the flour. Shake off the excess flour.
6. Dip the shrimp into the egg wash until all of the flour is wet.
7. Press the shrimp into the breading lightly with your hand.
8. Set the shrimp on a cookie sheet and continue until all the shrimp are coated. Be certain to spread the shrimp evenly on the cookie sheet. Do not stack them.
9. Refrigerate until frying.

FRYING

1 quart oil

When done properly, frying can be a very healthy method of cooking with very little oil absorbed into the food. Follow these guidelines:

1. Heat oil to 350 degrees. Do not let the temperature drop below 325 degrees. This results in the oil getting sucked into the breading and the shrimp will become greasy and unhealthy. Use a thermometer to watch the oil temperature and wait until the oil temperature recovers to 350 degrees before adding the second round of shrimp.
2. Use at least 1 quart of vegetable, canola or peanut oil. (You can use more oil if you are frying a lot of shrimp. A larger amount of oil will help in maintaining the proper temperature. The more oil you use, the slower the temperature will drop.) Don't try to fry too much at once. No more than 8 shrimp at a time.

ASSEMBLY

1. Place five shrimp on each dinner plate.
2. Drizzle the sauce on top.

129

Grilled Salmon in a
Gingered Corn and Herb Broth
atop Baby Bok Choy with Shrimp Dumplings

Serves 6

"A woman without a man is like a fish without a bicycle." —Gloria Steinem

This dish is our family dumplin' and we have Chef Robert Rhoades to thank.

For two years the restaurant had earned the number one spot with the Dale Rice yearly scorecard. Then, in the summer of 2003, we lost our number one spot and a star due to a plastic, walled-in porch addition and a tilting table. In 2004, Dale Rice came to Hudson's and spooned up some of this magic and suddenly the stars are shining upon us again! (All five of them!) Coincidentally, Jeff had returned that very day from his Alaskan cooking school and with the fresh salmon he had caught in the Nak Nek River, he was able to reel Dale back in with the fresh catch. This is the recipe that brought us back into favor.

Try this delicious combination of flavors and you will see the stars twinkling in the eyes of your diners. It worked for us! To Robert and this recipe we owe the stars and the moon.

VARIATIONS: Salmon could be replaced with tuna or swordfish
Cooked over a grill or a stovetop smoker
You can use a blend of garden herbs, anything you've got in your garden.

TIMING: Glaze can be made a day ahead.
Gingered corn stock can be made a day in advance
Dumplings can be made the morning of serving

 GARNISH: needs no garnish is very colorful with the corn and tomatoes. If you so desire put fresh garden herbs on top

TOOLS:
Medium saucepan
Large sauté pan
Medium stock pot
Food processor
Spoons
Sharp knife
Tongs
Food brush
Wood grill
Whisk
Strainer

HONEY CILANTRO AND GINGER GLAZE

(Recipe makes extra glaze, but, saves in refrigerator for weeks and is delicious on grilled fish, chicken, pork or wild game.)

1 1/2 cups honey
1/4 cup soy sauce
1/4 cup Worcestershire sauce
1/2 cup fresh ginger, minced
1/4 cup garlic, minced
1/4 cup shallots, minced
Salt and pepper to taste
1 bunch cilantro, rough chopped
1/4 pound sweet butter

1. With 1 tablespoon of butter in a medium sauce pan, soften the garlic, shallots, and ginger over medium heat for 7 minutes.
2. Add all of the remaining ingredients, except the butter, to the saucepan and bring to a simmer on medium heat. Simmer for another 10 minutes.
3. Remove from the heat and whisk in the butter.
4. Hold on warm, 160 degrees or less, so the butter does not separate.

GINGERED CORN STOCK

4 corn cobs
1/2 cup ginger root, sliced into nickel sized coins
1/2 pound butter
1 tablespoon sea salt
2 quarts cold water

1. Using a sharp knife, remove the corn kernels from the cob and hold the corn for the final assembly of the dish.
2. Put all ingredients in large pot and bring to a boil.
3. Simmer for 1 hour and strain.

SHRIMP DUMPLINGS

1 pound raw shrimp, peeled and deveined (size does not matter)
1/2 cup cornstarch
1 tablespoon fish sauce (located on the Asian aisle at your grocer. It is the Worcestershire sauce in the Asian kitchen)
1 bunch cilantro, rough chopped

1. Put all of the ingredients into a food processor and pulse until smooth.

2. Bring gingered corn stock to a simmer in preparation to poach the dumplings.

3. Shape the shrimp mixture into quarter sized dumplings with your hands. Practiced dumpling makers, if you know how to make quenelles (football shaped dumplings), using two spoons, go for it.

4. Drop the dumplings into the simmering gingered corn stock until dumplings float. This should take 3 to 4 minutes.

5. Remove and reserve for final assembly.

GRILLED SALMON

6 salmon filets, 6 ounces each, skin off

1. Over a hardwood fire or charcoal fire, grill your salmon to a medium rare center.

2. Hold in a warm oven at 200 degrees while the final broth is prepared.

HERB BROTH

1/4 cup garden herbs (Thai basil, thyme, arugula, or any combination of fresh herbs from your garden to add your own signature)

2 cups Ginger Corn stock

2 baby bok choys, cut into thirds lengthwise

2 cups cut corn

Shrimp Dumplings

1/2 cup grape tomatoes, cut in half

3 tablespoons butter

1. Put all of the ingredients, except the butter, into a large sauté pan and heat to a simmer.

2. Remove from heat and whisk in the butter.

3. Divide the herbed corn broth into 6 bowls.

4. Divide the bok choys, corn, tomatoes, and shrimp dumplings equally into the six bowls

5. Brush the salmon with the cilantro glaze and place a filet into each bowl.

6. Serve.

The rich buttery corn broth and the richness of the grilled salmon is complemented by the ginger glaze

131

Macadamia Nut
Crusted Red Snapper
with a Mango Butter Sauce

"Man come along with me lets fill our pockets with macadamia nuts" —Tom Waits

Serves 6

"Why does Sea World have a seafood restaurant?? I'm halfway through my fish burger and I realize, Oh my God....I could be eating a slow learner." —Lyndon Baines Johnson

VARIATIONS: Orange roughy, red fish, halibut. Use the freshest lightest flaky fish available through your fishmonger. It is important that the filets not be more than 3/4" thick.

TIMING: Sauce can be prepared 1 hour in advance. Breading can be made days in advance. Fish can be breaded the morning of your dinner.

GARNISH: Diced mangos and a little diced red, green, and orange bell pepper or chopped chives to break the monotony of orange

TOOLS:
Food processor
Medium saucepan
Large sauté pan
Blender
Sharp knife
Thermal pitcher
Whisk
Spatula
Zester
3 casseroles for breading station
Cookie sheet

We have a new obsession with macadamia nuts and oil. It is due to the fact that we love the richness and flavor of the nuts. They are monosaturates and are as healthy if not more so than extra virgin olive oils. According to the ever reliable source of *People Magazine,* the stars eat 2 tablespoons of macadamia nut oil a day to boost their metabolism. They are very heart healthy! What a bonus to find something this rich and tasty that is also good for your heart. If you have trouble finding the macadamia nut oil, go to www.macnutoil.com. It is a great item to keep on hand in your pantry.

The Chinese five spices are traditionally used with chicken and pork, but it adds a wonderful zing to our crust. The five spices are cinnamon, Szechwan peppercorns, star anise, clove, and ginger all ground into a powder.

MANGO BUTTER SAUCE

2 cups dry white wine, sauvignon blanc or chenin blanc
1 large shallot, rough chopped
4 cloves garlic, crushed
4 limes, juiced and zested
1/2 cup honey
1/2 cup heavy cream
3 mangos, pitted and peeled (one of these mangos is 1/4" diced and reserved for garnish)
1/2 teaspoon sea salt
1 jalapeño pepper
2 sticks butter, cubed at room temperature

1. In a medium saucepan, over high heat, reduce the wine to 1/4 cup of amber liquid.
2. Add the shallot, garlic, zest, lime juice, honey, cream, mangos, sea salt, and jalapeño pepper. Simmer for 5 minutes over medium heat.
3. Pour the simmering mixture from the saucepan into a blender. Be certain to vent the steam and then blend on high.
4. Add the butter, a couple of chunks at a time until all of the butter has been added.
5. Adjust the salt level and store in a thermal pitcher until serving.

MACADAMIA HERB CRUSTED RED SNAPPER

6 filets of red snapper, skinless and boneless (6 to 7 ounces each)
4 cups macadamia nuts
2 cups panko bread crumbs
3 tablespoons Chinese Five-Spice mix
1 1/2 tablespoons sea salt
Egg wash (3 eggs and 1 cup milk)
2 cups all-purpose flour
1/2 cup macadamia nut oil

1. Put macadamia nuts in a food processor with the S-blade and pulse until the nuts are corn kernel size. Some will be smaller.
2. Add the panko bread crumbs, Chinese Five-Spice mix and salt to the food processor. Pulse until blended. Do not over blend. You want some texture.
3. Set up your breading station.*
4. Bread the snapper filets using the standard breading procedure.
5. Heat a large sauté pan on medium high heat with the macadamia nut oil to 350 degrees. This temperature is reached just before the oil begins smoking. Hint: A small piece of lettuce will pop when it is dropped in the oil.

Sweet freshness of the fish surrounded by the rich warm macadamia nuts is offset by the citrus mango sauce.

6. Cook 2 filets at a time for about 4 minutes on each side until a rich golden brown.

7. Place the cooked filet on a cookie sheet in a warm oven (200 degrees) while you finish cooking the snapper.

*STANDARD BREADING PROCEDURE

1. You will need 3 casserole dishes or baking pans.

2. Put 2 cups of all-purpose flour in one baking pan.

3. Make your egg wash with 3 eggs and 1 cup of milk whisked together and put the mixture in the second baking pan.

4. The third container will hold the breading.

5. Bread one piece of snapper at a time. Begin by dragging the snapper through the flour. Shake off the excess flour.

6. Dip the snapper into the egg wash until all of the flour is wet.

7. Press the snapper into the breading lightly with your hand.

8. Set the snapper on a cookie sheet and continue until all the snapper are coated. Be certain to spread the snapper filets evenly on the cookie sheet. Do not stack them.

9. Unlike some of our breading recipes, this one can be done several hours in advance. Refrigerate until cooking time.

ASSEMBLY

1. Place the cooked snapper filets on the dinner plate.

2. Top with 3 ounces of sauce.

3. Garnish with diced mango and peppers.

133

Mahi Steamed in a Banana Leaf

with Herbed Lemon Wine

Serves 4

"I don't like to say that my kitchen is a religious place, but I would say that if I were a voodoo priestess, I would conduct my rituals there." —Pearl Bailey(1918-1990), Pearl's Kitchen (1973)

Banana leaves can be found in Shanny's backyard or in your gourmet grocery stores. In Austin, we have Central Market and Whole Foods to serve our gourmet needs. You can sometimes locate banana leaves in Asian markets, Mexican markets, or your neighbor's backyard.

Do you remember when a past president ate the cornhusks while dining on tamales? The banana leaves are to the mahi what the cornhusk is to the tamale. It's beneficial in the preparation of the seafood, but really detracts from the flavor of the dish if eaten, a bit too chewy and tough!

"You gone fishin'... Gone fishin' instead of just a-wishin'" —Louis Armstrong

 VARIATIONS: : If you are caught in a non tropical area or it is in the dead of winter on your island, 4 12" pieces of parchment paper can be used as a stand in for the banana leaves.
Other types of fishes can be used. As always, let fresh be your guide.

TIMING: The Herbed Lemon Wine sauce can be made earlier in the day. The fish should not be wrapped any sooner than 30 minutes prior to cooking. The lime in the sauce will turn your fish into ceviche.

GARNISH: The leaf does the trick.

TOOLS:
Steamer
Medium saucepan
Sharp knife
Zester
Whisk

HERBED LEMON WINE

3 cups dry white wine
3 lemons, juiced and zested
4 tablespoons butter
2 cloves garlic, minced
1 shallot, minced
1 teaspoon fresh lemon thyme, minced
1 teaspoon lemon balm, minced
1 teaspoon lemon basil, minced
1/2 teaspoon salt
1 chipotle pepper en adobo, minced
1 tablespoon dark brown sugar

1. In a medium saucepan, reduce the white wine to half a cup.
2. Add the lemon juice and zest, garlic, shallot, lemon thyme, lemon balm, lemon basil, salt, brown sugar and chipotle pepper to the saucepan and return to a simmer.
3. After a slow simmer begins, remove from heat and whisk in the butter.

ASSEMBLY

1 large banana leaf
4 mahi mahi filets, 6 ounces each
Butcher's twine or household string
4 tablespoons butter
Salt and pepper

1. Cut the banana leaf into 12" squares.
2. Lay them out on your countertop.
3. Place a tablespoon of butter into the center of each leaf.
4. Salt and pepper each mahi mahi filet.
5. Place the mahi mahi on the butter pat on the leaf.
6. Evenly distribute the Herbed Lemon Wine sauce on each filet.
7. Fold each leaf up in the same manner as you would when wrapping a gift.
8. Tie the leaf up with the twine in a decorative and secure manner.

STEAMING

Every culture has its own steamer. We prefer the Asian bamboo steamers, but a stainless vegetable steamer will work just fine.

1. Place the wrapped mahi in your steamer, with the folded side up to hold in the herbed lemon wine sauce.
2. Steam over high heat for 12 minutes.
3. Remove from the heat and serve.
4. Eating the banana leaf is optional, although not recommended. The string probably should not be eaten unless you're in need of roughage.

When cutting open the banana leaf wrap...
a perfume of herbs, garlic and ginger tickle
all of your culinary senses!

Really Expensive King Crab
Legs and Lobster Salad

Serves 6

> "Nouvelle Cuisine, roughly translated, means: I can't believe I paid ninety-six dollars and I'm still hungry."
> —Mike Kalin

One of Jeff's first encounters with a star was when he was given the opportunity to cater Jimmy Buffet's bachelor party. Doing a little research, he discovered that Jimmy's relatives were a "Cajun, Indian, wild people" with a "grandfather that was a sailing ship captain". Rather than serving "Cheeseburgers in Paradise", "Come Monday", Jeff decided on this salty, sailor pleasin' seafood dish and added "The Last Mango In Paradise". Jimmy didn't have to plea "Why Don't We Get Drunk", it was a given. This salad was the hit of the party, until Dr. Hunter S. Thompson handed out his 'gonzo' party favors. Suddenly, everyone's appetite evaporated!

VARIATIONS: Shrimp and scallops would be a delicious change.

TIMING: The dressing can be prepared a day in advance. But the salad assembly should be done no more than 2 hours in advance.

GARNISH: Chopped chives or lemon zest on top

TOOLS:
Blender
Sharp knife
Zester
Large bowl

DRESSING

2 egg yolks
1 tablespoon Dijon mustard
1/4 cup rice wine vinegar
3/4 cup macadamia nut oil or extra virgin olive oil
1/4 cup honey
3 lemons, juiced and zested
1/4 cup fresh basil leaves, finely chopped
2 cloves garlic, minced
1 shallot, minced
1 tablespoon salt

1. Put the 2 egg yolks into a blender with the honey, lemon juice, lemon zest, basil, garlic, shallot, mustard, salt, and rice wine vinegar.
2. Puree.
3. While still pureeing, slowly add the oil into the blender.
4. Set aside in refrigerator.

SEAFOOD

(Check with your fishmonger at your grocer for precooked lobster and Alaska king crab legs. All crab legs shipped out of Alaska are mandated by law to be cooked.)

8 ounces lobster meat (most good seafood shops will have precooked lobster available)
8 ounces of king crab leg meat

1/2 cup red bell pepper, 1/4" diced
1/2 cup poblano pepper, 1/4" diced
1/2 cup celery, 1/4" diced
1 cup mango, 1/4" diced
1 cup avocado, 1/4" diced

1. Cut the lobster and crab meat in to 1/2" diced pieces.
2. Mix the crab, lobster, peppers, mango, avocado, and celery together in a bowl.
3. Pour the dressing on the seafood and toss gently.

ASSEMBLY

1 head butter lettuce or Boston lettuce
6 radicchio lettuce leaves

1. Pull 6 leaves from each type of lettuce.
2. Rinse the lettuce and pat dry.
3. Using a jumbo martini glass or margarita glass, line the bottom of the glass with the lettuces.
4. Spoon the seafood salad into the glass on top of the lettuce.
5. Serve.

"A White Sport Coat and a Pink Crustacean"
—Jimmy Buffett

Sweetest meats of the sea partnered
with this zesty herb dressing

Sea Scallops Sautéed
with a Saffron Cream
in a Pumpkin Squash Cup

Serves 8

"One of the delights of life is eating with friends; second to that is talking about eating. And for an unsurpassed double whammy, there is talking about eating while you are eating with friends." —Laurie Colwin

Jeff's favorite saffron story is from the opening of the Fairmont Hotel in Dallas. The purchasing agent was ordering dried spices for the initial inventory for the five different kitchens. He ordered 5 pounds of this spice, 20 pounds of peppercorn, 10 pounds of another spice, you get the picture. Apparently, he had no knowledge of saffron and the fact that it is more expensive than gold. At any rate, he ordered several pounds of saffron. The salesman that took his order clearly was working on commission. He neglected to enlighten the purchaser of the deep debt into which he was about to enter. When the invoice arrived, the saffron cost was in excess of $20,000.00. When this bill hit the accounts payable office, the purchasing agent was ushered into the general manager's office for an herbal education. He was the talk of the hotel's accounts payable department for many weeks.

Here are 3 web suppliers if you are having trouble finding high quality saffron. www.saffron.com or www.wholespice.com or www.spanishtable.com

 VARIATIONS: Shrimp or lobster medallions can be substituted for the scallops.
There are several different types of minipumpkins on the market now. The most common is the Jack-Be-Little, but there are numerous choices of fall gourds that will make this a fun presentation. There are also ceramic pumpkins available at Crate & Barrel. If the pumpkins are not available, you can use large gourd type squashes.

TIMING: Prepare the pumpkins earlier in the day. Everything else must be done immediately prior to service to ensure the best results.

GARNISH: Pumpkin seeds

 TOOLS:
Large sauté pan
Sharp knife
Cookie sheet
Sturdy spoon

SEA SCALLOPS

8 minipumpkins, large enough to hold 4 large scallops
32 large sea scallops (diver hand-picked quality)
3 cups chardonnay
4 tablespoons shallots, minced
2 tablespoons garlic, minced
4 lemons, juiced and zested
1 cup scallions, 1/4" chopped
3 cups heavy cream
1 teaspoon saffron, crushed
1 teaspoon sea salt
1/2 teaspoon white pepper
1/2 cup pumpkin seeds, toasted and seasoned (reserve for garnish)

1. Cut the tops off the pumpkins, just like you would to carve a jack-o-lantern. Using a sturdy spoon, scrape the insides clean. Set aside until you are ready to warm in the oven.

2. Warm the pumpkin tops and bottoms in the oven at 250 degrees as you begin to prepare the sea scallops.

3. In a large saucepan over high heat, reduce the chardonnay to 2 tablespoons. It will be a golden color with a tart rich flavor.

4. Add the garlic, shallots, zest, lemon juice, salt, pepper, and crushed saffron. Simmer until the garlic and shallots are soft, approximately 3 minutes.

5. Add the cream and reduce by half.

6. Add the scallops and the scallions and simmer on medium heat for 5 minutes.

7. Adjust the salt.

8. Serve the scallops and saffron cream in the warmed pumpkins.

 *"Simply the Best" —Tina Turner*

The rich buttery scallop is balanced by the citron and the saffron.

Spicy and Crispy Fried Oysters
on a Bed of Spinach
in a Bacon, Mustard, and Honey Vinaigrette
Serves 4

*"I will not eat raw oysters.
I want my food dead.
Not sick, not wounded,
dead." —Woody Allen.*

Halloween is upon us in Austin, Texas and that first cold wind blows into town. If you stop and listen to this wind, you will clearly hear Mother Nature's recommendation: oysters. This is our favorite recipe for oysters. Your taste buds will be screaming and howling at the full autumn moon.

The vinaigrette offsets the briny oysters in this crispy crust. It is best to make the vinaigrette prior to frying the oysters. You can heat the vinaigrette and wilt the spinach as the last batch of oysters is cooking. Proper timing makes this dish a success! It is of the utmost importance that you not wilt the spinach until just before the last of the oysters are done.

SPICY AND CRISPY CRUSTED OYSTERS

32 fresh oysters (more if they are small)

1 quart oil for frying

1 cup corn flour

1/2 cup corn starch

1/2 cup semolina flour

1 teaspoon habanero powder (cayenne powder for those who don't view extreme heat as a good thing)

1 1/2 teaspoons sea salt

1. In a large saucepan, heat the oil to 350 degrees and hold at that temperature while breading the oysters.
2. Sift all the dry ingredients together in a bowl large enough to bread the oysters.
3. Drain the oysters in a colander.
4. Toss the oysters in the breading, evenly coating them.
5. Divide the oysters into 3 batches. Fry the oysters, one batch at a time. Make certain the oil does not drop below 330 degrees. Give the oil time to recover its heat between each batch.
6. Hold the cooked oysters in a warm (200 degrees) oven while the rest of the oysters are cooking.

WILTED SPINACH & VINAIGRETTE

4 large handfuls of baby spinach, rinsed and dried

1/2 pound smoked bacon, 1/4" diced (reserve enough bacon to make bacon bits for garnish)

1/4 cup honey mustard (we prefer Hudson's on the Bend mustard)

1/4 cup honey

1/4 cup rice wine vinegar

1. In a large sauté pan, cook the bacon over medium high heat until crispy. Drain half of the bacon fat and discard.
2. Add the mustard, honey, and vinegar to the sauté pan with the bacon. Mix while bringing it to a simmer.
3. Place the baby spinach in a large bowl. Pour the simmering hot vinaigrette over the spinach mixing it well.

ASSEMBLY

1 pear, julienned

1. Divide the spinach onto four serving plates.
2. Place the oysters atop the spinach.

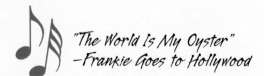

"The World Is My Oyster"
—Frankie Goes to Hollywood

VARIATIONS: There is no substitution for oysters unless you want to go with Viagra. We will give you the "go ahead" for shrimp.

 TIMING: Timing is of the utmost importance. Prepare vinaigrette first. Have spinach ready and set aside, waiting for the dressing. As the last batch of oysters are frying, wilt your spinach. This can be a meal gone bad if you wilt your spinach or fry your oysters too soon. Let the answering machine get the phone!

GARNISH: Crumbled bacon bits and matchsticks of pears.

TOOLS:
Large sauté pan
Large bowls
Large saucepan
Colander
Sifter
Sharp knife

Briny oysters in a crispy crust set against the tart vinaigrette and the smokiness of the bacon

141

Tea Smoked Tuna in a
Chipotle Gingered Shellac

Serves 4

"You can tune a piano, but you can't tuna fish."—Joe Walsh or like my friend Charlie says, "You can tell an alcoholic, but you can't tell him much."

This recipe comes from Jeff and Shanny's very own dinner table. Shanny is an avid fresh tuna fan! She likes it with a crunchy crust and a medium rare center. (Just like she likes her men.) Jeff likes that smoky grill flavor to fire up the little used bitter taste buds found at the back of the mouth. These taste buds are often forgotten by some, but never by Jeff! You can bring them back to life when foods are burnt or charred. So, to get the proper response from Bud, we like to use our stovetop smoker over high heat. With the flavors from the shellac, you will excite the sweet, sour, and salty tastes buds as well.

After all, that is what fired up cooking is all about! Getting all 11,000 taste buds responding at once. If you don't have a stovetop smoker, a hot grill will get the desired effect. If you do have a stovetop smoker, refer to the section on Grilling Meats.

VARIATIONS: You can use swordfish or salmon, but it has got to be sushi grade due to the rareness.

TIMING: Shellac can be made early in the day. The seasoning can be made several days in advance. Smoke the seafood just prior to service.

GARNISH: Pickled ginger or minced candied ginger

TOOLS:
Spice grinder
Medium skillet
Stainless bowl
Medium saucepan
Sharp knife
Stovetop smoker

*"Beloved Wife"
—Natalie Merchant*

CUMIN CILANTRO SEASONING

1 teaspoon cumin seed
3 tablespoons coriander seed
1 teaspoon chipotle chili powder
2 tablespoons lemon pepper
2 tablespoons sea salt

1. In a dry skillet, over medium high heat, toast the cumin and coriander seeds until they are light brown.
2. Using a spice grinder, grind the cumin and coriander seeds until they are almost powder, but not completely pulverized. We want a little crunch and texture.
3. Put the toasted and ground seeds in a bowl. Add the remaining ingredients and mix together.

CHIPOTLE GINGERED SHELLAC

1/4 cup fresh ginger, minced
1/4 cup hoisin sauce
1/4 cup soy sauce
1/4 cup fresh lime juice
1 cup dark brown sugar
4 cloves garlic, minced
2 chipotle chiles en adobe sauce, minced

1. Put all of the ingredients in a saucepan. Heat over medium high heat.
2. Simmer for 8 minutes, stirring occasionally.
3. Reserve for the smoked tuna.

SMOKING THE TUNA

24 ounce tuna loin, grade A, the freshest you can get! (A thick loin cut of number 1 grade tuna is needed for the best results. Buy 6 ounces per person. Smoking it as a large uncut loin works the best.)
1. Liberally coat the outside of the loin with the Cumin Cilantro Seasoning rub.

2. Remove the contents from 4 envelopes of orange pekoe tea and place underneath the rack in the stovetop smoker. The tea gives the tuna a wonderful flavor and keeps the dish on the Asian path.

3. Place the seasoned loin in the smoker.

4. When smoking 24 ounces of tuna, place the smoker over high heat for 8 to 10 minutes. The tuna will be a nice medium rare in the center. If you are one of those people who can't do the medium rare thing, smoke it for an additional 4 to 5 minutes.

5. Remove and slice into 1" thick medallions.

ASSEMBLY

1. Place the sliced tuna medallions on a dinner plate.

2. Brush with the shellac.

Smoky sweet tart and tangy... it's all here!

Texas Jumbo
Lump Crab Au gratin

Serves 4

Casserole of Life

(From Teri Yakimoto)

Life can only be
What you put into it
My life is my casserole
And I want to fill it with fun,
fun, fun, fun

The versatile diversity of casserole
is similar to living life
The ingredients are things that
you can't live without
Everybody's recipe is different
upon what you put in these are
the things that make my life
taste good

"Crab Dance"
—Cat Stevens

 VARIATIONS: Shrimp, crawfish, or lobster can be used or even fresh fish.

 TIMING: Casserole can be premade and refrigerated. You will just need to add 5 to 7 minutes to the baking time if it is cold when it goes into the oven.

GARNISH: None needed

TOOLS:
1 quart ovenproof casserole
Medium saucepan
Whisk
Zester
Sharp knife
2 mixing bowls
Wooden spoon

Lump Crab Au gratin

1 pound jumbo lump blue crab
2 cups dry white wine
6 egg yolks
2 cups heavy cream
2 limes, juiced and zested
1 cup grated Parmesan cheese
1 cup panko bread crumbs
1/2 cup soft goat cheese
1/4 cup garlic, minced
1/4 cup shallots, minced
1 jalapeño, seeded and minced (if you love the heat,…leave the seeds)
1 bunch of cilantro, finely chopped
1/2 cup red bell pepper, 1/4" diced
1 1/2 teaspoons salt

1. In a medium saucepan, over high heat, reduce white wine to 2 tablespoons of amber liquid.
2. Add the heavy cream, garlic, and shallots. Reduce by half.
3. Add the lime juice, jalapeño, bell pepper, and salt. Return to a simmer.
4. In a separate bowl, place your 6 egg yolks. Whisk them together.
5. Slowly whisk the simmering liquid into the egg yolks. It is very important that you add it slowly. Otherwise the hot liquid will scramble the eggs.
6. Return the mixture to the saucepan and simmer for 1 to 2 minutes, until sauce will coat the back of a spoon.
7. Immediately turn off the heat.
8. Add the crab meat and cilantro to the mixture.
9. Pour all of the contents into an ovenproof casserole.
10. Dot the top of the casserole with goat cheese.
11. Evenly spread the Parmesan cheese on top.
12. Evenly spread the panko bread crumbs on top.
13. Bake in the oven for 30 to 35 minutes at 375 degrees, or until the gratin has become crusty and the casserole is bubbly.

Gulf coastal comfort
in a casserole

Veggies
From the Grill & Garden

Abelito's Refried Beans

Backyard Ranch Beans

Eggplant a la Michael Reese

Green Chile Corn Pudding

Skewer of Summer Squash
with Avomole

Green Chile and Mexican
Crème Smashed Potatoes

Grilled Baby Bok Choy with
Spanish Vinegar and Olive Oil

Grilled Peaches with a
Spicy Lemon Honey

Hominy and Green Bean Casserole

Oven Roasted Rosemary Yukon
Gold Potatoes

Texas 1015 Onion Compote

Truffled Mac 'n Cheese

Cook what your mother taught you—but add 2 more jalepeños

Abelito's Refried Beans

Serves 8

Earthy old Mexico comfort food

 VARIATIONS: none

 TIMING: This can be made the day before.

 GARNISH: Cotija cheese crumbled atop Asiago cheese

 TOOLS:
5 quart pot
Rock picker
Sharp knife
Iron skillet
Large fork for mashing

During the early hours of the day, the magic of the restaurant begins to beat. Enter Abel. He is the first to arrive every day. He rhythmically marches through the restaurant and its herb gardens all day dispersing his magic. At noon, he prepares lunch for the staff. This menu always contains offerings from 'south of the border'. Refried beans, the magical fruit, are his staple. We think that is where all of his mystical powers come from— the bean!

Dining at the stainless prep table in the Hudson's kitchen at employee dinner time with Abel, Blas, and Jesus; you learn tricks you would never be privilege to elsewhere. Refried beans in the can should not be your only experience with this bean dish. We cannot emphasize enough what a gourmet treat you will be missing if you stop with the can!

Frying the beans in a large iron skillet brings out a world of flavors. The caramelization and the *el carbon* that occur in the skillet create and enrich the flavors. Instead of becoming a bland side dish the beans become an exciting complement to any southwestern dish.

REFRIED BEANS

4 cups of dried pinto beans
5 slices of smoked bacon, 1/4" diced
3 to 4 dried chipotle peppers
5 cloves of garlic, minced
1 large onion, roughly chopped
3 tablespoons chile powder*
1 tablespoon cumin
1 tablespoon Italian herb seasoning
2 tablespoons onion flakes
1 tablespoon garlic powder
Shredded Asiago cheese
Salt to taste
1 tablespoon olive oil

1. Pick the rocks and dirt from the dried beans and wash four or five times.
2. Place beans in a 5 quart pot and fill to within 2 inches of the top with water.
3. Add the bacon, onions, dried chipotle peppers, and garlic.
4. Bring the water to a boil.
5. Turn the heat to a simmer and add the seasonings.
6. Cover and cook for 4 or 5 hours, until beans are tender.

7. Stir occasionally and make sure the beans are always covered with plenty of water, adding boiling water when necessary to maintain level. It is important that the beans keep their soupy texture.
8. When the beans are fully cooked, salt to taste.
9. Now for the refry…Remove dried chile peppers and discard.
10. Season a large iron skillet with olive oil. Heat the skillet until the oil is just about to begin smoking. At this point, add the beans and liquid to the skillet.
11. Mash the beans with a fork and cook over medium-high heat.
12. Reduce to a simmer and cook until most of the liquid is boiled off.
13. Just before serving, top the beans with shredded Asiago cheese and melt slightly in oven.

*We blend our own chili powder, using equal parts chipotle, New Mexico, San Antonio, dried ancho, and guajillo chile powders. But any type of prepared chile powder works almost as well.

 "Mexico & Mariachis"
—Music from and inspired by Robert Rodriguez

"You are where you eat"
—Fanny Courington.

This recipe was developed for the Backyard. If you are an Austinite, you most likely have enjoyed the music venue at the Backyard on Highway 71. Jeff partnered with Tim O'Connor during the venue's setup to establish the restaurant half of the operation. It was an exciting mix! Tim, long-time owner of Direct Events, brought his passion for rock n roll, and Jeff Blank, owner of Hudson's, brought his immense passion for food to the Backyard table. One of Hudson's most influential chefs, Ron Brannon, did an executive chef gig at this restaurant. At the Backyard, it was quickly recognized that rock n roll and good food reacted like gasoline and water. They do not mix. Unfortunately, the partnership was not a successful recipe. Although the friendship survived, the partnership did not. The Backyard is to this day the most magical of all places to see your favorite musician. And Ron made it out alive...barely!

"You'll find your happiness lies
Right under your eyes
Back in your own
backyard"
—Billie Holliday

VARIATIONS: Change the beers. Jalapeños vary according to taste.

TIMING: This can be made the day before; it's better the second day.

GARNISH: Chopped cilantro and Cotija cheese

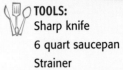

TOOLS:
Sharp knife
6 quart saucepan
Strainer

RANCH BEANS

2 pounds pinto beans, soaked overnight and cooked until tender and drained
1 medium white or yellow onion, minced
1 medium garlic cluster, minced
1 pound bacon, 1/4" diced, cooked and drained
2 ounces Lea and Perrins Worcestershire Sauce
2 medium jalapeños, seeded and minced
2 tablespoons chili powder
1 tablespoon cumin
3 tablespoons molasses
Salt to taste
1 cup cilantro, chopped
1 Shiner bock beer, 12 ounce bottle

1. Simmer all ingredients, except the beans. Continue to simmer until onions are soft. This should take approximately 15 to 20 minutes.
2. Add the cooked beans and simmer 20 to 30 minutes.
3. Add salt to taste.

In the pyramid of Texas food groups...this is the cornerstone.

Eggplant
a la Michael Reese

Serves 6

What can you say about Michael Reese? He does everything to perfection, from designing airplane interiors to cooking for his wonderful wife, Pam. After dining on this eggplant, you will have a complete understanding of what perfect is. Although it may seem lengthy, like everything that the Reeses do, the results are exhilarating!

 VARIATIONS: Don't mess with Mike Reese's eggplant. Why do you think it is called "a la Michael Reese"? This pasta sauce is the best...try it with any Italian pasta dish!

 TIMING: Make it earlier in the day and bake hour prior.

GARNISH: Parmesan

 TOOLS:
9" x 12" x 2" casserole dish
4 quart saucepan
Sharp knife
Peeler
Heavy skillet, 12" or bigger
Cheese grater
Saran Wrap or plastic film
Torch
Cookie sheet
Ziploc bag
Tupperware container
Cookie sheet

PASTA SAUCE

1 teaspoon rice wine vinegar
5 large Roma tomatoes
1 10 ounce can tomato sauce
1 medium onion, minced
3 cloves garlic, minced
3 slices Canadian bacon, roughly chopped
1 poblano or jalapeño pepper, chopped
1 teaspoon fresh basil, minced
1 teaspoon fresh oregano, minced
2 1/2 cups chicken stock (see our Stock Section)
3 teaspoons brown sugar
Salt and pepper to taste
Light olive oil (for sautéing)

1. Prepare the roma tomatoes as follows. Score an "x" on the end opposite the stem of each tomato.
2. Blanch the tomatoes in boiling water for 2 minutes.
3. Place the tomatoes in ice water for 5 minutes.
4. Remove from ice water.
5. Remove the skin, seeds, and stems from the tomatoes.
6. Place tomatoes in a glass bowl or Tupperware container.
7. Mix vinegar, oregano, and basil into tomatoes.
8. Refrigerate.

9. If you want to use the poblano or jalapeño pepper in this recipe, place the chile over an open flame or under an oven broiler until the skin turns black.
10. Remove and let cool.
11. Remove the skin, using paper towels.
12. Remove the stems and seeds and devein the chile.
13. Chop the chile finely.
14. Taste test the chile to see how hot it is. You should refer to this preference in step #20 of this recipe. Use according to your preference for heat.
15. Sauté finely chopped onion and Canadian bacon in olive oil, using a 4 quart saucepan for 4 to 5 minutes over medium heat.
16. Salt and pepper to taste.
17. Stir frequently.
18. Add finely chopped garlic to the pan and stir for another 1 to 2 minutes. Stir constantly to keep garlic from burning.
19. Drain excess olive oil from pan and return to burner.
20. Add 1/4 cup red wine and chiles to pan and reduce to 1 tablespoon.
21. Add 1 1/2 cups of chicken stock and reduce to 1 cup.
22. Add tomatoes, tomato sauce, and brown sugar to chicken stock.
23. Simmer lightly for 2 to 3 hours, stirring occasionally.
24. If the mixture begins to get too dry, add the remaining cup of chicken stock as needed.

It is a vacation in Tuscany!

EGGPLANT PREPARATION

1 medium eggplant
1 cup flour
1 tablespoon salt
1 teaspoon black pepper
1/2 teaspoon white pepper
1/2 teaspoon cayenne pepper
1 tablespoon paprika
1/4 cup olive oil for sautéing

1. Cut ends off of eggplant and remove skin with a potato peeler.
2. Cut the eggplant lengthwise into 1/8" to 1/4" thick slices. A mandoline slices them most easily.
3. Lay flat on Saran Wrap.
4. Salt both sides of eggplant slices.
5. Let sit for 30 minutes to remove bitter flavor.
6. Wash eggplant slices well with water and pat dry with paper towels.
7. In a 1 gallon Ziploc bag filled half full of flour, add salt, black pepper, white pepper, cayenne pepper, and paprika. Shake to mix well.
8. Add 1/4 cup of olive oil to heavy skillet and bring to a medium heat.
9. Put 4 or 5 pieces of sliced eggplant into the bag of seasoned flour and coat each piece well.
10. Shake off excess flour in bag and place eggplant in skillet.
11. Sauté until a light golden brown on each side (approximately 1 to 1 1/4 minutes per side).
12. Remove from skillet and sauté the remaining eggplant.
13. Cool on a cookie sheet.

ASSEMBLY

Prepare eggplant
Prepare sauce
1 package Parmesan cheese, grated
1 package Swedish Fontina cheese, thinly sliced
1 tablespoon olive oil

1. Lightly coat the casserole dish with olive oil.
2. Spoon a layer of tomato sauce about 1/4" deep into the casserole dish.
3. Cover the tomato sauce with a layer of eggplant.
4. Cover the eggplant with a layer of Fontina cheese and sprinkle parmesan cheese over this.
5. Repeat with another layer of sauce, eggplant, and cheese.
6. Cover with one final coat of tomato sauce.
7. Cook at 400 degrees for 1 hour in the oven.
8. Remove from oven and sprinkle parmesan cheese over the top.
9. Cook at 400 degrees for an additional 15 to 20 minutes.
10. Remove from oven and let cool.
11. Section, using a spatula. Let cool for 5 minutes before serving.

Green Chile
Corn Pudding

Serves 10–12

"It doesn't matter who you are, or what you've done, or think you can do. There's a confrontation with destiny awaiting you. Somewhere, there is a chile you cannot eat." —Daniel Pinkwater, "A Hot Time in Nairobi

Our corn pudding recipe is the restaurant's most requested. This recipe was in the *Cooking Fearlessly* cookbook and in all fairness to you, we knew we must include it in this cookbook as well. Predictably, we have changed the original recipe. We have added just a touch of our favorite—the green chiles from New Mexico!

Employees who have gone on to other careers always come back to visit. It's not the owner or the managers or the chefs they miss. It's the corn pudding that draws them back!

"She's sitting on the back steps, just shucking that corn.
That gal's been grinning since the day she was born"
—John Prine

VARIATIONS: One of the beauties of this recipe is that it is so flexible and sturdy that you can modify it any number of ways without altering its personality. Change the peppers to sun-dried tomatoes, if you please. Add different herbs like fresh basil, Mexican marigold mint, whatever you like. Try dried mushrooms, like porcinis or shitake. If Hatch chiles are not in season, use frozen or canned.

TIMING: You can make the batter the day before and store it in a bowl in the refrigerator. Just give it a whisk before putting it in a greased and floured casserole dish at baking time. This recipe is so sturdy you can bake it early and hold it on warm or in a chafing dish.

TOOLS:
9" x 9" casserole dish
Mixing bowls
Whisk or whip
Sharp knife

DRY MIX

1 1/4 cups flour
1/2 cup granulated sugar
2 tablespoons baking powder
1/2 teaspoon salt
1/2 teaspoon cayenne pepper

WET MIX

8 whole eggs
1 stick of butter, melted
1 cup sour cream
1/4 cup fresh squeezed lime juice
1 8 ounce can cream style corn

VEGGIE MIX

3 cups Hatch green chiles, roasted, peeled, seeded, and diced (if not in season, use frozen or canned—be sure to drain well)
1 pound fresh cut corn
1 bunch cilantro, rough chopped

1. Preheat oven to 350 degrees.
2. Combine all dry ingredients in a bowl. Mix well and set aside.
3. In a second bowl, whisk the eggs until blended and then add melted butter, sour cream, lime juice, and cream style corn.
4. Blend the dry ingredients into the wet ingredients using a wire whisk.
5. Add the fresh cut corn kernels and the diced peppers to the mixing bowl. Blend together.
6. Coat the casserole dish with butter or light vegetable oil and dust with flour.
7. Add the mix to the casserole dish. The depth can vary from 1 inch to 2 inches. If the mix is only 1 inch deep, it will cook 5 to 10 minutes faster.
8. Place in a preheated oven at 350 degrees and bake for 40 minutes or until golden brown and firm.

Skewer of Summer Squash with Avomole

Serves 6

"Be a safe eater and always use a condiment."
—unknown

Barefoot children running in the backyard, a summer thunderstorm heard in the distance, and summer squash on the grill. These are all blissful companions for the grilled steak and grilled chicken in the summer time. You should cook your skewers on the grill when you cook your meats. The "el carbon" flavors give the summer squash a new, exciting flavor.

The delightfully buttery, creamy avomole can be used for a gazillion different things. Try it with chips, on fish, as a salad dressing, a topping for chili and enchiladas, and so on. Some people simply like to lick it off of their fingers.

 VARIATIONS: Have a good time expressing yourself with the squash! Of course, let freshness be your guide.
You can add mushrooms and/or jicama for a different flair.

TIMING: Avomole can be made earlier in the day. The avomole will last 2 days if well refrigerated, of course. Squash can be cut and skewered earlier in the day.

 GARNISH: Needs none

TOOLS:
10" skewers
Sharp knife
Medium saucepan
Hot grill
Tongs
Blender

AVOMOLE

3 avocados
5 tomatillos
2 jalapeños
1 cup white onion, roughly chopped
1 bunch cilantro
1/2 cup heavy cream
1/3 cup fresh lime juice
Salt to taste

1. Blanch tomatillos and jalapeños in boiling water for 2 minutes. Shock them in ice water before the bright green color fades.
2. Place the remaining ingredients, except salt, into a blender and puree.
3. Flavor with salt to taste.
4. Chill.

SKEWERED SQUASH

We recommend picking three of the freshest summer squashes. Some of the varieties that we use are yellow crookneck, pattypan, zucchini, chayote or mirliton. You can use any combination you choose.

6 squash
1/2 cup olive oil
Salt and pepper to season
1 fresh lime

1. Cut the squash into 1 1/2" cubes.
2. Skewer the squash.
3. Coat the skewers in olive oil and salt them liberally.
4. Grill the skewers for 3-4 minutes, turning so that the squash is cooked evenly.
5. Squeeze fresh lime juice on the skewers just prior to serving.
6. Put 3-4 ounces of avomole on a dinner plate and place the skewer atop the sauce.

 "Summer lady" –Santana

Green Chile & Mexican Crème
Smashed Potatoes

Serves 8

> "What I'm doing here is seeking to offer protection from life, solely through the means of potato, butter and cream... there are times when only mashed potato will do."
> —Nigella Lawson

Warning to tourists. At the end of summer Austin celebrates the Hatch chiles' rolling into town. If you happen by Whole Foods, you might think they are having a gigantic hippie smoke-in. It is just the much anticipated Austin smell of Whole Foods roasting the Hatch chiles. Chuy's restaurant buys an entire crop and freezes them so they can have them all year long. They put them on everything, right down to the burgers.

There is a natural evolution of the chile's heat. The pepper is initially green. If it is left on the vine, it will slowly turn from green to orange to red. Pick when green for the hottest fire. When it turns red, it starts to lose its heat. The red chiles are commonly used to make wreaths—southwestern *ristras*. After the holidays, dry the chiles and grind them up into your very own homemade New Mexico chili powder.

 VARIATIONS: When Hatch chiles are not in season, go to frozen and then to can.

TIMING: Best to make fresh for dinner

 GARNISH: None needed

TOOLS:
Potato ricer or food mill
6 quart saucepan
Sharp knife
Nonreactive bowl
Plastic wrap

SMASHED POTATOES

6 large Idaho Baker potatoes
1 cup Hatch green chiles, fire roasted and peeled (canned or frozen will work)
1 bunch cilantro, fresh and chopped
1 cup Mexican Crème
1/2 cup Shiner Bock beer
1/2 pound butter
Salt and pepper to taste

1. Place the butter and Mexican Crème at room temperature for an hour. (Cold butter and cold sour cream will activate the gluten and cause the potatoes to become gummy.)
2. Simmer a bottle of Shiner Bock beer over medium heat until it reduces to a 1/2 cup. Keep it warm.
3. Peel and boil the potatoes in salted water until they are tender.
4. Drain the water and smash the potatoes with the ricer.
5. Combine the potatoes with the remaining ingredients.
6. Smash them together.
7. Serve or keep warm until served.

MEXICAN CRÈME

1 cup heavy cream
1/4 cup buttermilk (active buttermilk, not ultrapasteurized buttermilk)*

1. Mix the heavy cream and buttermilk together.
2. Let the mixture sit out overnight in a glass (nonreactive) bowl covered with plastic wrap. This is much like making yogurt.

*Active buttermilk is sold in the dairy section as buttermilk for baking. Modern dairies kill the bacteria in buttermilk. Bacteria is a must for most baking. With this active buttermilk, the French create a topping called crème fraische, Mexicans call it Mexican Crèma.

"Green Heaven"
—Red Hot Chili Peppers

The earthy flavors of taters and smoky Hatch peppers go together like Crosby, Stills, Nash and Young!

Grilled Baby Bok Choy
with Spanish Vinegar and Olive Oil

Spanish Dancer
—Patti Scialfa

Serves 6

"I'm a man. Men cook outside. Women make the three-bean salad. That's the way it is and always has been, since the first settlers of Levittown. That outdoor grilling is a manly pursuit has long been beyond question. If this wasn't firmly understood, you'd never get grown men to put on those aprons with pictures of dancing wienies and things on the front and messages like ' Come 'n' Get It'" —William Geist, New York Times Magazine

Until you try this preparation of bok choy you might see it as just a fancy cabbage.

Shanny proclaimed her dislike for bok choy, until she tasted it fresh off the grill. A special little magic occurs when the bok choy is grilled and it acquires the *el carbon* flavor. The *el carbon* treatment awakens the bitter taste buds that are located in the back of the mouth. Vegetables rarely hit this section of the buds.

Grilling summer vegetables can bring out seasonal flavors, but there's more good news. It also can simplify meal preparation, reduce utility bills, make short work of cleanup, and keep the kitchen cool on a hot summer day!

VARIATIONS: Substitute a balsamic vinegar in place of the Spanish vinegar for a sweeter flavor.

TIMING: This is meant to be cooked when you are cooking meat or seafood on the grill.

The bok choy should be the last thing to be put on the grill

GARNISH: Needs none

TOOLS:
Blender
Sharp knife
Hot grill
Zester

SPANISH VINAIGRETTE

1/2 cup Cepa Vieja Spanish vinegar (or top of the line Spanish vinegar)
2 lemons, juiced and zested
2 cloves garlic, minced
1 shallot, minced
1 teaspoon sea salt
1/2 teaspoon ground black pepper
1 cup extra virgin olive oil

1. Set olive oil aside.
2. Put the remaining ingredients, except the olive oil, into a blender and puree.
3. Slowly drizzle the olive oil into the blender.
4. Set aside until the bok choy is ready to be grilled.

BOK CHOY

6 whole baby bok choys

1. Cut each bok choy in half, lengthwise.
2. Dip each bok choy in the vinaigrette, completely covering the bok choy.
3. Place the bok choys on the grill.
4. Grill for approximately 1 minute on each side, totaling 2 to 3 minutes cooking time. Some of the leafier parts of the bok choy will be charred black. This is to be expected.
5. Remove from the grill and drizzle the vinaigrette over the bok choys and serve.

Grilled veggies with
a sharp vinaigrette...
mmmm

Grilled Peaches with a Spicy Lemon Honey

Serves 4

> "A Fredericksburg peach, a real Fredericksburg peach, a backyard great-grandmother's orchard peach, is as thickly furred as a sweater, and so fluent and sweet that once you bite through the flannel, it brings tears to your eyes."
> —Melissa Fay Greene

If it is a good season for peaches, we will cook them any way imaginable. Harvest time for these peaches begins in June, but the cling-free peaches don't show up at the market until early July. We always wait until the cling-free peaches appear; it's the only way to go!

Do you have problems with allergies? Dr. Jeff suggests that you always use regional honey because the bees get the pollen from whatever it is in your neck of the woods that makes you sneeze, wheeze, and itch. If you eat a little of the pollen that pesters you, it works as an antidote. We like Texas wildflower honey; and we always buy nonpasteurized honey. To this day, we don't know why people pasteurize honey. Pasteurization kills some of honey's beneficial qualities. Can you imagine Jeff's excitement when he found bee legs and wings in the honey while cooking in Ojinaga, Mexico!!! It doesn't get more organic than that. Honey is the only food that will never spoil.

 VARIATIONS: For dessert, use marscapone cheese rather than goat cheese for a spicy, healthy dessert!

 TIMING: Rub the peach flesh with lemon juice to avoid browning if you are not cooking immediately or better yet, cut just prior to cooking. Spicy lemon honey can be made a day in advance.

GARNISH: none

TOOLS:
Medium saucepan
Sharp knife
Hot grill
Whisk
Tongs

SPICY LEMON HONEY

1 cup honey
1/4 cup rice wine vinegar
3 lemons, juiced and zested
3 serrano peppers, minced (deseeding is optional, serranos are hotter than jalapeños)
1 teaspoon sea salt

1. Add all of the listed ingredients to a medium saucepan and bring to a low simmer.
2. Simmer for 5 minutes.
3. Set aside to use for the grilling.

GRILLED PEACHES

4 peaches, halved and pitted (peaches must be firm to hold up to the grilling process)
8 tablespoons goat cheese
2 tablespoons olive oil
Sea salt to taste

1. Cut a flat spot on the skin side of the peach about the size of a quarter so that it will sit still on the plate.
2. Salt the flesh side of the peach.
3. Rub the peaches with olive oil.
4. Place the peach fleshy side down on the grill. Grill for 2 minutes.
5. Flip the peaches over with the skin side down, and grill for 2 minutes.
6. While the skin side is grilling, put 1 tablespoon of goat cheese in the hole that once held the pit.
7. Place grilled peach on dinner plates and drizzle liberally with the spicy lemon honey. Salt to taste.

"Wild Honeycomb"
—Jeb Loy Nichols

Hominy and
Green Bean Casserole

Serves 8–10

*"String Bean
and Jean"*
*—Belle and
Sebastian*

> *"Vegetarianism is harmless enough,
> though it's apt to give a person
> wind and self-righteousness."*
> **—Sir Robert Hutchinson**

Perini Ranch in Buffalo Gap Texas,
top 10 in *Gourmet Magazine*.

In the beginning, Perini Ranch was out in the country
and far, far away from the eyes of the Department of
Agriculture. Lo and behold, in 2001 the *New York Times*
picked Tom's famous smoked tenderloins as one of the top
10 recommended gifts to ship to loved ones for Christmas.
But, as all celebrities can attest, along with fame comes
undesirable attention.

Everyone in the country started taking note of Tom's
tenders. The USDA called Tom to check on his type of
tenderloin and his method of smoking, and informed him
of the need for a permit to sell and transport tenders
across state lines. The USDA called on a daily basis.
Tom answered these daily phone calls in a high-pitched
woman's voice "Tom's not here".

Well, Tom discovered that you can run, but, you can't
hide from the USDA. He eventually walked the walk
through the maze of legal red tape and within several
weeks had a license to ship worldwide. Since then he has
cooked for Bush and Putin at the Ranch and has even
gone to Moscow to smoke his world famous tenderloins.

Tom is famous for his tenderloins. But it was his hominy
casserole that got our attention. We stole this little
side dish that he serves with the tenderloin. This recipe
is a twisted and turned version of Tom Perini's Hominy
Casserole.

We think our recipe is a wee bit more civilized. With
the "change three ingredients" rule, a recipe usually
ends up with an abundance of ingredients and
flavors. We think this one has acquired some unique
complexity in its flavor.

VARIATIONS: Leave
the bacon out for a
vegetarian dish, but, then
why do you have this
cookbook?

Wild boar would be really
good in this dish.

TIMING: Casserole
can be prepared
earlier in the day, baked
1 hour prior to service

GARNISH: Needs none

TOOLS:
9" x 12" casserole
2 large mixing bowls
Sharp knife

CASSEROLE

3 16 ounce cans yellow hominy
1 pound blanched* green beans cut into 1" lengths
1 pound bacon, cooked and drained
1 cup Hatch New Mexico chiles, roasted, peeled,
    seeded, and 1/4" diced
1 cup red onion, 1/4" diced
1/3 cup garlic, minced
1/2 tablespoon dark chili powder (ancho)
1/2 tablespoon cumin
1/2 tablespoon sage
1/2 tablespoon oregano
1 tablespoon salt
1/4 cup brown sugar
1 cup cheddar cheese
1 cup Monterey Jack cheese
2 cups Panko bread crumbs
10 whole eggs
*cooked in boiling salted water for 1 minute and then shock in
  ice water to preserve color and crispness

1. Preheat oven to 375 degrees.
2. Drain hominy
3. Chop cooked bacon into 1/4" pieces.
4. Mix hominy, green beans, onion, bacon, garlic, chili powder,
   Hatch chile, cumin, sage, brown sugar, oregano, and salt in a
   bowl.
5. Whisk 10 eggs.
6. Pour the whisked eggs into the hominy mixture.
7. Pour into 9"x 12" casserole.
8. Layer cheese on top and cover with Panko bread crumbs.
9. Bake at 375 degrees for 50 minutes.

Smoky bacon and sweet hominy...
you'll find yourself pickin'
at the crust!

Oven Roasted Rosemary
Yukon Gold Potatoes

Serves 4

"Where Rosemary flourished, the woman ruled." —Unknown

This recipe is one of our favorites because it is simple and fast. You will serve flavors to your family and friends that make them think you spent the entire day in the kitchen, when in fact it is a 5 minute process!

"There is a vulgar belief in Gloucestershire and other counties that rosemary will not grow well unless where the mistress is 'master'; and so touchy are some of the lords of creation upon this point, that we have more than once had reason to suspect them of privately injuring a growing rosemary in order to destroy this evidence of their want of authority."

The Treasury of Botany

"Come On-A My House"
—Rosemary Clooney

 VARIATIONS: Works with every variety of potato.

 TIMING: If you quarter your potatoes early, cover with water in a bowl to prevent oxidation. All of the ingredients can be prepared earlier in the day.

 GARNISH: None needed.

TOOLS:
Sharp knife
Cookie sheet
Bowl

OVEN ROASTED POTATOES

8 small Yukon gold potatoes, quartered
1/2 cup extra virgin olive oil
1/2 cup fresh rosemary leaves, removed from stems and roughly chopped
4 cloves garlic, minced
1 tablespoon salt
1 teaspoon ground black pepper

1. Preheat the oven to 400 degrees.
2. Place all the ingredients in a bowl and toss together. The potatoes should be completely covered with the olive oil and seasonings.
3. Bake for 15 to 20 minutes, until the potatoes are crisp on the outside and creamy on the inside.

Sharp garlic and pungent rosemary do the Texas 'Two Step' with the creamy potatoes.

Texas 1015
Onion Compote

Serves 8–10

> "Life is like an onion: You peel it off one layer at a time, and sometimes you weep." —Carl Sandburg

The fifteenth day of the tenth month of the year is planting day for this onion in Texas. Thus, it got its name, Texas 1015 onion. Don't let an onion make you cry! If you refrigerate your onions and wait until they are well chilled before slicing and dicing, you will find that it is no longer an emotional experience.

VARIATIONS: You can use sweet Vidalia onions from Macon, Georgia

Substitute 1 cup of a good balsamic vinegar for the sherry vinegar to make the dish sweet and tangy!

TIMING: You can prepare this 3 hours prior to service.

GARNISH: Place a big steak underneath the onions.

TOOLS:
Sharp knife
12" heavy skillet

ONION COMPOTE

6 1015 onions, cut in half and julienne
1 stick butter
1 pound butter, cut into 1" cubes (reserve to be used in step 4 to finish the compote)
1/4 cup olive oil
4 cups veal stock, reduced to 1 cup (refer to Stock Section)
4 tablespoons garlic
1 cup sherry vinegar (we recommend using a really good sherry vinegar such as "Vinegre de Jerez")
Salt and pepper to taste

1. In a large skillet, over high heat, add butter, oil, and onions and cook until the onions are fully caramelized. Depending upon the horse power of your flame top, this could take up to 20-30 minutes. The onions should be a rich golden brown.
2. Add sherry to deglaze the pan.
3. Add veal stock and garlic and continue cooking on high until almost dry.
4. Remove from heat and add butter cubes one at a time until the entire pound has been worked into sauce. Salt and pepper to taste.
5. Hold in a warm place until service.

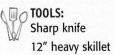

"Vidalia, Vidalia
Girl won't you tell me why
Sweet Vadalia
You always gotta make me cry"
—Sammy Kershaw

Truffled Mac 'n Cheese

Serves 10–12

"Take a bowl of macaroni and cheese and call me in the morning."
—mac 'n cheese website

Immediately after 9/11, everyone was craving comfort food. This one appeared on our menu as a result of Becky's need to comfort the world with her God-given talents. She elevated the lowly mac 'n cheese to a gourmet level. Though the veal meatloaf with a foi gras center and the buffalo hamburger did not survive on our menu, the Truffled Mac 'n Cheese lives on at Hudson's.

Rich, earthy gooey!!!!!

 VARIATIONS: Choice of pasta is entirely up to you. Replace pecarino cheese for Parmesan.

Boursin cheese can be replaced with any soft herb cheese.

TIMING: This can be prepared in advance, refrigerated, and baked at the last minute.

GARNISH: Truffle slices or more grated cheese

 TOOLS:
6 quart saucepan
4 quart saucepan
Cheese grater
Sharp knife
Large kitchen spoon for mixing
9 x 9 ovenproof casserole
Truffle slicer
Colander

MAC 'N CHEESE

1 pound dried pasta (macaroni, penne, cavatappi)
1/4 cup truffle oil
1 quart heavy cream
1/2 stick of butter
6 tablespoons all-purpose flour
Dash cayenne pepper
Salt and pepper to taste
1 cup grated Parmesan
1 cup Boursin cheese
1 truffle
1 cup bread crumbs
1 tablespoon truffle oil
3 tablespoons melted butter
2 tablespoons fresh herbs (parsley and chives)

1. Cook pasta in a large pot of boiling salted water, until just tender.
2. Cool pasta with ice and then drain in colander.
3. Toss pasta with 1/4 cup truffle oil.
4. Melt 1/2 stick butter in a heavy bottomed saucepan.
5. Stir in flour to make a blonde roux. Don't brown.
6. Add heavy cream and simmer mixture until it thickens.
7. Season with cayenne, salt, and pepper.
8. Remove from heat and add pasta and cheeses.
9. Stir to combine.
10. Taste mixture and adjust salt and pepper if needed.
11. Pour into a buttered ovenproof casserole dish.
12. In a bowl, combine bread crumbs, melted butter, 1 tablespoon of truffle oil, and herbs.
13. Pour bread crumbs over the pasta cheese mixture.
14. Bake until golden brown at 400 to 425 degrees for approximately 25 minutes.
15. Garnish with truffle slices. (Optional, if you would rather avoid the expense.)

"Comfort You"
—Van Morrison

Desserts

Bread Puddin' with Sour Mash Sauce

Hill Country Peach and White Chocolate Towers

Mimi's Peach Beehives with a Vanilla Rum Glaze

Passion Fruit Curd Crepes Topped with Cajeta Sauce

Peach and Dewberry Cobbler

Pumpkin Cranberry Crème Brûlée

Roger's Margarita Passion Fruit Tart Pie!

The Little Tart's Tarte Tatin

The World's Richest Dreamsicle

Way South of the Border Ancho Pepper Pecan Pie

*The best way to deal
with temptation is to give into it.*

Bread Puddin'
with Sour Mash Sauce

Serves 8

"Always serve too much bourbon sauce on bread puddin'. It makes people overjoyed, and puts them in your debt." —Anonymous

This recipe was created on the banks of the Rio Grande by Chad and Amber Burns, a husband and wife team. They have such a happy marriage that they have practically become one! Jeff found himself entering their kitchen in the Ocotillo Restaurant and calling for them as Chamber. It worked, the two would look up and reply in unison.

One of Chamber's favorite marketing tactics in their Ocotillo Restaurant kitchen was to send out a complimentary bread pudding. As the smells went a bubblin' and a waftin' through the room... it sold itself. Chamber couldn't keep up with the incoming puddin' orders!

" If you don't eat yer meat, you can't have any pudding. How can you have any pudding if you don't eat yer meat?"
—Pink Floyd

VARIATIONS: Use Hudson's on the Bend Bourbon Vanilla Praline Sauce (www.hudsonsonthebend.com).

TIMING: Sour Mash Sauce can be made well in advance. The bread puddin' is always good reheated for many desserts following.

GARNISH: The sauce and a scoop of ice cream are the perfect garnish.

TOOLS:
9" x 12" casserole
Large mixing bowl
Whisk
Sharp knife
Ladle
Large sauce pot
   (recommended serving in a cast iron skillet or some sort of individual metal casserole)

BREAD PUDDIN'

6 eggs
2 1/2 cups heavy cream
2 tablespoons vanilla paste
1 teaspoon cinnamon
1/2 teaspoon salt
4 cups stale bread cut into 1" cubes (pumpkin, apple, raisin, and nut breads or Danish pastries and croissants add more flavor)
1 cup brown sugar
1/2 cup dark rum
1/2 cup sour cherries
1/2 cup dates, chopped
1 cup white chocolate chips

1. In a large bowl, beat the eggs.
2. Mix all of the other ingredients, with the exception of the bread, in the large bowl with the eggs.
3. Place the bread in a casserole dish.
4. Pour the wet mixture on top of the bread and mix.
5. Bake at 375 degrees for 40 minutes.

SOUR MASH SAUCE

1 cup Jack Daniel's sour mash bourbon
1/2 pound butter
2 tablespoons vanilla bean paste
1/2 tablespoon cinnamon
1 cup rum
1 cup heavy cream
2 cups dark brown sugar
1/2 teaspoon nutmeg

1. Heat the rum and the sour mash bourbon over high heat. (Caution, two cups of burning alcohol can produce a 4 foot flame on your stove top! It would probably be safer to burn 1 cup of alcohol at a time.)
2. Reduce by half.
3. Add all the remaining ingredients, except for the butter.
4. Bring to a rolling boil for 7 minutes.
5. Remove from the heat and whisk in the butter.
6. Set aside for final assembly.

You can taste this dessert from 10 paces....

ASSEMBLY

1. Preheat 6 iron skillets or ovenproof dishes (5" to 6" dishes) in an oven at 400 degrees. This is optional; you can serve it on a plate.

2. In each skillet, place a large spoonful of hot pudding.

3. Top with 3 ounces of the Sour Mash Sauce.

4. Top with a scoop of vanilla ice cream.

5. Run to the table while it is bubbling! Serve it on trivet or charger to protect your tabletop.

Hill Country Peach and White Chocolate Towers

Serves 8

"Strength is the capacity to break a chocolate bar into four pieces with your bare hands — and then eat just one of the pieces." —Judith Viorst (1931—)

The Mayan people were some of the first to grow large plantations of cacao as early as 600 AD. Early explorers brought chocolate to Europe. It was later brought to North America. During World War II, soldiers got chocolate candy bars as part of their rations.

Given the ancient Mayan's great intelligence and their profound religious fervor, it was inevitable that they would create their own religious architecture. We too have our own religious adoration for the peach and we have created this tower of peaches to worship!

*"It's party time for the guys in the tower"
—Elton John*

 VARIATIONS: When peach season is not to be, a really ripe nectarine will work

 TIMING: The white chocolate cream can be made that morning, but assembly must be just prior to serving.

8 large peaches, ripe
16 ounces white chocolate (best quality you can buy)
6 cups heavy cream
3 tablespoons vanilla bean paste
1/3 cup confectioner's sugar
1/2 cup cinnamon sugar (2 tablespoons cinnamon mixed with 1/2 cup sugar)
16 wonton wrappers
16 ounces mascarpone cheese (softened at room temperature for 1 hour)
2 cups canola oil
2 lemons
2 tablespoons Gran-Marnier
Zest of 1 orange for garnish

1. Chop or break the white chocolate into small bits.
2. Bring 2 cups of the heavy cream to a rolling boil.
3. Mix the chocolate bits and the heated heavy cream together in a mixing bowl. Whisk until the chocolate is melted.
4. Whisk in the Grand Marnier.
5. Refrigerate until well chilled.
6. Whisk the vanilla bean paste and confectioners sugar with four cups of heavy cream until stiff.
7. Add 1/4 cup mascarpone cheese and whisk.
8. Remove the chilled white chocolate cream from refrigerator.

GARNISH: Orange zest

TOOLS:
4 quart saucepan
Sharp knife
Mixing bowls
12" skillet
2 whisks
Tongs
Pastry bag with star tip

9. Whisk the two creams together until well blended.
10. Refrigerate while preparing wontons.
11. In a large skillet, bring the canola to 325 degrees.
12. Lightly fry the wontons, until a golden brown.
13. Dust the wontons with the cinnamon sugar and cool.
14. Leaving the skins on the peaches, remove the pits and slice the peaches.
15. Squeeze the juice of the lemons over the peaches and refrigerate.

ASSEMBLY

1. Using a pastry bag with a star tip, fill the bag with the whipped cream.
2. Lay a wonton on a plate to make your first layer.
3. Squeeze the cream around the edge of the wonton to make your second layer.
4. To form your third layer, cover the cream with sliced peaches.
5. Top the peaches with more cream and then top that with another wonton.
6. Repeat this process as many times as you dare. We have never gone higher than two stories.
7. Top your finished tower with a decorative dollop of white chocolate cream!

A hill country summer is captured in the perfume of tree ripened peaches.

Mimi's Peach Beehives
with a Vanilla Rum Glaze

Serves 6

*"Comfort me with peaches:
for I am sick of love."*
—The Song of Solomon 2:5

This recipe came to us from Hill Country peach lover and foodie extraordinaire, Russell Lewis. His mother, who is known as Mimi to her grandkids, was kind enough to share her San Angelo based recipe. Some of our greatest treasures have come from San Angelo! That is the birthplace of Earl the Girl, Los Lonely Boys, and Fess Parker.

We of course changed several of the ingredients. (The law of possession requires changing at least 3 ingredients!)

This dessert is better than mom's peach pie because it has this decadent glaze poured over the top just before service. Feel free to nestle a scoop of your favorite homemade ice cream next to the peach.

We have found that you can prepare the beehive the day before. Be sure to use a firm peach. We prefer the cling free variety. If you place the peach beehives in a 400 degree oven at the beginning of your meal, you should have a golden brown delight at the end of your meal.

GLAZE

2 sticks unsweetened butter at
   room temperature
1 whole egg
2 tablespoons vanilla bean paste
1/4 tablespoon nutmeg
1/2 tablespoon cinnamon
2 cups powdered sugar
2 ounces rum
1 tablespoon rum extract
Dash of salt

1. In a mixer, cream the butter and sugar until it is pale.
2. Add the egg and blend.
3. Add all the remaining ingredients and blend.
4. In a saucepan, warm the glaze to a liquid before topping the peaches.
5. Set aside to be used for a topping for the peaches.

CINNAMON SUGAR

1 tablespoon cinnamon
4 tablespoons granulated sugar

1. Mix cinnamon and sugar together.
2. Set aside.

EGG WASH

1 egg
1/4 cup milk

1. Whisk the two together.

ASSEMBLY

6 firm peaches
2 pie shells

1. Prepare your favorite pie dough recipe. You will find ours in the dairy case at the store.
2. Roll the dough out and cut it into 1/2" strips.
3. Place your firm peach, stem side down and wrap the pastry strips around the unpeeled peach. Coat the dough with the egg wash and wrap the dough around the peach. It will act as food glue and will add a golden crust to the final outcome. Overlap each row until you have covered the peach so it looks like a cartoon beehive.
4. Sprinkle the cinnamon sugar on the dough covered peach.
5. Place the peaches on a baking sheet and bake at 400 degrees for 35 minutes, or until golden brown.
6. Remove and place on a service plate.
7. Drizzle the glaze on top of each peach.
8. A hot skillet adds a little drama as the glaze begins to trickle down and bubble!

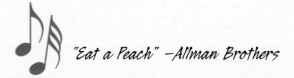

"Eat a Peach" —Allman Brothers

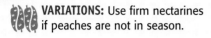

VARIATIONS: Use firm nectarines if peaches are not in season.

TIMING: Peach beehives can be wrapped with the pastry that morning but, bake them at the beginning of the meal. Glaze can be made in the morning as well.

GARNISH: Glaze and a scoop of ice cream.

TOOLS:
Mixer
Rolling pin
Sharp knife
Baking sheet
Whisk
Ladle
Saucepan
Mixing bowls

One can taste this dish before it gets to the table— baked peaches, cinnamon, vanilla, rum and brandy all vaporizing into the air.

Passion Fruit Curd Crepes
Topped with Cajeta Sauce

Serves 6

*"I drive way too fast
to worry about cholesterol."*
—Steven Wright.

An egg-shaped tropical fruit that is also called a purple granadilla, the passion fruit has a brittle, wrinkled, purple-brown rind enclosing flesh-covered seeds, something like a pomegranate (*granadilla* means "little pomegranate" in Spanish). The seeds are edible, so you can eat the orange pulp straight from the shell. Passion fruit is more commonly sieved, and its highly aromatic pulp and juice are used as a flavoring for beverages and sauces.

Native to Brazil, passion fruits are grown in Hawaii, Florida, and California. These crops, along with imports from New Zealand, keep passion fruit on the market all year. Choose large, heavy fruits. If the skin is not deeply wrinkled, keep the fruit at room temperature until it is: the leathery rind, however, will not soften much. Ripe passion fruit can be refrigerated for a few days.

This web site will ship to you over night. www.perfectpuree.com

♪♪ *"Passion"* —JJ Cale

VARIATIONS: If you don't want to make the cajeta sauce, you can use a caramel sauce.

TIMING: Curd should be made at least 6 hours prior, so it can chill and firm up. Rolling of crepes should be done no more than 2 hours prior to dinner.

GARNISH: Fresh fruit and powdered sugar sprinkled on plate.

TOOLS:
2 large bowls
Strainer
6" Teflon saucepan for crepe making
Blender
Parchment paper
Spatula
6 quart saucepan
Whisk
1 ounce ladle

FILLING

1/2 pound butter

1 cup passion fruit puree concentrate (www.perfectpuree.com)

10 egg yolks

1 3/4 cups sugar

1 tablespoon and 2 teaspoons cornstarch

1/4 cup heavy cream

1. In a large bowl, combine sugar, cornstarch, and egg yolk and whisk together until well blended.
2. Bring passion fruit puree and melted butter to a boil in a saucepan.
3. Slowly add the heated puree to the egg mixture. Remember to do this very slowly, add a small amount at a time. If you add all of the hot puree mixture to the eggs at once, the eggs will scramble. They need to adjust to the heat very slowly.
4. Return mixture to saucepan and stir constantly on low heat until thickened.
5. Cool the mixture slightly.
6. Add the heavy cream to the mixture and whisk together.
7. Pass curd through a fine strainer.
8. Chill curd completely. Approximately 1 hour.

CREPES

(Dessert crepes can be found in the dairy case in your grocery store)

7 eggs

2 1/2 cups milk

2 cups all-purpose flour

4 tablespoons confectioner's sugar

1/2 teaspoon salt

3 tablespoons vanilla bean paste

1/2 teaspoon ground cinnamon

Vegetable oil for crepe preparation

1. Combine all ingredients in blender.
2. Blend until smooth.
3. For best results, allow batter to rest 1 to 2 hours before making. It allows the gluten to relax.
4. Heat 8" Teflon pan and 1/2 teaspoon of vegetable oil until almost smoking.
5. Pour in one ladle of crepe mixture.
6. Roll the mixture in the pan, evenly coating the bottom.
7. Loosen crepe with spatula and turn over to cook the other side.
8. Slide off onto a plate.
9. Layer each crepe with a piece of parchment paper.
10. Repeat until you have made 12 crepes.

CAJETA SAUCE

1 quart goat's milk

1 cup sugar

1/8 cup light corn syrup

1 cinnamon stick

1/4 teaspoon baking soda, dissolved in 1 tablespoon hot water

1 ounce rum

1. Combine the milk, sugar, corn syrup, and cinnamon in a saucepan.
2. Bring to a boil.
3. Remove from the heat and add the baking soda/water mixture and stir.
4. Return to the heat and simmer over medium high until golden brown and has reduced to a thick syrup consistency. The volume should reduce by 75%.
5. Add the rum to thin the sauce to a light syrup like consistency.
6. Remove the cinnamon stick and reserve the sauce for topping.

ASSEMBLY

1. Put 2 to 3 ounces of the mixture on the center of the crepe.
2. Roll the crepe.
3. Ladle the warm sauce atop the crepe.

A tart curd embraced by a light crepe and topped with a rum caramel sauce.

Peach and Dewberry Cobbler

Serves 12

> *"The devil has put a penalty on all things we enjoy in life. Either we suffer in health or we suffer in soul or we get fat."* —Albert Einstein

Food snobs, take a hike. We're tired of designer food. We want something real and we want a lot of it, the kind of dessert Grandma would pull out of the oven and serve with big scoops of ice cream melting over the top. We want the ultimate comfort food, an old-fashioned cobbler made with real butter and lots of juicy, fresh fruit!

In the Texas Hill Country the last two weeks of June, the wild dewberries are abundant and delicious.

"All I wanna do is have some fun"
—Sheryl Crow

VARIATIONS: Good tart blackberry instead of a dewberry.

TIMING: The cobbler should be done and put in the oven at the beginning of the meal.

GARNISH: Ice cream

TOOLS:
Bowls
9" x 12" casserole
Whisk

COBBLER

1 cup butter, melted
2 cups flour
1 tablespoon baking powder
3 cups sugar
1 1/2 cups milk
4 cups sliced peaches
3 cups dewberries
1/4 cup cornstarch
1 teaspoon cinnamon
3/4 cup boiling water

1. Preheat oven to 400 degrees.
2. Combine flour, baking powder, and 2 cups of sugar in a bowl.
3. Whisk in milk and melted butter until well blended.
4. Place fruit in a 12" x 9" casserole dish.
5. Cover top of fruit with batter.
6. Combine cornstarch, 1 cup of sugar, and cinnamon.
7. Sprinkle over batter.
8. Bake at 400 degrees for 15 minutes.
9. Remove from oven and pour boiling water over the top. Continue to bake an additional 30 minutes, or until brown and bubbly.

Juicy,
fruity,
crunchy
and sweet!

Pumpkin Cranberry
Crème brûlée

Serves 6

"Ideas are a dime a dozen, people who implement them are priceless" —Mary Kay Ash

Several years ago, Jeff and Shanny were sitting in the Santa Café in New Mexico with a good friend (a wonderful restaurant, not to be missed if you are in the area). He turned to Jeff and said "You know you just can't get enough crème brûlée". With that comment and a smile on his face he ordered more crème brûlée.

After returning to Austin, crème brûlée was added to the dessert menu. In typical Hudson's style, it wasn't *PLAIN* crème brûlée! Fall was in the air and Thanksgiving was just around the corner. Inspired by the sights, sounds, and smells of autumn, we put a cranberry twist to the traditional French custard. This is the typical reaction and interaction at Hudson's that creates our style of menu.

This recipe can be made a day or two ahead of time and stored in the refrigerator. Then all you have to do is caramelize the sugar layer on top just prior to service. This recipe is for 6, but it doubles with great success for 12 and "hey, you can't get enough crème brûlée"!

"She was sittin' in the corner of a café In the burnin' heart of downtown Santa Fe Pickin' on a Gibson and singin' "Baby, Can't You See""

"Santa Fe"—Shawn Mullins

 VARIATIONS: Sour cherries, golden raisins

 TIMING: This can be made a day or two ahead of time and caramelized prior to service.

GARNISH: Burnt sugar is garnish

 TOOLS:
Torch
6 quart saucepan
2 large bowls
Wire sieve
6 – 4 ounce ramekins or crème brûlée cups
12" x 12" water bath pan
Whisk

2 cups heavy cream
1/2 cup and 2 tablespoons sugar
1/4 teaspoon cinnamon
1/4 teaspoon ginger, minced
1/8 teaspoon nutmeg
1/8 teaspoon allspice
1 tablespoon vanilla paste
6 large egg yolks
6 tablespoons dried cranberries (craisins)
1/2 cup pumpkin puree (canned)

1. Preheat oven to 300 degrees.
2. Combine cream, sugar, spices, and vanilla paste in a large heavy bottomed sauce pot over medium high heat and bring to a boil.
3. While that is heating to boil, in a separate bowl combine yolks and pumpkin puree and blend with a whisk.
4. After the cream mixture comes to a boil, slowly add 1/2 of the mixture to the egg mixture. Remember to add the hot cream mixture very slowly and a little bit at a time. If you pour the hot mixture into the eggs all at once, you will scramble the egg mixture!
5. Pour all the combined egg and cream mixture into the remaining half of the hot cream in the large pot and cook until it coats the back of a spoon (this will occur just before it begins to boil).
6. Remove from the heat and strain through a sieve.
7. Fill six 4 ounce ramekins or small mold type cups (make sure they are oven proof) with 1 tablespoon of dried cranberries.
8. Pour the crème brûlée liquid mixture on top of the cranberries, filling the ramekins.
9. Set the molds in a deep baking pan. Pour hot water into the baking pan. The water should be deep enough to cover the bottom fourth of the sides of the ramekins.
10. Bake for 25 to 30 minutes or until they are set.
11. To test for doneness, tap the side with a spoon. If it ripples it is not quite set.
12. When done, remove and cool on a wire rack at room temperature.
13. Refrigerate overnight.
14. Just prior to service, sprinkle granulated sugar evenly across the top of each custard and caramelize the sugar into a dark brown thin sheet. This can be done in a preheated broiler, but you must be very careful not to burn them. We prefer to use a propane torch; it's very quick and will not heat the custard. It will melt the sugar evenly and leave the custard chilled.

Creamy rich pumpkin is offset by tart cranberries with a sugar crunch!

Roger's Margarita Passion
Fruit Tart Pie!

Serves 6

Jesse Lemos was a recent graduate of the CIA and was working for our good friend Roger Joseph. Although Roger is an entertainer and very entertaining, he was unable to keep Jesse employed full time, so we welcomed Jesse to our staff.

Roger's 10th anniversary of his 50th birthday was rapidly approaching. (You can do the math.) We wanted to create a sweet for our sweetie on his special day, and this came to be Jesse's first creative contribution to Hudson's on the Bend.

Jesse decided to marry two of Roger's great loves, passion fruit and tequila! Chemically, passion fruit defies the thickening of eggs. So Jesse had to triple the amount of eggs. Voila! Roger's Passionate Margarita Pie!

♪♫ "Never Grow Old" —Toots and the Maytalls

TIMING: This can be made a day in advance so it can be well chilled and gelled.

GARNISH: Meringue topping torched in the most decorative fashion you can imagine.

 TOOLS:
9" pie pan
Whisk
Mixing bowls
Food processor
Mixer or whisk with really strong arms
Pastry bag with star tip

CRUST

1/2 cup slivered almonds
1 cup graham cracker crumbs
1/2 cup sugar
3 tablespoons melted butter

1. Toast the almonds in a 350 degree oven until they are golden brown.
2. Combine the almonds, graham cracker crumbs, and sugar in a food processor.
3. Pulse to chop the almonds and blend the crust mixture. Texture is best for this crust. Do not over chop.
4. Add the melted butter and blend.
5. Place the crust mixture into a pie pan.
6. Press the crust firmly.

FILLING

8 egg yolks
1 1/2 cups sweetened condensed milk
3/4 cup passion fruit juice
3/4 cup of tequila

1. Combine filling ingredients.
2. Pour into the crust.
3. Bake at 350 degrees for 10 to 12 minutes.
4. Remove and chill.

MERINGUE

3 egg whites from large or jumbo eggs, at room temperature
1 1/2 cups sugar
1/2 teaspoon vanilla paste
1/2 teaspoon cream of tartar

1. Beat the egg whites at high speed with an electric mixer until soft peaks form.
2. With mixer running, add the cream of tartar. Gradually add the sugar one tablespoon at a time, and beat until stiff peaks are formed. If there is any question, beat some more. The firmer, the better!
3. Beat in the vanilla.
4. Fill the pastry bag with the meringue and express your artistic talent by decorating the top of the pie.
5. Using a blow torch, brown the meringue topping.
Note: Meringue pies cut better with a wet, hot knife blade.
6. Refrigerate until service.

A tart passion fruit margarita transformed into a pie!

The Little Tart's
Tarte Tatin

Serves 6–8

"Tart"
–Elvis Costello

> "I prefer Hostess fruit pies to pop-up toaster tarts because they don't require as much cooking." —Carrie Snow (comedienne, actress)

The Little Tart's Tarte Tatin invokes thoughts of Becky Barsch Fisher. If you have been reading the accompanying stories with the recipes, you are probably desperate to meet this "Becky"!

Becky started in the bowels of the culinary world (the kitchen) when it was still somewhat of a frontier for women. She is deceptively the tiniest, cutest little woman, with twinkling eyes and a pixie smile. Her petite frame is 100% muscle. She is a sailor, a princess, a butcher, a nurse, a marathon woman, and our hero. She has always fancied herself to be quite the tart. No one dares to argue with her. Becky holds her own and everybody else's.

While making the tart of the day, Becky could tell stories that made the dishwashers blush and run! Thanks for the memories!

VARIATIONS: Pears would make a wonderful tart. If you have a favorite pie dough recipe, you can use that instead of the puff pastry.

TIMING: This can be done an hour before dinner. Keep in a warm place.

GARNISH: Ice cream

TOOLS:
10" sauté pan
12" round platter
Paring knife

10 Granny Smith apples, peeled, cored, and quartered
1/2 cup unsalted butter
1 cup sugar
2 tablespoons vanilla bean paste
Pinch of salt
Splash of brandy, Calvados, or rum
1 12" sheet of puff pastry (found in the dairy case in your grocery store)

1. Preheat oven to 375 degrees.
2. In a heavy bottomed 10" sauté pan, melt the butter, add sugar, salt, liquor, and vanilla bean paste. Cook until it is a rich amber brown color.
3. Arrange apples tightly in pan.
4. Cook over medium high heat.
5. Apples will begin to shrink. Continue to add apples until you just can't fit in anymore.
6. Cook over medium high heat until sugar begins to caramelize the apples.
7. Remove from heat. Cover the top of the sauté pan with pastry and seal edges by pinching the pastry over the edge of the sauté pan with your fingers.
8. Place sauté pan in the oven and bake approximately 35 minutes or until pastry is crisp and browned.
9. Remove from oven and allow to cool slightly, approximately 20 to 30 minutes
10. Release the pastry from the edge of the sauté pan with the blade of a paring knife. Place a 12" platter on top of the sauté pan. Invert tart onto large platter.
11. Slice into 8 wedges.
12. Serve with a scoop of vanilla ice cream.

*Less is more,
simple is best!*

The World's Richest Dreamsicle

Serves 6

"I doubt the world holds for anyone a more soul-stirring surprise than the first adventure with ice cream." —Heywood Broun

Do you remember when public schools did not have air conditioning? Remember the sound of the fans? Do you remember wishing you were the lucky student in the chair closest to the gust of air? Now, do you remember going to the cafeteria and finishing everything in your plaid lunch box? After wolfing down the pbj and reaching the bottom of the box, if your mother really loved you, there was a dime.

Dreamsicle, dreamsicle, oh cool me down, dear dreamsicle. Do you remember gleefully handing that dime over to the cafeteria lady in exchange for an afternoon delight! Make this dreamsicle for your kids and tell them how it was back in the old days!

 "Dreamsicle"
—Jimmy Buffett

 VARIATIONS: It won't be a dreamsicle, but you can use your favorite juice concentrate i.e. pineapple, passion fruit, and cranberry.
You can go to William Sonoma or Sur la Tab for fancy molds if the Dixie cups don't do it for you.

TIMING: These take at least 4 hours to freeze.

GARNISH: Wooden Popsicle stick.

TOOLS:
Bowl
Whisk
Sharp knife
Saucepan
Sieve
Wooden spoon
Dixie cups
Popsicle sticks

CRÈME ANGLAISE

8 egg yolks
8 ounces heavy cream
2 cups milk
2 tablespoons vanilla bean paste
2 cups sugar

1. Place egg yolks into a mixing bowl and set aside.
2. Combine cream, milk, vanilla bean paste, and sugar in a large heavy bottomed pot. Bring to a boil.
3. Slowly add the hot mixture to the egg yolks, a little at a time, while whisking vigorously until you have added approximately 2/3 of the mixture to the yolks. Be sure to add the hot mixture very slowly so that the egg yolks can adapt to the heat. If you pour all of the hot mixture into the egg yolks at once, you will have scrambled eggs.
4. Return the 2/3 egg yolk and cream mixture to the remaining 1/3 of the hot mixture in the original pot and cook until you see the first bubble break the surface or until it will evenly coat the back side of a wooden spoon.
5. Remove from heat and strain through a wire sieve to remove any lumps.
6. Cool.

ASSEMBLY

2 cups orange juice concentrate (no water added)

1. Mix 2 cups orange juice concentrate with the crème anglaise.
2. Pour into molds, add popsicle sticks and freeze overnight. (A small Dixie cup works as well as a mold.)
3. Dip in warm water to release from the molds.

Summertime delight!

Way South of the Border
Ancho Pepper Pecan Pie

Serves 8

"The South is dry and will vote dry. That is, everybody sober enough to stagger to the polls will."
—Will Rogers (1879-1935)

The quiet little pecan, delicately sweet and so rich tasting, is as American as pecan pie! Well, stand back boys! We have taken the quiet little pecan and turned it into a screaming meemy, so ancho that! We have cracked it, chopped it, and made it sizzling and sweet.

When we heard about the El Paso Diablos baseball club making the largest pecan pie in the world (41,586 pounds and 50 feet in diameter) back in May of 1999, we knew we were beaten on the size front. So we took the challenge and have made the 'phattest' pie. We have proven that great things come in 9" packages!

"South of the Border"
—Patsy Cline

VARIATIONS: You can use guajillo chile pepper puree and Jack Daniel's instead of Southern Comfort or even a rum would be good.

TIMING: This should be made at least 6 hours ahead of time so it has time to gel and cool.

GARNISH: Dollop of Mexican Crème or ice cream.

TOOLS:
Large mixing bowl
Whisk
Mixer
6 quart saucepan
Baking sheet to place pie on so it doesn't bubble on top of your oven

PECAN PIE

1 9" deep dish pie shell from the dairy case in your grocery store
7 egg yolks
1/2 cup light corn syrup
1 cup granulated sugar
1/2 cup unsweetened cocoa
1 cup dark brown sugar, firmly packed
1/2 stick butter, melted
3 cups Southern Comfort bourbon
2 cups pecan halves
1 cup ancho pepper puree (refer to Salt & Seasonings Section, pg. 33)
1 pinch of salt
4 tablespoons all-purpose flour
2 tablespoons vanilla bean paste

1. Preheat oven to 300 degrees.
2. In a saucepan, over high heat, reduce Southern Comfort to 1/4 cup. Caution: When heating alcohol, a 3 foot flame can result.
3. In a sauté pan, add both sugars and corn syrup and bring to a boil.
4. Add the reduced Southern Comfort, ancho paste, cocoa, salt, vanilla and butter to the boiling sugars and continue to boil.
5. Whisk the egg yolks in a bowl. Slowly add the bubbling sugar mixture to the eggs. Do this very slowly, adding just a small amount at a time as you will scramble the eggs if done too quickly.
6. Remove from heat and whisk in the flour.
7. Place pecan halves in pie shell.
8. Pour filling into pie shell.
9. Place on a sheet tray and bake for 40 minutes at 300 degrees.

Chiles and sugar and sweet heat and how we like to do that!

187

Hill Country Libations

Basil Mojito

Burning Pear Martini

Café Hudson's

Fredericksburg Peach Bellini

Hudson's Tequila Fizzzz

Jay's Holiday Eggnog

Prickly Pear Margaritas

Rosi's Jamaica Lime-Aid

Smoked Heirloom Tomato Bloody Mary

Remembrance of Wines Past

"If you drink, don't drive, don't even putt."
—Dean Martin

Libations

"I'd rather have a bottle in front of me than a frontal labotomy ." —Tom Waites

BASIL MOJITO

serves 1

Pronounced (Moh-HEE-toh) this is a popular classic "club" drink from Cuba. We have replaced the classic fresh mint with the tasty basil. When the mojito became popular, we happened to be short on mint, yet long on basil. Being that the basil is from the mint family, we just grabbed a clump and made it Italiano.

2 ounces simple syrup or 3
    teaspoons sugar
1/2 lime
10 fresh basil leaves
1/2 cup fresh ice
1 1/2 ounces rum
2 ounces club soda
1 sprig basil for garnish
1 lime wedge for garnish

1. Juice the 1/2 lime into a tall glass.
2. 2. Cut the remaining lime into quarters and add them to the glass.
3. Muddle the basil leaves with the lime and syrup (or sugar), crushing the leaves to extract their flavor.
4. Add the ice, rum, and club soda and stir well to blend.
5. Garnish with the lime wedge and basil sprig.

"Babalu" –Desi Arnaz

BURNING PEAR MARTINI

Makes 1 martini

Pear is the name of the fruit of the cactus. Oftentimes, during the droughts of the Texas summers, the cattle have no grass to feed upon. The ranchers' solution to this dangerous problem is to go out on the range and burn the prickles off of the cacti and the pears so the cows can eat them. We have concocted a recipe for human consumption with this delicacy. If you are not in the desert region, you can order the prickly pear juice from www.perfectpuree.com.

1/2 cup ice cubes
3 ounces citrus-flavored vodka
2 ounces prickly pear juice*
Lime peel twist

1. Put ice, vodka, and pear juice into a shaker.
2. Shake until really well chilled.
3. Strain into a martini glass.
4. Garnish with lime peel, twisting and wiping rim of glass with the zesty peel.

*www.perfectpuree.com

"I Did It My Way"
—Frank Sinatra

CAFÉ HUDSON'S

serves 1

"Only Irish coffee provides in a single glass all four essential food groups: alcohol, caffeine, sugar, and fat."
—Alex Levine

This after-dinner java drink found it's beginnings in our restaurant in Aspen, Colorado in 1972 (aka Café Pierre). In actuality, this is another victim of thievery! We borrowed this clever application of the after-dinner coffee from Pierre Casselli. Pierre was one of Jeff's first employers in the restaurant biz. Pierre's son-in-law, Phillip Dubov, has been serving the contraband at Hudson's for the past 7 years!

Lemon wedge
Sugar bowl and sugar
1 ounce 151 rum
1 ounce kahlua
1 ounce of tuaca
Whipped cream
3 ounces of coffee

1. Rub a lemon wedge along the rim of the glass.
2. Dip the glass in the sugar bowl, coating the rim with about 1" of sugar.
3. Add 151 rum.
4. Flame until sugar is brown and bubbly.
5. Add kahlua and tuaca.
6. Fill with coffee, leaving room for whipped cream
7. Top with whipped cream.

FREDERICKSBURG PEACH BELLINI serves 8

Although the Hill Country peach crop lasts from late May until early August, imported peaches from all corners of the world make this not just a seasonal drink. Try peaches from Australia or Chile. A food processor will work, but, it is best to use a blender to get the proper emulsion.

1 lemon, juiced
1/2 to 3/4 pounds ripe Fredericksburg peaches
2 teaspoons sugar
1 bottle champagne
1/2 cup ice

1. Peel, pit, and slice the peaches.
2. In a blender, puree the peaches with the sugar, lemon juice and ice. Use more sugar if the peaches are tart. Bear in mind this is not a sweet drink.

3. If the peaches don't have red veins, add a few raspberries to the blend for a rosy color.
4. After well blended, pour cold peach mixture into a serving pitcher.
5. Add one bottle of chilled champagne.
6. Stir gently.
7. Serve!

"Eating the Peach"— Randy Newman (From James and the Giant Peach Soundtrack)

HUDSON'S TEQUILA FIZZZZ

serves 1

This drink is a variation of the Ramos Gin Fizz. The original fizz was created in New Orleans by restaurant owner Henry Ramos in the late 1800's. Rumor has it that the drink was so popular Ramos had to hire the New Orleans street people to shake the drinks to keep up with the demand.

We added our Tex-Mex twist to Henry's concoction. We recommend it as a complement to your brunch menu. FYI: The orange flower water literally is a tincture of orange blossoms and can be found at all liquor stores.

2 ounces tequila
2 teaspoons lemon juice
2 teaspoons sugar
2 teaspoons heavy cream
2 teaspoons lime juice
1 egg white
2-3 drops orange flower water
6 ounces crushed ice
Club soda

1. Combine everything except the soda in a blender. Blend at high speed for a few seconds.
2. Strain and fill with club soda.

"Ai Viva Tequila" —Tex Ritter

JAY'S HOLIDAY EGGNOG serves 12–16

Jay Moore, chef/owner of Aransazu Restaurant in Rockport, Texas, shared this fabulous holiday concoction with us many years ago. Jay coauthored *Cooking Fearlessly*, our first cookbook, with Jeff Blank and was the Executive Chef at Hudson's for 10 years.

Jay is a CIA graduate and created this nog while at the Institute. Those culinary students are always looking for new ways to libate and celebrate! For their holiday party, they combined three recipes to create this delicious eggnog.

If you are wondering about the inclusion of the cream of tartar, it helps stabilize the egg whites. FYI: Cream of tartar is thrown off of red wine while it is distilling in casks. After the wine is taken out of the casks, the Cream of Tartar is scraped off.

Make the base one day in advance and chill. A few hours before needed, whip cream and beat egg whites and fold into base. Keep refrigerated.

12 eggs, separated
1 1/2 cups sugar
4 cups milk
6 cups cream
2 cups bourbon
1 cup dark rum
Pinch of cream of tartar

1. Beat yolks until pale in mixer.
2. Add sugar and continue to beat until thick and smooth.
3. Add milk, 4 cups of cream, bourbon and rum.
4. Mix well and refrigerate overnight.
5. To serve, beat whites and cream of tartar to soft peak.
6. Fold into refrigerated base mixture.
7. Beat 2 cups heavy cream to soft peaks and fold in.
8. Cheers!

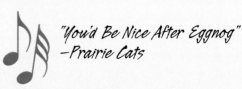
"You'd Be Nice After Eggnog" —Prairie Cats

PRICKLY PEAR MARGARITAS

serves 1

This has become a favorite at Hudson's on the Bend Cooking School. The contrast of the fuchsia ritas with the twinkling blue of the Lake Travis view is guaranteed to be a shaker of fun with sweetness on the rim. During the late summer or early fall, you can harvest your own prickly pears. These cacti can be found just south of Austin on the highway to Llano. Be sure to take a pair of tongs and a thick pair of rubber gloves. After you have collected a bucket full of cacti pears. Put them into the blender with a little lime juice to aid the blending. Puree and strain. Running short on time or just not interested in the needle-y adventure, go to www.pureeperfect.com to order the prickly pear concentrate.

3 ounces tequila
1 1/2 ounces Cointreau liqueur or Gran Marnier
4 ounces fresh-squeezed lime juice
2 tablespoons sugar
1 ounce fresh-squeezed prickly pear juice
1 ounce fresh-squeezed orange juice
1 cactus pad, julienned to make Napalito stir stick (We recommend that you burn the spines off the pear with a torch or over the stove top.)

1. Vigorously shake all ingredients together.
2. Rim the glass with salt.
3. Garnish with Cactus Napilito stir stick.

"Margarita"
–Traveling Wilburys

ROSI'S JAMAICA LIME-AID

Non alcoholic just like Rosi
serves 8–10

Not only is Jamaica a country, it is also the dried Mexican hibiscus flower. Jeff was invited to cook in Acapulco during the summer of 2004. While cooking in 100 degree weather, the kitchen crew made Jamaica punch with these dried blossoms.

After doing a little reading about Jamaica, we have found that it has more electrolytes than a bottle of gator aid. So if you are perspiring in the hot Texas summers, a glass of Rosi's Jamaica Lime-aid will quench your thirst and recharge your body chemistry.

Following is the recipe for our version of the miraculous thirst quencher.

20 hibiscus blossoms (www.nilevalleyherbs.com)
Juice of 6 limes
1/2 cup sugar
Club soda
Hibiscus flower for garnish

1. Brew tea with a quart of water and 20 hibiscus blossoms or Jamaica blossoms.
2. Add the lime juice and sugar to a 1 quart of brewed tea and stir well.
3. Fill tall glass with ice.
4. Pour 2/3 full with tea mixture.
5. Fill the remaining 1/3 of the glass with sparkling water..
6. Garnish with hibiscus flower.

"White Hibiscus in the Moonlight"
–Lyrics & Music: Bernie Kaai

SMOKED HEIRLOOM TOMATO BLOODY MARY

serves 4

After doing 250 episodes of cooking on Austin's News 8 "Dinner at Eight", Jeff was looking for a new path to take. As he was assembling ingredients for his upcoming shoot, Chuy Caballero was smoking tomatoes for our tomato sauce when he thought, "hmmm." Sometimes things are created from others' ideas, sometimes they come from mistakes, and sometimes boredom will ignite the creativity. For this recipe, you have to break out the stovetop smoker. If you put the 'maters on the grill you will get a very comparable flavor.

4 cups Smoked Heirloom Tomato juice (8 tomatoes)
1 tablespoon celery salt
Pepper; to taste
3 limes, juiced
Salt; to taste
2 tablespoons Worcestershire sauce
2 jalapeños
1 1/2 ounces vodka

1. Smoke heirloom tomatoes and jalapeños in stove top smoker for 8 minutes.
2. In a blender puree tomatoes, jalapeños, lime juice, celery salt and Worcestershire Sauce.
3. Rim glass with salt.
4. Fill glass with ice and pour 1 1/2 ounces of vodka over ice.
5. Top the glass off with the bloody mary mixture.
6. Garnish with a lime wedge and celery stalk.

"Bloody Mary Morning"
–Willie Nelson

Remembrance
of Wines Past

When Jeff approached me and asked me to contribute a small piece on food and wine pairing for the upcoming second cookbook, my mind flashed to the graphs and articles I have encountered in my exploration of wine. Most of them just did not connect in a meaningful way. Frank Zappa has a quote about writing about music; he thought that writing about music was kind of like dancing about architecture. Music is an experience, as is wine. We assimilate a lot of useful information through reading, but it is important to sometimes put down the books and just enjoy more wine in your life. There is something magical about enjoying a glass of wine. It transforms—I watch peoples' faces soften up as they relax, drop their guard, and open up to life.

As the sommelier at Hudson's on the Bend Restaurant, I'm always asked, "What should I drink?" And I always ask, "What do you like?" That is where the journey begins for us. Together we begin our travels across the landscape of the wine list. But for everyone the experience is different. I try to interpret where they want to go. I try to encourage them to leave their comfort zones and go somewhere new.

I recently started dining regularly with a friend and she considered herself a cabernet sauvignon drinker. Initially, that is what she drank. But we have not drunk cabernet in a long time. She trusted me to be her guide on the voyage as there is a sea of interesting wines waiting to be explored.

Let your wine connection, be it myself or others in the trade, offer suggestions. Take a short vacation to Italy, Germany, or Oregon. When was the last time you drank something from the Alsace? Seek out wines that have a sense of place and character.

Sometimes when I am suggesting wines, people tell me that they don't like pinot noirs, or rieslings, or other wines. You may have had a bad experience with a wine in the past. Give the wine a second chance. If you are not open to sampling wines from the vast tapestry of life, you are missing out.

My last wine epiphany involved a 2001 Fritz Haag Brauneberger Juffer-Sonnenuhr Spatlese, from the Mosel region in Germany. The following experience took place the day after the wine had been opened. I was drinking it with some very spicy food. All of the tumblers fell into place, the clouds parted, and I was allowed to enter into the kingdom of glorious synchronicity; it was magical. Sometimes it just clicks. I wanted to call someone and share the experience, but I refrained. It was my experience. No point in dancing about architecture. You just had to be there.

Most food and wine experiences are good. When the great ones happen, bow down and be thankful. The factors that go into making those moments are many and varied. Like music, you can listen to the same recording at different times and have a completely different experience. How you feel, what you think, where you are, and who you are with all influence your experience.

"There is something magical about enjoying a glass of wine. It transforms—I watch peoples' faces soften up as they relax, drop their guard, and open up to life."
—John Seibels

"LA PARILLA, THE MEXICAN GRILL"
by Reed Hearon

TAMALES
Curra's Grill
614 E. Oltorf
512.444.0012

Dos Gringos Tamales
www.dosgringostamales@yahoo.com
512.249.5947

MEXICAN FOODS
MexGrocer.com, LLC
7445 Girard Ave.
Suite 6
La Jolla, CA 92037
Phone: 858.459.0577
Fax: 858.459.0595
www.MexGrocer.com is a nationwide online grocery store for authentic Mexican food, Mexican recipes, cookbooks, cooking tips, and utensils.

QUAIL
Whole quail, de– boned quail and quail breasts
Diamond H Ranch
5322 Hwy 16 N.
Bandera, TX 78003
Phone: 830.460.8406
Fax: 830.460.7705
email: quail@texasgourmetquail.com
www.texasgourmetquail.com

WILD GAME
Broken Arrow Ranch
America's provider of free– ranging venison, antelope, and wild boar.
Located in the heart of the Texas Hill Country, Broken Arrow Ranch harvests axis deer, fallow deer, sika deer, and South Texas (nilgai) Antelope
Broken Arrow Ranch
P.O. Box 530
Ingram, TX 78025
830.367.5871
www.brokenarrowranch.com

MACADAMIA NUT OIL
www.macnut oil.com

SAUCES
COOKING CLASSES
STOVE TOP SMOKERS
Hudson's on the Bend
3509 RR 620
Austin, TX 78734
512.266.1369
www.hudsonsonthebend.com

JAPANESE KNIVES
www.japaneseknives.com

THE PERFECT PUREES OF NAPA VALLEY
Hayward Enterprises, Inc.
2700 Napa Valley Corporate Dr.
Suite L
Napa, CA 94558
800.556.3707
707.261.5100
www.perfectpuree.com

ORIENTAL FOOD PRODUCTS
www.orientalmarket.com

SPANISH FOOD PRODUCTS
www.spanishtable.com

SAFFRON
www.saffron.com
www.wholespice.com

Glossary

 A

ACHIOTE PASTE—This moist, brick-colored seasoning paste is available in most Mexican and Latin American food markets. It is a blend of the annatto seeds of the annatto tree, garlic, salt, onion, and oregano. It keeps almost indefinitely, tightly covered, at room temperature.

ACTIVE BUTTERMILK—This is sold in the dairy section as "buttermilk for baking." It has active bacteria and is not ultrapasteurized.

AIOLI—A strongly flavored garlic mayonnaise.

ANAHEIM CHILE—This long, green chile is the most widely grown mild chile. Pale green and five to seven inches long, it can be a bit anemic in flavor but is much improved by roasting, particularly over a wood fire.

ANCHO CHILE—This broad, dried chile is three to four inches long and a deep reddish brown; it ranges in flavor from mild to pungent. The rich, slightly fruit-flavored ancho is the sweetest of the dried chilies. In its fresh, green state, the ancho is called a poblano chile.

ANCHO CHILE POWDER—Made from ground ancho chiles, this powder can be found in most good Mexican groceries. To make your own, fry ancho chiles in 1 tablespoon vegetable oil over medium high heat until puffed and browned, 5 to 10 seconds. Drain well on paper towels. Grind into a powder in a blender or food processor.

ANCHO PUREE—Ancho chilies pureed. (See Salt and Seasoning section.)

APPLE WOOD SMOKED BACON—Bacon cured with apple wood smoke.

ARBOL—Usually the dried version of the ripe serrano, the skinny, reddish-brown chile de arbol varies from one to three inches long. It is hot but also has a pleasant nutty, rich flavor when toasted.

Often toasted and used whole in soups or stews, when crushed or ground these chiles can pack a real wallop. These are widely available and often sold whole as "red chiles."

ARTICHOKE HEARTS—Hint … the smaller the artichoke, the more tender it will be; the rounder it is, the larger its heart.

ARUGULA—Also called rocket lettuce, a bitterish, aromatic salad green with a peppery mustard flavor.

ASIAGO CHEESE—A semifirm Italian cheese with a rich, nutty flavor. It is made from whole or part skim cow's milk.

B

BABY BACK RIBS—Pork ribs. 2 1/4 pounds or less per rack qualifies them as baby back.

BANANA LEAF—The large, pliable leaves of the banana plant, used in the cooking of Mexico, Central and South America, the Caribbean, and Southeast Asia to wrap food to be baked or steamed.

BALSAMIC VINEGAR—Italian vinegar made from white Trebbiano grape juice; it gets its dark color and pungent sweetness from aging in barrels over a period of years.

BAY LEAVES—This aromatic herb comes from the evergreen bay laurel tree. They are used to flavor soups, stews, vegetables, and meats.

BLACK TRUFFLE PIECES—The black truffle is the most desirable truffle of the seventy known varieties. Its extremely pungent flesh is black with white striations.

BLACKENING SEASONING—A cooking technique made famous by New Orleans's chef Paul Prudhomme. The seasoning is customarily a Cajun spice mixture.

BLANCH—To plunge food into boiling water briefly, then into cold water to stop the cooking process.

BLEU CHEESE—This genre of cheese has been treated with molds that form blue or green veins throughout and give the cheese its characteristic flavor.

BONING KNIFE—Designed for cutting meat away from the bone, trimming excess fat, or preparing thin cutlets. Use it to filet an entire fish or to prepare a crown roast.

BOSC PEARS—A large winter pear with a slender neck and a russeted yellow skin. The Bosc is available from October through April. It has an agreeably sweet-tart flavor and is delicious fresh or cooked.

BOURSIN CHEESE—White and smooth with a buttery texture, this triple cream cheese is often flavored with herbs, garlic, or cracked pepper.

BUTTERNUT SQUASH—This large cylindrical winter squash looks rather like a pear-shaped bat. It is eight to twelve inches long, three to five inches at its widest point, and can weigh two to three pounds. The color of the smooth shell ranges from yellow to camel; the flesh is sweet and orange. It can be baked, steamed, or simmered.

C

CABRITO—Young goat meat. Cabrito has little to no fat. For optimum flavor and texture, cook with a slow, moist heat and avoid overcooking.

CARAMELIZE—To heat sugar until it liquefies and becomes a clear syrup. Caramelized sugar is also referred to as burnt sugar.

CEVICHE—An appetizer popular in Latin America, consisting of raw fish marinated in citrus (usually lime) juice. The action of the acid in the lime juice "cooks" the fish. Onions, tomatoes, and green peppers are added to the marinade.

CHAMBORD LIQUEUR—A French liqueur with a rich garnet color and an intense black raspberry flavor.

CHAMPAGNE VINEGAR—Made from fine champagne prepared for drinking. Each year a limited portion of the champagne is drawn from bottles and placed in oak barrels where it is aged for twelve to eighteen months. To ensure its longevity, it is aged to a grain of 65 (6.5%) acidity. This method produces a superior vinegar with an inviting bouquet and the crisp taste of champagne.

CHILES—More than thirty different varieties of chiles have been identified, with literally hundreds of subtypes. Chiles, like wine grapes, reflect the soil, climate, and growing conditions where they were cultivated. Connoisseurs pay high prices for chiles grown in certain regions or dried under special conditions. As you familiarize yourself with chiles, you will come to understand why. Each chile brings much more than heat to a dish. Smokey, sweet, sharp, astringent—every variety has a unique flavor. The most important things to know are whether the chile is fresh or dried and how hot it is.

CHILI POWDER—Chili powder is a mixture of chile powder and other spices, usually garlic, oregano, coriander, cumin, and cloves.

CHINESE FIVE SPICE—Can be found ground and premixed on the Asian foods aisle in your grocer. (See macadamia nut snapper.)

CHIPOTLE AIOLI—Aioli flavored with the chipotle chile.

CHIPOTLE CHILE—This is the dried, ripe version of a particular type of jalapeño and one of my favorite chiles. It is slowly cured over peat fires, giving it a smoky, rich flavor. Ranging from three to four inches long and dusty brown, chipotles are perhaps better known in the canned condiment chipotle en adobo (chiles

simmered in adobo sauce). This is very hot! Those who can stand the heat will appreciate the wonderful rich flavor.

CHIPOTLE EN ADOBO—Of Mexican origin, this dark red rather piquant sauce is made from ground chiles, herbs, and vinegar. It's used as a marinade as well as a serving sauce. Chipotle chiles are often marketed packed in adobo sauce.

CHOLULA HOT SAUCE—This is an excellent-tasting hot sauce that isn't overpowered by heat or the vinegar tast,e as sauces like Tabasco or Louisiana Joe's. It is mild enough for eggs and complements without masking flavors.

CILANTRO—The bright green leaves of the coriander plant. Cilantro has a lively, pungent fragrance that some describe as soapy.

COCO LOPEZ—The original Cream of Coconut. It is made from the coconut meat and blended with natural cane sugar. This can be found in the bar section of your grocery store.

COOKING WITH WINE—Whenever we say cooking with wine, we mean a type of wine that you would drink at a mature age versus that stuff you drank in college.

CORIANDER SEED—The tiny yellow-tan seeds are lightly ridged. They are mildly fragrant and have an aromatic flavor akin to a combination of lemon, sage, and caraway.

CORN HUSKS—These papery husks from corn are used primarily in making tamales. Latin markets sell packaged corn husks, which must be softened before use. To do so, soak husks in very hot water for about thirty minutes; then drain, pat dry, and use.

CORNSTARCH SLURRY—Cornstarch is most commonly used as a thickening agent for puddings, sauces, soups, and so forth. Because it tends to form lumps, cornstarch is generally mixed

with a small amount of cold liquid to form a thin paste before being stirred into a hot mixture.

COTIJA CHEESE—Queso cotija. Named for the town of Cotija, Michoacan, where it originated, this is a sharp, crumbly goat cheese. It has been called "the Parmesan of Mexico" and is usually served over beans and salads.

CRÈME ANGLAISE—A creamy dessert sauce.

CRÈME FRAICHE—This matured, thickened cream has a slightly tangy, nutty flavor and a velvety rich texture. In America, where all commercial cream is pasteurized, the fermenting agents necessary for crème fraiche can be obtained by adding buttermilk or sour cream.

CREAM OF TARTAR—A fine, white powder derived from a crystalline acid deposited on the inside of wine barrels. Cream of tartar is added to candy and frosting mixtures for a creamier consistency and to egg whites before beating to improve stability and volume. It's also used as the acid ingredient in some baking powders.

CREPE PAN—Shallow, Teflon-coated skillet used to make the delicate crepes.

CRIMINI MUSHROOMS—Crimini mushrooms are similar in shape and appearance to white mushrooms, to which they are related. Crimini mushrooms have a pale coffee-colored cap and a firm texture. These mushrooms have a dense, earthy flavor.

CUMIN—Cumin is the dried fruit of a plant in the parsley family. Its aromatic, nutty flavored seeds come in three colors: amber, white, and black. Cumin is available in seed and ground forms. It's used to make curries and chili powders.

CURD—When it coagulates, milk separates into a semisolid portion (curd) and a watery liquid (whey). Cheese is made from the curd. A creamy mixture is made from juice, sugar, butter, and egg yolks. The ingredients are cooked together until the mixture becomes quite thick. When cool, the lemon curd becomes thick enough to spread and is used as a topping for breads and other baked goods.

D

DE GLAZE—Taking a liquid (wine or liquor) and adding that to an almost dry pan that has little flavored nubbets sticking to the bottom. The wine releases them from the bottom and into the recipe you are making, like when Grandma made the gravy.

DRIED MEXICAN OREGANO—Mexican oregano has a flavor distinct from Greek oregano. Greek oregano tastes like pizza, while Mexican oregano tastes like Mexican food. Do not substitute one for the other. It is easily found in Mexican and Latin American markets. Mexican oregano develops its full flavor when toasted in a dry skillet until fragrant.

DURUM FLOUR—Durum wheat is not good for baking. Instead, it's most often ground into semolina, the basis for excellent pasta.

E

EGG ROLL WRAPPERS—Paper-thin squares of dough made with flour, water, and salt. They are larger than wonton skins and are used to make egg rolls and spring rolls. They can be purchased packaged in Asian markets and some supermarkets.

EGG WASH—Egg yolk or egg white mixed with a small amount of water or milk. In this book, it is the first step of the standard breading procedure.

EPAZOTE—On its own, epazote, a deep green herb with serrated leaves, has a strange medicinal smell, almost like kerosene. It is essential in a wide range of dishes, including a large number of Vera Cruz specialties as well as black beans. The herb should

always be used fresh. The flavor of the dried version bears no resemblance to the fresh. Epazote is becoming more widely available, especially in Southern California and Texas.

F

FIGS—There are hundreds of varieties of figs, all having in common a soft flesh with a plentitude of tiny edible seeds. They range in color from purple black to almost white and in shape from round to oval.

FISH SAUCE—Fish sauce can be any of various mixtures based on the liquid from salted, fermented fish. It's used as a condiment and flavoring, much as soy sauce would be used. Fish sauces can be found in Asian markets and some grocery stores.

FOIE GRAS—The literal translation from French is "fat liver." Foie gras is the term generally used for the enlarged liver from a goose or duck. This is a specialty of Alsace and Perigord.

FRITTATA—An Italian omelet that usually has the ingredients mixed with the eggs rather than being folded inside, as with a French omelet. It can be flipped or the top can be finished under a broiling unit. An omelet is cooked quickly over moderately high heat and, after folding, has a flat-sided half oval shape. A frittata is firmer because it's cooked very slowly over low heat and round because it isn't folded.

G

GEWURTZTRAMINER WINE—The German word Gewurz means "spicy," and this white wine is knows for its crisp, spicy characteristics.

GINGER/GINGERROOT—A plant from tropical and subtropical regions that's grown for its gnarled and bumpy root. The flavor is peppery and slightly sweet, while the aroma is pungent and spicy.

GOAT CHEESE—Goat's milk cheese can range in texture from moist and creamy

to dry and semifirm. They are often coated in edible ash or leaves, herbs, or pepper. We get ours from the Pure Luck Dairy Farm in Dripping Springs, Texas.

GRAND MARNIER—A rich, amber-colored cognac-based liqueur flavored with the peels of Haitian bitter oranges, exotic spices, and vanilla.

GRAPESEED OIL—Extracted from grape seeds. Some grape seed oils have a light grapey flavor and fragrance. It can be used for salad dressings and is also good for sautéing due to its high smoke point. This oil is available in gourmet food stores and some grocery stores.

GREEN ONION—Scallions that can be chopped and used in salads, soups, and a multitude of other dishes for flavor.

GREEN PEPPERCORN—The soft underripe berry that is usually preserved in brine. It has a fresh flavor that is less pungent than the berry in its other forms.

GUAJILLO—This is the dried version of the Mexican (unhybridized) version of the New Mexico–type red chile. It is about four inches long, reddish brown, and smooth skinned. Its medium heat and nutty flavor make it a versatile chile for salsas and moles. Use it in conjunction with chipotles or moritas for a complex layering of flavor and heat.

H

HABANERO—This small, round chile is purported to be the hottest in the world. It is a different species than all other chiles commonly eaten in this country. Aside from its remarkable heat, it has an elusive floral-citrusy flavor that makes it highly prized as a component to many salsas. This chile is still rare in the United States. If you see it, buy some and see what all the fuss is about. It is available in green, yellow, and orange, reflecting different degrees of ripeness.

HATCH CHILE—A fresh chile, a close relative of the New Mexico green chile.

HEARTS OF PALM—The edible inner portion of the stem of the cabbage palm tree. They are slender, ivory colored, delicately flavored, and expensive.

HIERBA SANTA/HOJA SANTA/HOYA SANTOS—Hierba means "herb" and hoja means "leaf." This large, heart-shaped leaf adds an incomparable exotic aroma hinting of anise, camphor, or even sassafras to Oaxacan and Veracruzano dishes. It is becoming more widely available in the United States but is still difficult to find. It is best when fresh, but the dried herb makes a good substitute. Refresh the dried herb before using by soaking in warm water a few minutes. Squeeze out excess water before proceeding with the recipe.

HOISIN SAUCE—This thick, reddish-brown sauce is sweet and spicy and widely used in Chinese cooking. It's a mixture of soybeans, garlic, chile peppers, and various spices. Hoisin is mainly used as a table condiment and as a flavoring agent for many meat, poultry, and shellfish dishes. It can be found in Asian markets and many large supermarkets.

I

ITALIAN HERB SEASONING—A blend of Mediterranean herbs and a hint of black pepper to add a true Italian flavor to most savory dishes. This can be purchased in the spice aisle in your grocery store.

J

JALAPEÑO—This is probably the most familiar and popular hot chile. Ranging from two to three inches in length, with a fat shape and dark, shiny green skin, the fresh jalapeño, the chipotle, is dried by slowly smoking it over peat. It adds a wonderful smoky savor to soups and salsas.

JICAMA—A large bulbous root vegetable with a thin brown skin and white crunchy flesh. Its sweet, nutty flavor is good both and raw and cooked.

Jicama ranges in size from about four ounces up to six pounds. It is available year round and can be purchased in Latin American markets and most supermarkets.

K

KALAMATA OLIVES—An almond-shaped Greek olive with a dark eggplant color. They have a flavor that can be rich and fruity.

KEY LIME JUICE—A lime from Florida that is smaller and rounder and has a color more yellow than green. The key lime is usually found only in specialty produce markets and some supermarkets that carry gourmet produce.

L

LEMON GRASS—One of the most important flavorings in Thai and Vietnamese cooking. This herb has long, thin, gray-green leaves and a woody scallion-like base. It has a sour lemon flavor and fragrance.

M

MACADAMIA NUT OIL—The macadamia nut makes a fabulous oil. It has a beautiful color, a subtle but rich flavor, and a light finish. With its high smoke point it is uniquely versatile, and its uses are endless.

MADAGASCAR PEPPERCORN SAUCE—Peppercorn sauce offered at Hudson's on the Bend Restaurant and used on meats and as a marinade. Order at www.cookingfearlessly.com.

MANDOLINE—A compact, hand-operated machine with various adjustable blades for thin to thick slicing and for julienne and French fry cutting. Mandolins have folding legs and come in both wood and stainless steel frame models. They are used to cut firm vegetables and fruits with uniformity and precision. On most machines, the food is held in a metal carriage on guides so that fingers aren't in danger.

MANGO JALAPENO SAUCE—A spicy sweet sauce offered at Hudson's on the Bend Restaurant. Order at www.hudsonsonthebend.com.

MASCARPONE CHEESE—A buttery rich double cream to triple cream cheese made from cow's milk.

MASA—Masa is the dough used for corn tortillas. Masa flour or masa harina is dried masa. Many supermarkets now carry masa harina. You could also check in Hispanic markets in your area.

MEXICAN CRÈME—See Crème fraische.

MIRIN SWEET RICE WINE—A low-alcohol, sweet, golden wine made from glutinous rice. Essential to the Japanese cook, mirin adds sweetness and flavor to a variety of dishes, sauces, and glazes. It's available in all Japanese markets and in the gourmet section of some supermarkets. Mirin is also referred to simply as rice wine.

MOJITO—A cocktail made by combining lime juice, sugar, and mint leaves in a tall glass, then crushing the mint slightly with the back of a spoon. The glass is then filled with crushed ice, a jigger of rum, and sometimes a spritz of soda.

MOLE—A rich, dark, reddish-brown sauce usually served with poultry. Generally, mole is a smooth cooked blend of onion, garlic, several varieties of chiles, ground seeds, and a small amount of Mexican chocolate, its best-known ingredient. The chocolate contributes richness to the sauce without adding overt sweetness.

MORITA—This chile is like the smaller brother of the chipotle. It, too, is a smoked, dried chile made from a small jalapeño grown in the state of Michoacan. It is very hot but not as hot as the chipotle and, also like the chipotle, is often sold canned as chipotle en adobo. It is a small chile, about one inch long and reddish.

MR. PIBB—Soft drink with a taste similar to root beer.

Glossary

N

NOPALES—The flat, dark-green leaf or paddle of the nopal cactus, also known as the prickly pear cactus, is widely eaten in Mexico. It has a pleasant, sappy, almost green-bean flavor. The only problem is that the nopal comes with small needles that will stick in your hands as you clean the leaves. In Mexico, seemingly every market sells neat little bags of already cleaned, whole nopal paddles. Unfortunately, here you must usually clean them. But don't fear. Put on an old pair of gardening gloves, take a small paring knife, and cut off each of the little bumps that contains the needles. Fresh, whole nopales are fairly widely available in supermarkets throughout the Southwest.

P

PANKO BREAD CRUMBS—Bread crumbs used in Japanese cooking for coating fried foods. They are coarser than those normally used in the United States and create a deliciously crunchy crust. Panko is sold in Asian markets.

PASILLA—This is a blackish chile, five to eight inches long, with a deep cocoalike flavor. Unfortunately, the name pasilla is used in parts of the United States to refer not to a dried chile but instead to the fresh poblano.

PASSION FRUIT—This tropical fruit is said to be named not for the passionate propensity it promotes but because particular parts of the plant's flowers resemble different symbols of Christ's crucifixion, such as the crown of thorns. When ripe, it has a dimpled, deep purple skin and a soft golden flesh generously punctuated with tiny edible black seeds. The flavor is seductively sweet-tart, and the fragrance is tropical and perfumey. The fruit is available from March through September in Latin markets. It contains a small amount of vitamins A and C.

PINE NUTS—This high-fat nut comes from several varieties of pine trees. The nuts are actually inside the pinecone. Pine nuts can be found in bulk in natural food stores and packaged in many supermarkets. Because of their high fat content, pine nuts turn rancid quickly.

POBLANO CHILE—A dark green chile with a rich flavor that varies from mild to snappy. The very best poblanos are found in central Mexico. This is the preferred chile of chiles rellenos—big (about five inches long), heart shaped, dark green, meaty, and mildly spicy. Poblanos are wonderful roasted, and, if you are careful and do not overly blacken the skin, you do not have to peel them. Just pull off the stem and with it will come the seed core. Milder Anaheims are the best substitute. The poblano, especially in California, is often incorrectly labeled a pasilla chile. Ancho chiles are dried poblanos.

PROBE THERMOMETER—This is an instant meat thermometer that takes the reading in just a few seconds; these are inserted into the meat toward the end of the cooking time. Always insert a meat thermometer as near to the center of the meat as possible, avoiding bone or gristle areas.

Q

QUENELLES—Quenelles are shaped in small balls or between tablespoons, making an oval, or by forcing the mixture through a pastry bag on buttered paper. They are cooked in boiling salted water or stock and are served as a garnish to soups or other dishes.

R

RADICCHIO LETTUCE—This red-leafed Italian chicory is most often used as a salad green.

RICE VINEGAR—There are Japanese as well as Chinese rice wine vinegars. Both are made from fermented rice and both are slightly milder than most Western vinegars.

ROUX—A mixture of flour and fat that, after being slowly cooked over low heat, is used to thicken mixtures such as soups and sauces. There are three classic roux—white, blond, and brown.

S

SAFFRON—The world's most expensive spice. The yellow orange stigmas are picked from a small purple crocus. Each flower provides only three stigmas, which must be carefully hand picked. It takes 14,000 of these tiny stigmas for each ounce of saffron.

SCOTCH BONNET—Scotch bonnet pepper. Called wiri wiri in Jamaica, the Scotch bonnet is grown and used in the Caribbean. Like a lantern-shaped walnut in a rainbow of colors, and distinguished by its namesake wrinkled crown, the fiery hot Scotch bonnet scorches the tongue, occupying the top of the pepper heat scale with the related but distinct Mexican habanera used in the Americas. See more here, especially on handling this pepper.

SEMOLINA FLOUR—Durum wheat that is more coarsely ground than normal wheat flours, a result that is often obtained by sifting out the finer flour. Most good pasta is made from semolina. It is also used to make gnocchi, puddings, and soups and in various confections.

SERRANO—This small, light-green chile is skinny and pointed, about two inches long. It has a bright, clean heat and flavor and can be significantly hotter than the jalapeño. Always use the seeds. They are vital to the serrano's flavor.

SESAME OIL—Expressed from sesame seeds, sesame oil comes in two basic types. One is light in color and flavor and has a deliciously nutty nuance. The darker Asian sesame oil has a much stronger flavor and fragrance and is used as a flavor accent for some Asian dishes. Sesame oil is high in polyunsaturated fats, ranking fourth behind safflower, soybean, and corn oils. Its average smoke point is 410 degrees, making it excellent for frying.

SHALLOTS—Shallots are formed more like garlic than onions, with a head composed of multiple cloves, each covered with a thin papery skin. They are in the onion family.

SHERRY VINEGAR—A very special vinegar made from a very special drink. Spanish sherry is wonderful, both to drink and to cook with, and the vinegar from the sherry grape has its own delightfully rich, sweet, nutty flavor. Though quite different from balsamic, it is equally good sprinkled over salads and cooked vegetables just by itself.

SHITAKE MUSHROOM (SHE—TAH— kee)—Mushrooms may be a new item in many American markets, but they have been a staple of the Asian diet for centuries. Shiitakes are the second most consumed mushrooms in the world. Their pungent, woodsy flavor, nutritional value, and health benefits attract gardeners, gourmets, and mushroom lovers, even at $12–$26 a pound. Shiitakes ("shii" is Japanese for oak and "take" means mushroom) are delicious, with a meaty texture and four times the flavor of white button mushrooms. Shiitakes provide high levels of protein (18% by mass), potassium, niacin, B vitamins, calcium, magnesium, and phosphorus. The mushroom has all essential amino acids. Shiitakes have natural antiviral and immunity-boosting properties and are used nutritionally to fight viruses, lower cholesterol, and regulate blood pressure. Researchers Suzuki and Oshima found that a raw shiitake eaten daily for one week lowered serum cholesterol by 12%. Concentrated forms of lentinan, a shiitake extract, have been used to treat cancer, AIDS, diabetes, fibrocystic breast disease, and other conditions with impressive results. The very best shiitakes are grown on natural hardwood logs, such as oak.

SIL PAT—Nonstick fiberglass and silicone sheet pan liner.

SMOKE POINT—The stage at which heated fat begins to emit smoke and acrid odors and impart an unpleasant flavor to foods. The higher the smoke point, the better suited a fat is for frying.

SQUIRT BOTTLE—Used to paint, design, or express yourself with sauces by squirting a thin stream onto a plate. It is the old diner ketchup bottles with the cone top. Can be purchased in restaurant supply stores and some grocery stores.

STANDARD BREADING PROCEDURE—The organized method of preparation with which to implement the breading process—flour to egg wash to breading.

STOVETOP SMOKER—A smoker used on your stovetop.

THERMAL PITCHER—A thermos like you would find at the IHOP used to keep coffee warm, but in the culinary world (sorry IHOP) it is used to keep delicate sauces warm.

TOMATILLOS—This fruit belongs to the same nightshade family as the tomato. They are used while still green and quite firm. Their flavor has hints of lemon, apple, and herbs. They are available sporadically year round in specialty produce stores, Latin American markets, and some supermarkets.

V

VANILLA PASTE—Paste extracted from the vanilla bean that adds a gourmet flavor to any recipe.

WHITE TRUFFLE OIL—Oil that is flavored with scraps of white truffles.

WONTON WRAPPERS—Paper-thin squares of dough made from flour, water, eggs, and salt. They can be purchased prepackaged in some supermarkets and in most Chinese markets.

WORCESTERSHIRE SAUCE—There was an Englishman who said, "What's this here sauce?" and thus the name. Really, though, this condiment was originally developed in India by the English, and it takes its name from the fact that it was first bottled in Worcester, England. It's a thin, dark, rather piquant sauce used to season meats, gravies, soups, and vegetable juices and as a table condiment.

Z

ZESTER—The stainless steel cutting edge of this kitchen tool has five tiny cutting holes that, when the zester is pulled across the surface of a lemon or orange, create threadlike strips of peel. The zester removes only the colored outer portion of the peel, leaving the pale bitter path.

Index

Index

All Done